APPLYING PSYCHOLOGY

PSYCHOLOGY

to health

PHILIP BANYARD

Series Editor: **ROB McILVEEN**

Hodder & Stoughton

A MEMBER OF THE HODDER HEADLINE GROUP

British Library Cataloguing in Publication Data

Banyard, Philip
Applying Psychology to Health. –
(Applying Psychology to. . . Series)
I. Title II. Series
610.19

ISBN 0-340-64756-6

First published 1996
Impression number   10 9 8 7 6 5 4 3 2 1
Year   1999 1998 1997 1996

Typeset by Transet Ltd, Coventry, England.
Printed in Great Britain for Hodder & Stoughton Educational, a division of Hodder Headline Plc, 338 Euston Road, London NW1 3BH by Redwood Books, Trowbridge, Wiltshire

CONTENTS

PREFACE

The aim of *Applying Psychology to Health* is to give you an introduction into the wide range of links that have been made between psychology and the study of health and health care. I hope that the book provides a framework that enables you to go and study the subject in more detail, and I hope it is written in an interesting enough way to encourage you to do this. To read this book, you do not need to have a detailed knowledge of psychology, though it would be helpful if you are aware of the basic concepts of psychology.

The book is divided up into 12 chapters which deal with the current concerns of health psychology. These concerns have developed from the problems of health and health care, rather than from the research areas of psychology. The traditional approach to psychology has divided the subject into specialist areas such as cognitive psychology and physiological psychology. The approach in health psychology, on the other hand, is to use whatever psychology is useful. This means that evidence is often used from a wide range of psychological approaches when dealing with a health problem.

A lot of the published information on health and psychology is from the USA and so the evidence is largely from studies that are carried out on the other side of the Atlantic. This book tries, wherever possible, to use British health figures and British evidence. It also make extensive reference to *The Health of the Nation*, which is the policy document for health produced by the British government.

Each chapter is divided into four sections. The first section puts the chapter content in a context, either of traditional psychology or contemporary evidence. The following two sections look at a range of psychological contributions to this health problem, and take a more detailed look at one special issue. It is not possible to cover all the possible issues in depth, so I have tried to select a range of special issues to show the breadth of evidence that can be used in discussions on health. The final sections look at applications that psychologists use to help with the health problem under discussion.

This book developed out of a series of lectures on the Health Studies degree at the Nottingham Trent University. These lectures were designed to give students a broad overview of the field and to encourage individual reading and individual research. In keeping with this approach, I have tried to provide a number of references in this book that will be useful for further reading and research. I have not, however, provided a long list of the various studies that support different positions in health psychology. I hope that readers will be able to go from this text to the more specialised works that are referred to, and also to the primary research if they are interested in a particular question.

It is a convention in psychology texts to write them in a dispassionate voice as if the author does not have a personal bias. I have always been uncomfortable with this tradition, and I think it is not possible to write a book about human affairs without showing your bias. It is my belief that a society should protect and care for its citizens and should aim to offer universal health care for people regardless of their financial circumstances, class, gender or race. This value guides the way I view psychology and health.

Finally, this book is meant to be relatively easy to read while still covering a wide range of important issues. I hope that you enjoy reading it.

ACKNOWLEDGEMENTS

I would like to acknowledge my colleagues at The Nottingham Trent University who help create a supportive working environment. I would also like to acknowledge the colleagues and friends who have read and commented on various parts of the text, and provided useful information. In particular, I would like to thank Mark Griffiths, Lesley Phair, Patrick Hylton, Nicky Hayes and Wendy Wood. If there are any mistakes in the text, I blame them.

chapter one

INTRODUCTION TO HEALTH PSYCHOLOGY

CHAPTER OVERVIEW

The INTRODUCTION looks at definitions of health and asks how we can tell illness from health. MODELS OF HEALTH looks at the traditional approach of the biomedical model. It goes on to explore the changing view of health, and considers the more recent approach of the biopsychosocial model which takes a systems approach to health. The SPECIAL ISSUE is a brief review of the *Health of the Nation* policy document produced by the British government. PSYCHOLOGY AND HEALTH contains a brief description of the content and methods of psychology, looking at how, for example, we can investigate sexual behaviour through interview research. The chapter concludes with a review of the concerns of health psychology.

INTRODUCTION

What is health?

The first question we have to look at is what do we mean by health. This is by no means as straightforward as it sounds. Before reading on, try the exercise in Box 1.1.

Box 1.1 The distinction between health and illness

Draw the boxes in the figure overleaf and under them list the features of illness and health.

This is much harder than you would think, so try to do this answering the questions, 'How do I feel when I am healthy?', and 'How do I feel when I am ill?' You could try to list the *signs* of health and illness, the *symptoms* of health and illness, the different *cognitions* (the way you think and make judgements) in health and illness, the different *behaviours* in health and illness, and the different *emotions* in health and illness.

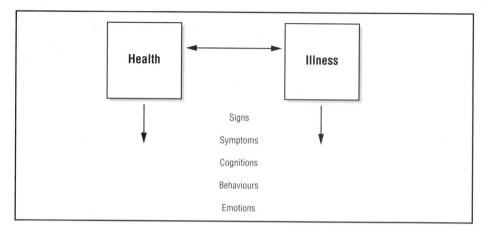

Our personal sense of being healthy or being ill is quite difficult to define. It is affected by a number of things, including our ideas about:

- how we *normally* feel
- how we *could* feel
- what the cause of our present condition is
- how we think other people feel
- how other people respond to us
- how our friends, family and culture describe our symptoms, behaviour and feelings.

For example, if I drink too much alcohol on a Friday night then I might feel very unwell on Saturday morning, but am I ill? I know that I have brought on my own condition and that I will feel better fairly quickly. I also know that I will receive no sympathy for my condition and I will be expected to carry out my normal tasks. In fact, I might feel much worse than when I have a heavy cold, but when I have a cold I describe myself as being ill, and I receive sympathy, Lemsip and time off from work and other responsibilities. So although I feel worse with a drink reaction than I do with a cold, I describe myself as 'ill' with the cold and not with the drink.

Another confusing example is provided by chronic disorders, for example insulin-dependent diabetes. This is a life-threatening disorder, but one which can be successfully controlled so that diabetics can lead active and normal lives with the exception that they have to take regular insulin injections. Can a diabetic be healthy? If we define good health as the absence of any disease or physical disorder, then the answer must be 'no', but most diabetics lead a very healthy life. Clearly defining health and illness is not going to be easy.

Defining 'health'

The word *health* comes from an Anglo-Saxon term meaning 'wholeness'. The same root-word gives us the words *whole* and *holy*. It is interesting that the religious idea of being spiritually holy has a similar origin to the medical notion of being physically healthy. Before the development of modern Western medicine the role of physical healing was often closely connected with the role of spiritual healing, and religious people were involved in the care of the sick. In many parts of the world today, spiritual health is still associated with physical health.

If we are looking for a modern definition of health, then a commonly quoted example was provided by the World Health Organisation in 1948: 'a state of complete physical, mental, and social well-being and ... not merely the absence of disease or infirmity'.

The strength of this definition is that it acknowledges that there is more to health than getting rid of spots and rashes and pains. However, when I look at that definition I am inclined to think that I have never had a day of good health in my life. It suggests that I should be in a state of complete well-being, and that is rather difficult to achieve. The definition suggests that to be healthy, people must live in good social, political and economic conditions, and must be able to love, to work and to create. However, for many people in the world, daily life is about getting by, rather than aspiring to a state of complete well-being. Another problem with the World Health Organisation definition is that it suggests that people who are not fulfilled in life, people who engage in dissent, and people who live rebel lifestyles, are all somehow not healthy.

The wellness continuum

It would seem that a clear definition of health and illness is not possible. There is, however, some general agreement that health is not just a matter of the absence of illness. There is also some general agreement that the attempt to categorise people as sick or healthy is not particularly helpful. Instead, it is suggested that we place people somewhere on a wellness continuum (see Figure 1.1). This continuum acknowledges that nearly everyone could improve their health, and the health of every living person can also deteriorate. If we can place ourselves on the continuum then we can set about trying to improve our health and prevent illness.

FIGURE 1.1 *The wellness continuum. Where would you place yourself on this continuum today?*

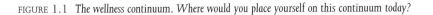

MODELS OF HEALTH

When we think of health care, some of the first images that spring to mind are of doctors and nurses dashing around high-tech hospitals pushing trolleys loaded up with machines that go 'ping!' Health is associated with doing something physical to the patient, such as cutting something out of the body, or administering some chemicals. This is at the heart of the biomedical model of health. This model has been the cornerstone of Western medicine for 300 years, and it is based on the idea that illness can be explained by looking at the workings of the body such as biochemical imbalances or abnormalities in nervous system activity.

The biomedical model

The biomedical model asks us to look at people as if they are biological machines. If something is going wrong then we need to fix the machine in the same way we might fix a car. We make observations and diagnose the faulty bit, then we can repair it if possible, or replace it if necessary. Sometimes we might benefit from a general overhaul and sometimes from a few minor adjustments. This biomedical model has some appeal because we are clearly made up of biological bits, and also some biomedical treatments produce dramatic improvements in health.

The biomedical model has a number of key features:

1 **Reductionism**
   The model tries to reduce explanations of illness to the simplest possible process. For example, it will look for explanations in disordered cells rather than psychological or social processes.
2 **Single-factor causes**
   The biomedical model looks for the cause of a disorder rather than looking for a range of contributory factors. For example, there are numerous attempts to explain complex disorders in terms of a simple genetic effect. Also, there is a tendency to describe smoking as the cause of coronary heart disease, yet many smokers do not develop the disease and many non-smokers do. The process would seem to have more than one cause and more than one contributory factor.
3 **Mind–body distinction**
   Dating back to the French philosopher René Descartes, Western science has made a distinction between the mind and the body. In some ways this is a religious distinction and encourages us see people as split into two parts – a ghost and a biological machine. (This is often referred to as the *Cartesian dualism* – *Cartesian* after Descartes, and *dualism* because it proposes a split into two.) In many ways this is a comforting idea especially when

someone we love changes their personality and behaviour due to their poor health. For example, when someone develops Alzheimer's disease they become unrecognisable from the person they were throughout much of their life. It is comforting to think that the original person is still there but trapped in a decaying body.

4 **Illness not health**

'If it ain't broke don't fix it' might well be the motto of the biomedical model. It deals with illness and the development of illness rather than the promotion of good health.

The changing view of health

There are three main changes that have led to dissatisfaction with the bio-medical model. First, throughout the twentieth century there has been a decline in the incidence of infectious, single cause diseases. In the United States of America the three most common causes of death in 1900 were:

1 Influenza and pneumonia
2 Tuberculosis
3 Gastro-enteritis

Theses are all caused by micro-organisms and respond to relatively simple medical interventions such as anti-biotics.

On the other hand, in 1986, the three most common causes of death were:

1 Heart disease
2 Cancer
3 Accidents

None of these has a known simple cause, and the medical interventions are often drastic and costly, and have only limited success. The general picture is that large-scale infections (caused by simple micro-organisms such as bacteria) which were common in the early part of this century have been replaced by chronic diseases (such as cancer) which have multiple causes.

Secondly, there has been a dramatic increase in the specialist technology and an equally dramatic increase in the cost of health care. The costs of treating someone who is ill are now prohibitively high so there is a major incentive to prevent people getting ill in the first place. The third change is a growing emphasis on quality of life. People are developing an expectation that they should have a healthy, enjoyable and active life. These three factors have changed the general view of health from one where we deal with illness to one where we promote good health.

It is important to add that this description of the changing priorities of health only applies to the technologically advanced countries. In other parts of the world, infectious diseases still cause many deaths despite there being relatively easy and cheap medication for them. For example, tuberculosis (TB) was a major cause of death world wide until the development of a near perfect cure about 35 years ago. The entire course of this treatment (which is known as 'directly observed treatment short-course' or DOTS) can cost as little as £10. However, the World Health Organisation (cited in the October 1995 issue of the *New Internationalist*) estimates that nearly 2 million people died of TB in 1990. (Some other issues relating to culture and health are dealt with in Chapter 8.)

The biopsychosocial model

An alternative approach to the biomedical model is look at all the biological, psychological and social factors that are associated with health and illness. This is referred to as the biopsychosocial model. It is a real mouthful of a name but it does have the advantage of telling you exactly what it refers to.

In contrast to the biomedical model, the biopsychosocial model is not reductionist. Instead it looks at all levels of explanation from the micro level (for example changes in body chemicals) to the macro level (for example the culture that someone lives within). The biopsychosocial model does not look for single causes but starts from the assumption that health and illness have many causes, and also produce many effects. The model does not make the distinction between mind and body but instead looks at the connections between mental events and biological changes. Finally, the biopsychosocial model is concerned as much with health as it is with illness.

The biopsychosocial model is a systems theory. This means that it recognises that there are a number of different systems at all levels of organisation and these systems are linked. Figure 1.2 shows some of the systems involved in human life. At one end of the scale, we exist within an ecological system which includes the planet we live on, the life we have developed from and the species we are part of. At the other end of the scale we are made up of the

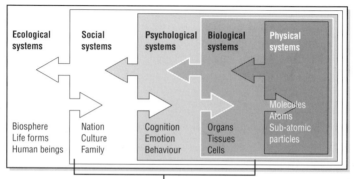

The biopsychosocial model

FIGURE 1.2 *Systems*

basic units of the universe – molecules, atoms and various sub-atomic parti-cles with a range of dodgy names.

In between these two systems, the biopsychosocial model looks at three sys-tems which are all separate from each other yet are also connected to each other – systems within systems. We live within a social system that includes our country, our culture and our family. We also experience a psychological system of cognitions, emotions and behaviour, and we are affected by a bio-logical system of organs, tissues and cells.

One biological system that has received a lot of attention from psychologists and physicians is the immune system, which is a collection of responses that allow the body to neutralise, eliminate or control the factors that produce disease. It seems possible that there are connections between the immune system and the experience of stress which would fit into our psychological systems. The experience of stress is also affected by the social systems we live in – for example, our family. When we look at it this way, we can see there is no single cause for ill-health that brings out a simple response, but rather there are a mass of connections that create a complex series of changes with-in us.

The development of this biopsychosocial view of health and illness moves the emphasis away from traditional Western medicine and towards psychology. However, before we get to the psychology we will look at how changes in social policy have also brought psychology into focus.

The Health of the Nation

The Health of the Nation is the British government's strategy for health which was published in 1992 (see the Special Issue below). The strategy emphasises dis-ease prevention and health promotion while acknowledging that improve-ments in treatment are also important. It identifies five key areas where sub-stantial improvement can be achieved and sets national targets that mainly refer to the year 2000. The key areas are:

- coronary heart disease and stroke
- cancers
- mental illness
- HIV/AIDS and sexual health
- accidents.

The striking thing about this list is that the route to improvement in all the key areas is psychological. The main risk factors with coronary heart disease and stroke are diet and smoking. These factors are also important in the development of some cancers. A further behavioural issue with cancers is encouraging people to attend for screening. One of the targets for mental health is to reduce the incidence of suicide and this also requires psychological rather than medical interventions. The issue with sexual health is to encourage people to have safer sex, and with accidents there is a need to understand why some environments are more dangerous than others and why some people are more susceptible to accidents than others (see Chapter 10). All these issues require changes in behaviour rather than new treatments by doctors.

There is barely a single medical intervention suggested within the key areas of the strategy. The strategy also mentions a number of other areas for attention including diabetes and breastfeeding, both of which require mainly psychological interventions. It is clear that the medical model has little to offer in these areas and the key issues are to do with personal change, behavioural change, and the health beliefs of the general public.

All of this leads us towards psychology and how it can be applied to health. Our approach to health has been changing so that the medical model is no longer so important, and the health needs of the nation have changed so that we now need to look at prevention rather than cure.

SPECIAL ISSUE:
The Health of the Nation

In 1992 the British Government published *The Health of the Nation*, which is its strategy for health in England. The strategy selects five key areas for action and sets national objectives and targets for these key areas. *The Health of the Nation* states that its overall goal is to encourage improvement in the general health of the population of England by:

adding years to life: an increase in life expectancy and reduction in premature death; and

adding life to years: increasing years lived free from ill-health, reducing or minimising the adverse effects of illness and disability, promoting healthy lifestyles, physical and social environments and, overall, improving quality of life. (from page 13)

The report states that success will come from (a) public policies, (b) healthy surroundings, (c) healthy lifestyles, and (d) high-quality health services. The report recognises that the government has a responsibility to promote good health in the general population as well as providing high-quality health care facilities.

The objectives for the five key areas are:

1 **Coronary heart disease and stroke:** to reduce the level of ill-health and death caused by coron-

ary heart disease and stroke, and the risk factors associated with them.

2 **Cancers:** to reduce ill-health and death caused by breast, cervical and skin cancer; to reduce ill-health and death caused by lung cancer – and other conditions associated with tobacco use – by reducing smoking prevalence and tobacco consumption throughout the population.

3 **Mental illness:** to reduce ill-health caused by mental illness.

4 **HIV/AIDS and sexual health:** to reduce the incidence of HIV infection; to reduce the incidence of other sexually transmitted diseases (STDs); to strengthen monitoring and surveillance; to provide effective services for diagnosis and treatment of HIV and other STDs; to reduce the number of unwanted pregnancies; to ensure the provision of effective family planning services for those who want them.

5 **Accidents:** to reduce ill-health, disability and death caused by accidents or unintentional injuries.

Each of the objectives is followed by a short list of main targets and a strategy for how these targets might be achieved. For example, one of the targets on coronary heart disease is 'to reduce death rates for both CHD and stroke in people under 65 by at least 40% by the year 2000' (page 18). This target has a number of risk factor targets including for example, 'to reduce the percentages of men and women who are obese by at least 25% for men and at least 33% for women by 2005' (page 20).

The targets and strategies include specific mention of alcohol consumption (it should go down) and the proportion of fat in food (it should also go down). Targets are set for various cancers, and smoking is heavily targeted for attention. There is a clear target for suicide reduction and for a reduction in accident deaths in particular age groups. Some of these targets appear quite attainable because the trend is already going in the appropriate direction. For example, the incidence of sexually transmitted disease (see Figure 1.3) has been falling steadily in recent years. Other targets, however, might be harder to achieve because the trend is in the opposite direction. For example, the incidence of suicide in young men is showing a steady rise all over the Western world.

The Health of the Nation is an important statement of health policy, and is relatively unique in the way it has outlined specific national targets. These targets will make it easy to evaluate the strategy because they are very specific and also have a clear time limit.

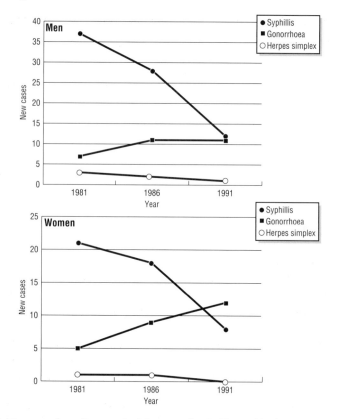

FIGURE 1.3 *New cases of sexually transmitted diseases in the UK (thousands). (Source: Social Trends, 1994. Crown copyright (1994)/Office for National Statistics)*

PSYCHOLOGY AND HEALTH

Psychology

Psychology is commonly defined as the scientific study of behaviour and experience. The term *scientific* refers to the way that psychology collects its evidence, which is through research, testing and verification. Psychology is concerned with what a person does (their behaviour) and what sense they make of the world (their experience).

Psychology has been developing as a subject for around 100 years, and the last 30 years have seen a very large growth in research activity and student numbers. The early psychologists such as William James and John Watson had very wide interests and explored a range of human activity. As the subject developed, the various fields within psychology became more specialised and more focused on restricted areas. These areas include:

- cognitive psychology which looks at mental processes such as perception, memory and thinking
- biological psychology which looks at the relationship between biological changes and psychological responses
- social cognition which looks at the how we make judgements about people and events
- developmental psychology which looks at how people grow up and change from the cradle to the grave
- social psychology which looks at our interactions and relationships
- individual differences which attempts to categorise and define people in terms of their personal qualities.

Psychology and health

Psychology has two special features that it brings to the study of health. The first feature is the breadth of the subject. The brief list above gives a flavour of the broad interests of psychologists. Within the same university department you might find one psychologist strapping magnets to a pigeon's head to see if it can navigate without information about the earth's magnetic fields, and another psychologist exploring the various behaviours associated with opening and closing doors. The study of health requires us to consider a broad range of issues and consider evidence from a wide range of sources.

The second important feature of psychology is its methodology. Psychology has 100 years of experience in trying to record and measure human behaviour and experience, and it has developed a wide range of useful methods that can be applied to health issues. The key areas of The Health of the Nation all require us to discover the following information – what do people do?, why do they do it?, how do they explain their behaviour?, and what would encourage them to change their behaviour? These are the sort of questions that psychologists are concerned with, so it has been a natural progression for them to become more involved in health.

The changing role of psychology in health was brought into sharper focus with the discovery of HIV/AIDS in the early 1980s. This disease poses a challenge for psychologists. Put bluntly, if you never have sex, and you never take intravenous drugs, and you never have blood transfusions, then, provided your mother was not infected when she carried you, you will not get AIDS. Solved that one then! Well, not quite, but the message is clear: you have to do something to get AIDS, and this is where psychologists come in. The disorder is transmitted behaviourally, and once you have the infection there is, as yet, no known cure. So, if we are to slow down the spread of HIV/AIDS, then we must change our behaviour and the behaviour of other people.

AIDS was always going to be different to other diseases. It made us discuss taboo topics like sex and drugs, it made us watch embarrassing television demonstrations of how to put a condom on a carrot, and it made us accept that the only protection from it is to change our behaviour. It also made us realise how little we know about human behaviour, and in particular human sexual behaviour (see Box 1.2).

Box 1.2 Interviews and sexual behaviour

The most important risk behaviours in the transmission of HIV/AIDS are sexual behaviour and drug-taking behaviour. The big problem is that we have very sketchy knowledge about these behaviours. The obvious way to get information is to interview people or give them questionnaires, but there are a number of problems in investigating personal issues like these.

The first systematic study of sexual behaviour was conducted by Kinsey (Kinsey, 1948, 1953) who used interviews to find out the sexual histories of five thousand men and five thousand women, from a mainly white American population. The interviews were mainly concerned with who people had sexual contact with, how often they did it and what they did. The publication of the results caused considerable controversy because they did not fit in with what people expected or what people thought of as acceptable. For example, the study showed that there was a much higher incidence of pre-marital sex, fetishism and homosexuality than society had expected. The hostile reaction to Kinsey's research led to him being virtually ostracised, yet his only crime was that he had applied systematic methods of sampling and data collection to an area which society deemed to be taboo. So, we have two problems when we want to find out about sexual behaviour: first, we do not have many reseach findings on it; and secondly, we probably don't want to know the answer anyway. A further problem arises because people are unwilling to disclose aspects of their sexual life. Imagine it from a personal point of view. Would you tell a researcher about the intimate details of your sexual behaviour? I have to admit that I would not.

Perhaps as a result of Kinsey's experience, the area of sexual behaviour has been much discussed but, until the incidence of AIDS, relatively little researched. The health messages surrounding HIV and AIDS, however, are all about changing sexual behaviour, but if we do not know how people conduct their sexual lives and how they negotiate sex with another person, it is very difficult to design health education programmes to change it.

A recent study of sexual behaviour in young people looked at the behaviours that have greatest risk of HIV/AIDS transmission (Breakwell, 1994). The researchers asked their sample a number of questions including whether they had any experience of heterosexual anal intercourse. Very little is known about this behaviour, probably because it is difficult to ask such a question, since this behaviour breaks a number of taboos and goes against our expectations of romantic love. (Just imagine how you would respond if someone asked you that question.) Breakwell and her associates found that by the age of 19, around 14% of their sample reported the behaviour. If this finding represents behaviour in the general population, then it might account for some of the transmission of HIV/AIDS in heterosexual sex.

> What psychologists have to face as scientists, and we have to face as people, is that when we look at human behaviour we will find out things that will make us very uncomfortable. The threat of HIV/AIDS has made us find out more information about risk behavious, and has broadened our understanding of human sexual behaviour.

Health psychology

Health psychology has developed as an area of research within psychology. It is very different from the traditional areas because instead of focusing on more and more detailed issues, it takes particular health problems and looks at the range of psychology that can be applied.

Health psychology is defined as:

> the educational, scientific, and professional contributions of the discipline of psychology to the promotion and maintenance of health, the prevention and treatment of illness, the identification of etiology and diagnostic correlates of health, illness and related dysfunction, and the improvement of the health care system and health policy formation. (Matarazzo, 1982)

Health psychology provides a basis for making sense of isolated and confusing bits of data. For example, it is difficult for doctors to understand why a large proportion of patients fail to adhere to certain aspects of their treatment programmes (Taylor, 1990; see Chapter 5 on compliance). Models from social psychology throw some light on this and suggest ways of responding to it.

Health psychology also provides models that point to new research areas and point directly to interventions that can improve the practice of health behaviour or the adjustment to illness.

Health psychology takes the position that all stages of health and illness are affected by biological, psychological and social factors – the biopsychosocial model.

The concerns of health psychology

Health psychology has been developing since about 1980 and it has developed a wide range of interests within health. What follows is a brief review of the concerns of health psychology.

Health promotion

The key question for health promotion is how we can encourage people to change their behaviour to enhance their health and prevent illness. Health promotion has usually concentrated on trying to change our attitudes, and you are probably familiar with various campaigns about healthy eating and unhealthy smoking. Many of these campaigns are based on the idea that our attitudes (or opinions) are the most important thing in our behaviour. Unfortunately, this is not the case and social psychology discovered that there is a poor relationship between our attitudes and our behaviour, so these campaigns are unlikely to be very successful.

Psychology can help health promotion with its theories of communication and research findings on how to get a message across. It can also help with its theories of behavioural change and decision-making. For example, why does a person with a heart condition continue to smoke despite believing that smoking is seriously damaging their health? The psychological models of change, such as the Health Belief Model (see pages 68–70) offer some suggestions for explaining this puzzle.

One problem in investigating health habits is the low correlation between health behaviours. Just because someone makes healthy choices in one area does not mean that they *usually* make healthy choices. For example, an athlete may train hard, watch his diet, and may not smoke, but he may drink to excess every weekend. One reason for this inconsistency is that each habit has a complex history of development, and a complex pattern of maintenance, change and relapse. The reason we develop a particular habit, such as smoking, is not the same as the reason for carrying on smoking or the reason for not giving up.

The message for health promotion is that it is not enough to appeal to everyone's common sense. It is necessary to understand why people make the choices they do and how they can be supported in changing them.

Do psychological states cause illness?

Or, to put it another way, is there a disease-prone personality type? The underlying psychological questions include:

1 Do people have consistent personalities?
2 Can psychologists measure these personalities?
3 Do these measurements predict health vulnerability?

Psychology has a long history of studying the first and second points, and it has created numerous personality tests for every conceivable personal quality.

A major research area has been around Friedman and Rosenman's description of the Type A behaviour syndrome (see pages 82–84) which is characterised by competitive drive, impatience, hostility and rapid speech and motor movements. This was thought to be associated with coronary heart disease, though recent research has found the connection to be weaker than originally thought.

Cognitive factors in health and illness

The cognitive factors that psychologists have looked at include the common-sense representations that we make about health, our attributions (explanations for behaviour or events), and our locus of control (see pages 174–176).

Research suggests that people have general ideas of illness against which they evaluate their particular symptoms and disorders. These common-sense representations of illness include the following dimensions:

- identity (the label of the illness and its symptoms)
- cause ('How did I get it?')
- consequences ('What will happen to me?')
- time frame ('How long will it take to get better?')
- cure ('What will make me better?')
  (Leventhal, 1982, cited in Taylor, 1990)

Whenever we feel unwell, we develop some ideas and explanations about what is wrong with us. We want a name for the illness, we want to blame someone for giving it to us, and we want to know what we've got to do to get better. When people are able to match their symptoms to their representations of illness then they are likely to take appropriate illness behaviour, like seeking treatment. If the match is not made, then the person is likely to delay doing anything about it, unlikely to carry out healthy behaviours and to follow the recommendations of health practitioners.

Stress and coping

The early work in psychology looked at the fight-or-flight response to danger, and took a largely biological approach. More recently there has been a growing interest in the psychological judgements we make that affect our experience of stress. For example, the same event might be exhilarating to one person and stressful to another because of the different ways they interpret what is going on. A classic example of this is shopping in a crowded shopping mall. I know many people who adore this activity, but it makes me feel homicidal.

Psychologists look at stress, how we respond to it, how we make sense of it and how we cope with it. They have tried to develop ways of reducing stress and ways of enhancing people's ability to cope. As well as looking at stress itself, psychologists also look at how stress affects the development of other illnesses. All these issues are dealt with in more detail in Chapters 2 and 3.

Lifestyle and health

There are numerous factors in the way we live that contribute to ill-health. Some, such as risk-taking, are defined by our social reference group. Many are difficult to investigate because of the complex way we conduct our everyday lives. Some of the issues examined under this heading include substance use, nutrition, exercise, and accidents.

Using the health services

The way that we use the health services is an area of study in itself. Some of the important issues are:

- (non)compliance with health requests (see Chapter 5)
- patient–health worker interactions, for example, the consultation between doctor and patient (see Chapter 9)
- hospitals, and how they are experienced by the consumer.

Pain

Pain is a common and costly health problem. There are a number of theories of pain, the most popular of which is the Gate Control Theory proposed by Melzack and Wall in 1965. One of the problems in pain research is measurement, and psychologists have developed a number of measuring instruments. As we will see in Chapter 11, pain is very difficult to define and it is even more difficult to identify how and why we experience it.

Psychologists have been involved in improving our understanding of pain and also developing procedures for pain control that go beyond the simple administration of drugs.

Issues associated with chronic diseases

Chronic diseases bring their own array of psychological issues. Some of the issues are shared with a range of diseases, but each disease has its own special concerns. For example, having to adjust to a new body image is a feature of many disorders – for example, losing a limb in a car accident, or developing the disfiguring scars of Kaposi's sarcoma (a common feature of AIDS). These two conditions share the problem of adjusting to a different appearance, but they differ on a range of other psychological variables, for example, the way that family and friends deal with this change in the patient's appearance.

In this text it is not possible to do anything but scratch the surface of this vast area of research, but I hope that you are able to see some of the psychological variables that influence the development, experience and treatment of chronic disorders.

SUMMARY

Health psychology is a relatively new discipline, and has really only developed since the early 1980s. It aims to contribute to all aspects of health care, though clearly it is most valuable in the areas of preventive medicine and adjustment to serious illness. The biopsychosocial model provides a way of combining the advances of medical science with the insights of psychological theory and practice.

chapter two

STRESS

CHAPTER OVERVIEW

The CONTEXT looks at the various definitions of stress and reviews some of the early work by psychologists. This work includes studies of arousal such as the fight-or-flight syndrome and also the Yerkes–Dodson Law. It also includes the general adaptation syndrome first described by Hans Selye. The PSYCHOLOGICAL CONTRIBUTIONS include the models of stress – for example, the work of Folkman and Lazarus – and also the personal qualities thought to have an influence on stress such as hardiness. The SPECIAL ISSUE looks at post-traumatic stress disorder and the disaster of *The Herald of Free Enterprise*, the P&O ferry that sank in Zeebrugge harbour with massive loss of life. APPLICATIONS: MEASURING STRESS looks at the problems of trying to quantify how stressed people are, and considers a number of attempts to do this including the measurement of stressful life events.

CONTEXT

Stress – who needs it? Well the strange answer is that we probably all do. We seek it out as much as we avoid it. Nearly everyone could have an easier life if they didn't work so hard, play so hard, do so much or think so much. So what is this feeling of stress and why do we have it?

One of the first things to do is to define our terms. As ever in psychology, this is not an easy task, but it is helpful to think of the stress experience as being made up of two major components: *stressors* and the *stress response*.

Stressors are stimuli that require a person to make some form of adaptation or adjustment. These stressors usually bring out a relatively stereotyped set of biological and psychological responses – the stress response.

Stressors can be external, for example, environmental changes such as heat, crowding, or noise. They can also be social situations such as difficulties with a loved one, or contact with a hated one. These are events that happen outside of yourself but have a stressful effect. On the other hand, stressors can be internal (inside yourself); for example, pain can create a stress response, as can your thoughts and your feelings.

The relationship between stressors, the stress response and our experience of stress is not straightforward. We might suggest that heat is a stressor that will bring out a stress response so that we feel under stress. However, those of you who have ever chased the sun on your holidays will know that heat, a beach and a cool drink are blissfully relaxing. So the effect of stressors is affected by the situation we are in and the sense we make of what is happening. The position is further complicated by the fact that some stressors can be viewed as positive, for example, many people seek out big crowds to enhance their sense of excitement. Also, there are large individual differences in our responses to stressors. One person might dissolve into a flood of tears when they miss a train whereas another person might shrug their shoulders and have a beer while they wait for the next one.

All this means that it will not be simple to define and measure stressors. Likewise, the stress response is quite complex and is made up of numerous physiological, cognitive, affective and behavioural components

Early work on stress

Psychology's early work on stress concentrated on the biological aspects, and in particular, on the process of arousal, the fight or flight response and the general adaptation syndrome.

Arousal

The concept of arousal is very important to our understanding of stress. It is concerned with the activities of the sympathetic division of the autonomic nervous system, and how they affect our bodies and our experience. The function of the sympathetic division is to stimulate the body into action, and it does this by activating a number of physiological processes. These processes create or maintain alertness and energy by, for example, releasing stored sugar into the bloodstream to fuel muscle activity, increasing the heart rate so that blood reaches the muscles more quickly, and stimulating the release of the hormone adrenaline, which then acts to maintain this level of activity in the body.

States of arousal are often accompanied by highly emotional and highly active states. When we feel very angry, or very frightened, then we are likely to be in a state of bodily arousal. The feelings and the arousal tend to interact with each other, so that the arousal enhances our feelings and our feelings enhance our arousal. A similar state of arousal is also associated with less active emotions such as anxiety and worry, with the level of anxiety linking closely with the level of arousal.

Our level of arousal has an affect on our performance at a variety of tasks. If we are too relaxed (under-aroused) then we do not perform well, and if we are too anxious (over-aroused) then our performance will also suffer. There would seem to be an optimum level of arousal for our behaviour to be successful. This is often referred to as the Yerkes–Dodson Law (see Figure 2.1) which simply states that arousal improves performance, but only up to a point. Beyond that point, performance will decline. The optimal level of arousal varies for different tasks, with complex tasks showing an earlier performance decrement than simple tasks for the same level of arousal.

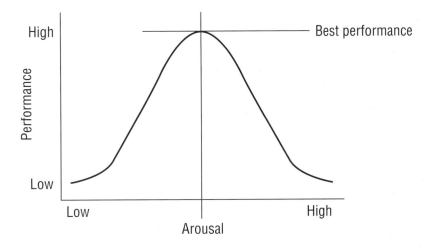

FIGURE 2.1 *The Yerkes–Dodson Law*

The fight-or-flight response

When we are confronted with a very stressful situation, for example, witnessing a road accident, then we experience an immediate physiological response. We can feel the blood drain from our faces (this is very visible in white people), our stomachs feel as if they have turned over, and our muscles tense. This is sometimes known as the fight-or-flight response, because our body is now prepared for activity – either by fighting to defend ourselves or by running away.

The response develops very quickly but it takes a long time to subside. This means that we are likely to remain in a heightened state of arousal and anxiety for some time after the initial event. Also, a person might become more susceptible to an arousal response following an unpleasant event. For example, after someone has been burgled they may find it too difficult to sleep and find that every noise at night produces a feeling of anxiety. This means that some people stay in a state of heightened arousal for a considerable time, and this might have some long-term consequences.

The general adaptation syndrome

From his early observations in the 1920s, Hans Selye suggested that we have the same bodily reactions to a range of stressful circumstances. He observed that when someone suffers from severe loss of blood, or an infectious disease, or from cancer, then they lose their appetite, their muscular strength and their ambition to do anything. They are likely to lose weight and also to 'look ill'. Originally he thought of this as a 'syndrome of just being sick' (Selye, 1973), but later in his research he developed the concept of the General Adaptation Syndrome.

This syndrome suggests that there are three stages that describe the response to long-term stress – the alarm reaction, the stage of resistance, and finally, the stage of exhaustion (see Box 2.1). This suggests that following our initial strong reaction to a threatening event, we are able to adjust to a higher level of arousal in order to resist the threat. However, there is a limit to how long we can maintain this arousal and eventually our body will take no more and we become exhausted (see Figure 2.2). This explanation has some appeal because it does seem to describe many people's experience of long-term stress, and it is also supported by some observations of biological changes that take place under stress. However, the main weakness of the idea of the general adaptation syndrome is that it does not take any psychological or behavioural variables into account and these are very important in our experience of stress.

Box 2.1 The general adaptation syndrome

1 Alarm

Like the fight-or-flight response, the function of this stage is to mobilise the body's resources. Initially, arousal drops below normal, then it rapidly rises above normal. The body cannot sustain the alarm reaction for long, and if it continues unabated then the organism will die within days or even hours.

2 Resistance

The body adapts to the stressor. Physiological arousal declines but is still above normal. The organism shows few outward signs of stress, but the ability to resist new stressors is impaired and the organism becomes vulnerable to diseases of adaptation such as ulcers and high blood pressure. People also experience feelings of fatigue and general weakness. Long-term psychological effects that have been identified include increased irritability and a tendency towards a pessimistic outlook.

3 Exhaustion

Eventually the body's energy reserves become depleted and the ability to resist declines. If stress continues, then disease, damage and death can follow.

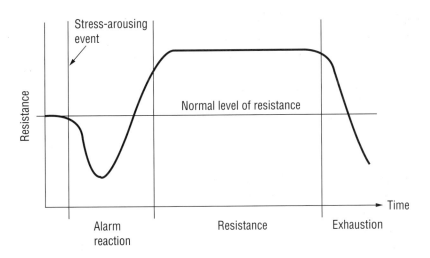

FIGURE 2.2 *The general adaptation syndrome*

The early work on stress looked mainly at biological responses in the person and so adopted the medical model (see Chapter 1). More recently psychology has taken a very different approach that looks at the interaction between these biological responses and the psychological changes within a person and also the social context in which they are living (the biopsychosocial model).

PSYCHOLOGICAL CONTRIBUTIONS

Models of stress

Sarafino (1994) defines stress as '... the condition that results when the person/environment transaction lead the individual to perceive a discrepancy – whether real or not – between the demands of a situation and the resources of the person's biological, psychological and social systems.' (page 74).

This definition looks beyond the biological changes and includes the social and psychological changes as well. One of the key features of this approach is to look at the gap between what we think we have to do to deal with a situation and what we think we are able to do. This gap depends on how we appraise a situation and how we appraise ourselves. Lazarus and Folkman (1984) suggest that we make two cognitive appraisals: first, whether the stressor or event poses a threat (the primary appraisal) and, second, whether we will be able to cope with it (the secondary appraisal) – see Figure 2.3 overleaf.

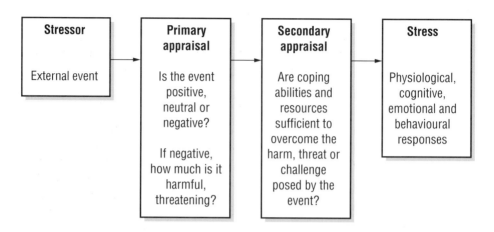

FIGURE 2.3 *The experience of stress*

Cognitive appraisal

In the primary appraisal we judge whether the event is positive, negative or neutral. So, developing a cold one evening might be positive (because you won't have to go to work or college tomorrow), it might be neutral (because you will be able to carry on with whatever you intended to do whether you have a cold or not), or it might be stressful (because you have an examination or interview tomorrow and you think you will not be able to do your best).

If we judge that the event is negative, then we make further judgements on three issues: first, how much *harm* has already occurred ('Oh no, it's already a nightmare!'); second, what is the *threat* of further harm ('Tomorrow will be a disaster!'); and, third, what sort of *challenge* does this event offer ('I'll boldly go where no one has gone before!').

In the secondary appraisal we have to make judgements about our own abilities and our current state of mind and health. It doesn't necessarily follow on after the primary appraisal and it sometimes might even affect the primary appraisal, so if you make the assessment that you are in a poor state of mind (secondary appraisal of coping ability), this might lead you to see a normally safe event as being quite threatening (primary appraisal). For example, if you don't feel able to cope with people today, then a visit to the newsagent for your *Daily Mirror* could appear quite taxing.

Personal qualities affecting appraisal of stress

Our appraisal of stress can be affected by our personal qualities, our personal circumstances, and also by the type of event that is causing the stress. Among the personal qualities that psychologists have studied is how *hardy* we are. Kobasa (1979) suggests that we can identify personality characteristics that separate out people who get ill under stress and people who remain healthy.

She calls the collection of these characteristics *hardiness*.

Hardiness is made up of three components – control, commitment and challenge. *Control* refers to the belief that a person can influence events in their life (see the section on locus of control on pages 174–176), *commitment* refers to a person's sense of purpose or involvement in their life, and *challenge* refers to the tendency to see problems as an opportunity for personal growth.

Support for the connection between hardiness and health came from a study by Kobasa (1979) who looked at the health of executives in a large American corporation. She used a questionnaire to divide the executives into two groups, one which had experienced a high level of stress and a high level of illness, and one which had experienced high stress but without much illness. When she assessed the hardiness of all the executives she found that the low illness group appeared to be hardier than the high illness group.

Although relating personal qualities to stress potential is quite appealing there are a number of problems with it. First, the many attempts within psychology to identify personality all run into difficulties because of the complexity and the changing nature of an individual's personality. It does not seem to be possible to put people into neat boxes and say 'You are a ***** type of person', and it is not very useful to try to do this. Second, much of the work on hardiness has been carried out on one narrow group of people – white, professional, American men – and it is not clear whether other groups would show similar results.

Other factors affecting appraisal of stress

There are a number of factors in our personal circumstances that will affect our appraisal of a stressful event. These include the amount of social support we experience, and the amount of resources we think we have at our disposal. These issues are discussed further on pages 36–40.

There are a number of dimensions of a stressful event that are thought to have an influence on how we appraise it, including whether it is negative, controllable or predictable, and whether it is ambiguous. It is generally thought that negative events are more likely to be experienced as stressful than positive events. For example, it is probably more taxing getting married than it is getting a divorce but the latter is more likely to be described as stressful. It is also thought that ambiguous events are experienced as more stressful than clear-cut events. If you are not sure of what is really going on, and therefore unclear about what you can do to affect the situation, then you are likely to experience more stress.

Feelings of control and predictability can relieve the stressful quality of an unpleasant event. An example of this is a study of commuters by Lundberg (1976). Lundberg studied male passengers on a commuter train, comparing their responses during journeys made in crowded and uncrowded trains, and measuring arousal by analysing levels of adrenaline in urine. Despite the fact that even under the most crowded conditions there were seats available for everyone, he found that levels of adrenaline increased as more people rode the train, indicating that people were becoming more aroused.

On the issue of control, Lundberg also discovered that the level of adrenaline was not just to do with the number of people on the train, but was also to do with when the passenger joined it. Those who got on the train at the first stop experienced fewer negative reactions than passengers who joined the train halfway to the city, despite the fact that the early boarders had a longer journey (over an hour compared to just over half an hour). The important issue here seemed to have everything to do with choice of seat: passengers who could choose where they sat experienced less stress than those who could not. So it seems that having some control over their environment made the horrors of commuter travel easier to bear.

SPECIAL ISSUE:
Post-traumatic stress disorder and The Herald of Free Enterprise

Dramatic events sometimes leave people with very unpleasant stress reactions. This has been observed for a long time, though only recently has it been identified as a serious condition and given the label 'post-traumatic stress disorder'. During the First World War (1914–18), a number of soldiers were discovered away from their positions, disorientated and seemingly confused. Many were treated as deserters and shot by their own military authorities. It is now thought that many were suffering from shell-shock, which is an example of post-traumatic stress disorder.

An example of a disaster that created post-traumatic stress disorder is the sinking of *The Herald of Free Enterprise*. On 6 March 1987, a 'roll-on/roll-off' ferry owned by the British company P&O sailed from Zeebrugge harbour on route for Dover. She left port without securing her bow doors and immediately began to take in water. When she made a hard turn in the harbour, the water in the hold destabilised the ship and it rolled over, with the loss of 188 lives. The events leading up to the sinking are a psychological case study in themselves (see Appendix 1), but it is the reactions of the other passengers and the relatives of the victims that we are interested in here. These reactions are reviewed by Hodgkinson and Stewart (1991) and the points below all come from this source.

Post-traumatic stress disorder was first described in the third edition of the Diagnostic and Statistical Manual of Mental Disorders of the American Psychiatric Association (DSM-III) in 1980. The description attempts to provide criteria so that it is possible to distinguish between a 'normal' reaction to an unpleasant event and an 'abnormal' reaction. It is defined as having three main groups of symptoms:

1 Re-experiencing phenomena, for example recurrent and intrusive distressing memories of the traumatic event or situation. It was originally thought that children do not experience intrusive imagery but most of the children involved in the *Herald of Free Enterprise* disaster reported intrusive thoughts and some experienced full-blown flashbacks.

2 Avoidance or numbing reactions, such as efforts to avoid the thoughts or feelings associated with the trauma, and feeling detached or estranged from other people. Many survivors of the ferry 'not only shunned the prospect of ferry travel again but could not even bear to see the sea, and in the immediate aftermath of the disaster could not face taking a bath or shower.' (page 14)

3 Symptoms of increased arousal, such as difficulty in staying asleep, irritability and outbursts of anger.

Post-traumatic stress disorder is cyclical and the symptoms can disappear and reappear. They can also appear some time after the event, even several months or years later, and the delayed versions of the condition are no less severe.

The victims of the *Herald* disaster who were assessed for compensation purposes during the first year after the disaster all showed high levels of distress. 'All were found to be suffering from "recognisable psychological distress", with 53 per cent assessed as moderately to severely depressed, and 90 per cent as suffering from PTSD' (page 41). Common wisdom suggests that counselling is a 'good thing' in these circumstances, but there is a considerable amount of controversy as to whether therapy for disaster victims offers any benefit. For example, a follow-up study of the survivors and the bereaved from the *Herald* disaster asked for an evaluation of the quality of the social support after the disaster. The people who reported that the support was 'mixed' or 'unhelpful' fared no worse than the people who reported it as 'helpful'.

APPLICATIONS: MEASURING STRESS

One of the most important contributions that psychology can make is the development of measuring techniques. If we want to investigate stress and we want to develop stress reduction techniques then we need to have some way of measuring how much stress people are experiencing. If we continue with the division of the stress experience into stressors and the stress response then we can look at measures for these in turn.

Measuring stressors

There have been numerous attempts to measure how stressful particular events are, including the following three ways:

1 Measuring the effects of stressors by looking at performance on simple behavioural tasks, or by using self-report scales (asking people to rate how stressful an event was)
2 Stressful life events (see below)
3 Social environment or social climate.

Moos (1973) suggested that social environments, like people, have unique 'personalities' – some are supportive and others are more controlling. All environments will have physiological, psychological and behavioural effects on the people interacting with them. Moos and Moos (1981) looked at a number of social climates including psychiatric wards, college dormitories, prisons, work groups, and families, and described the general characteristics of the environments. A summary of their general findings is shown in Box 2.2. Research has suggested that positive environments will enhance normal development and reduce recovery time from illness, but responsibility, work pressure and change can increase the likelihood of illness or subjective distress.

Box 2.2 Work environment scale: dimension descriptions

	Relationship dimensions
Involvement	the extent to which employees are concerned about and committed to their jobs
Peer cohesion	the extent to which employees are friendly and supportive to one another
Supervisor support	the extent to which management is supportive of employees and encourages employees to be supportive of one another
	Personal growth
Autonomy	the extent to which employees are encouraged to be self-sufficient and make their own decisions
Task orientation	the degree of emphasis on good planning, efficiency and getting the job done
Work pressure	the degree to which the pressure of work and time dominate the job milieu

	Systems maintenance and systems change
Clarity	the extent to which employees know what to expect in their daily routine and how explicitly rules and policies are communicated
Control	the extent to which management uses rules and pressures to keep employees under control
Innovation	the degree of emphasis on variety, change and new approaches physical comfort
Physical comfort	the extent to which the physical surroundings contribute to a pleasant work environment

Source: R.H. Moos and Moos (1981), cited in Feuerstein, Labbe and Kuczmierczyk (1986)

Stressful life events

The starting point for most discussions on stressful life events is the Social Readjustment Rating Scale developed by Holmes and Rahe (1967). They looked at what events and experiences affect our level of stress, and they developed a scale to measure this. The scale looks at the stress caused by major life events (the sort of events that we experience as difficult to deal with) and is based on previous research which had found that some social events requiring a change in lifestyle were associated with the onset of illness. They developed the scale by asking nearly 400 adults to rate 43 different life events for the amount of adjustment needed to deal with them (Table 2.1).

The researchers compared the responses of the different groups of people within their sample and found a startling degree of agreement. They compared the responses of different age groups, men and women, Catholics and Protestants, and in all cases found very high correlations in their ratings of stressful events. The one exception was the correlation of black subjects with white subjects which, although still quite high, was much lower than the other correlations.

To measure your personal stress score with the Social Readjustment Rating Scale, you tick off the events that have occurred to you in a given time, usually 12 months or 24 months, and add up the readjustment values. According to Holmes and Rahe, the higher the number you end up with, the more chance you have of developing an illness. A number of studies, by Holmes and Rahe in particular, have shown a connection between high ratings and subsequent illness and accident, though according to Sarafino (1994) the correlation between rating and illness is really quite weak ($r = 0.3$).

There are a number of problems with this method of measuring stress, and before reading on you might like to look at the scale and see what criticisms you can make of it as an attempt to measure stressful life events.

Table 2.1 Social Readjustment Rating Scale

Rank	Life event	Mean value
1	Death of spouse	100
2	Divorce	73
3	Marital separation	65
4	Jail term	63
5	Death of close family member	63
6	Personal injury or illness	53
7	Marriage	50
8	Fired at work	47
9	Marital reconciliation	45
10	Retirement	45
11	Change in health of family member	44
12	Pregnancy	40
13	Sex difficulties	39
14	Gain of new family member	39
15	Business readjustment	39
16	Change in financial state	38
17	Death of close friend	37
18	Change to different line of work	36
19	Change in number of arguments with spouse	35
20	Mortgage over $10,000	31
21	Foreclosure of mortgage or loan	30
22	Change in responsibilities at work	29
23	Son or daughter leaving home	29
24	Trouble with in-laws	29
25	Outstanding personal achievement	28
26	Wife begins or stops work	26
27	Begin or end school	26
28	Change in living conditions	25
29	Revision of personal habits	24
30	Trouble with boss	23
31	Change in work hours or conditions	20
32	Change in residence	20
33	Change in schools	20
34	Change in recreation	19
35	Change in church activities	19
36	Change in social activities	18
37	Mortgage or loan less than $10,000	17
38	Change in sleeping habits	16
39	Change in number of family get-togethers	15
40	Change in eating habits	15
41	Vacation	13
42	Christmas	12
43	Minor violations of the law	11

Source: Holmes and Rahe (1967)

Problems with the Social Readjustment Rating Scale

- Major life events are quite rare and many people will score near to zero.
- Some of the items in the scale are vague or ambiguous.
- Some of the items will have greater value for some groups in society rather than others.
- There are large individual differences in our ability to cope with stressful events.
- There are large cultural and sub-cultural differences in our experience of events.
- The value of events changes with time and changing social customs

It is worth noting, however, that the measurement of psychological phenomena is a singularly difficult enterprise, and it is usually easier to come up with criticisms of existing attempts than to devise better ways of doing things.

The study of the affect of life events on stress and illness generated a considerable amount of research, not least because the Social Readjustment Rating Scale developed by Holmes and Rahe provides a relatively straightforward way of measuring stress. It also conforms to everyday notions of the effect of dramatic events in our lives. In accounts of personal experience recorded in news reports, it is not unknown for people to say how a particular event, such as unexpected bereavement, or desertion by a loved one, has 'shattered my life'. Kanner et al. (1981), however, argue that the minor stressors and pleasures of everyday life might have a more significant effect on health than the big, traumatic events assessed by the Holmes and Rahe scale, particularly in view of the cumulative nature of stress.

Kanner et al. (1981) developed a scale to explore these small events, which they called the Hassles and Uplifts Scale (see Box 2.3). They administered the checklist to 100 middle-aged adults once a month for ten months. The Hassles Scale was found to be a better predictor of psychological problems than life event scores, both at the time and later. Scores on the Uplifts Scale, however, only seemed to relate to symptoms in women. The men in the study seemed relatively unaffected by uplifts.

Box 2.3   The Hassles and Uplifts of middle-aged adults

Ten most frequently expressed hassles of middle-aged adults

1 Concerns about weight
2 Health of a family member
3 Rising prices of common goods
4 Home maintenance
5 Too many things to do
6 Misplacing or losing things
7 Outside home maintenance

8 Property, investment or taxes
9 Crime
10 Physical appearance

Ten most frequently expressed uplifts of middle-aged adults

1 Relating well to spouse or lover
2 Relating well with friends
3 Completing a task
4 Feeling healthy
5 Getting enough sleep
6 Eating out
7 Meeting your responsibilities
8 Visiting, phoning or writing to someone
9 Spending time with the family
10 Home pleasing to you

Source: Kanner et al. (1981)

Measuring the stress response

The attempts to measure various aspects of our responses to stress include biochemical measures, behavioural observation, and cognitive measures.

The *biochemical research* has looked at the effects of stress on various processes in the body, such as those associated with adrenaline, noradrenaline and also the immune system. *Behavioural observation* has included work on specific behaviours such as facial expressions, rate of speech, posture and nail biting. It has also included a number of self-report measures on topics as diverse as marital satisfaction and frequency of urination. The *cognitive measures* have looked at the perceived control someone experiences over their life, their perceived level of arousal (often different to the actual level of physiological arousal), mood and attitudes.

In health psychology, there have been a number of stress measures developed to investigate the response to illness, injuries, and medical treatments. An example of this approach is the Perceived Stress Scale (Cohen, Kamarck and Mermelstein, 1983) which asks people to rate 14 items on a five-point scale for frequency of feeling stress during the previous month. For example, one of the items is 'In the last month, how often did you have to deal with irritating life hassles?'

The general problem with self-report measures such as this is that they ask for simple responses from people and so are unable to capture the richness of human experience. The alternative is to use interviewing techniques and sophisticated coding of people's responses. One of the best-known measures in this field is the Life Events and Difficulties Schedule (Brown and Harris,

1989). This schedule looks at a range of issues to do with health, employ-ment, social role, etc., but requires trained interviewers and trained judges to operate it.

Other methods of measuring stress

There have been numerous attempts to measure stress, and the items described above just give a flavour of this effort. They are all limited in some way but they all provide some clues to the experience we have of stress. One of the problems with many stress measures is that they make just one record-ing (a snapshot) of the stress level. However, the experience of stress is very variable throughout the day, and also from day to day. In order to find out the pattern of changes in stress, psychologists have tried a number of techniques, such as diary methods, where people make a number of recordings over a period of time of their feelings of stress, or responses to stress. For example, Gulian et al. (1990) carried out a study of the pattern of stress in British dri-vers. The drivers completed a number of psychometric tests (for example Rotter's Internal-External Locus of Control Scale) and filled in a diary of their feelings while driving over five days. They found that drivers experienced more stress in the evening and midweek. They also found that daily driving stress varied with age and experience, as well as with health condition, sleep quality, and driving conditions, and it was also affected by the driver's overall perception of driving as a stressful activity.

Sometimes psychologists try to combine a variety of methods to obtain a clearer picture of stress. An example of this is a study by Douglas et al. (1988), who used a diary method and physiological measures to look at stress in fire-fighters. They studied a stratified sample of 100 fire-fighters from 12 different fire stations. The heart rhythm of each fire-fighter was recorded for at least 48 hours while they were at work using a portable elec-trocardiogram, and the results were analysed to give a 'ventricular cardiac strain score'. They were also asked to keep a diary during this time of stress-ful events. Higher scores were found in those under stress due to the number of call-outs, their level of seniority, and the stressful events they recorded in their diaries.

SUMMARY

Stress is a part of our everyday vocabulary but it is difficult for us to accurately define and measure this quality. It is clear, however, that biological responses to threatening events, and our personal experience of stress, have an affect on our general level of health. In some of the following chapters you will see how stress is thought to be a factor in a wide range of health disorders.

chapter three

Chapter Overview

The CONTEXT looks at Freud's description of defence mechanisms and goes on to explore modern descriptions of coping strategies such as the one offered by Billings and Moos. The PSYCHOLOGICAL CONTRIBUTIONS include a review of our resources for coping, and a discussion on social support and how it affects our health. The SPECIAL ISSUE looks at the way we cope with bereavement, and the gap between everyday explanations of the grieving process and the findings of psychological research. APPLICATIONS: IMPROVING COPING AND REDUCING STRESS contains descriptions of a variety of techniques including biofeedback, mental imagery, rational emotive therapy, and stress inoculation.

Context

'I can handle it' we might say when we are confronted with a horrible event. We mean that we have the psychological defences to protect ourselves from whatever is going on. The concept of psychological protection can be traced back to the work of Freud (1856–1939), who suggested that we have a number of defence mechanisms that protect us from anxiety and relieve tensions. According to Freud these processes deny or distort reality and operate in our unconscious mind. He believed that they were basically unhealthy processes that created emotional problems and self-defeating behaviour. Some of the major defence mechanisms identified by Freud and his associates are shown in Figure 3.1, and it is interesting to note how much we still use these terms in modern descriptions of coping – for example, 'displacement' and 'denial'.

The recent work on coping mainly uses the model of stress proposed by Lazarus and Folkman (1989) which is described in Chapter 2. They suggest that we assess stress by appraising the threat of the stressful event and also our ability to cope with it. They define coping as the '...cognitive and behavioural efforts to manage specific external and/or internal demands that are appraised as taxing or exceeding the resources of the person' (Folkman and Lazarus, 1990).

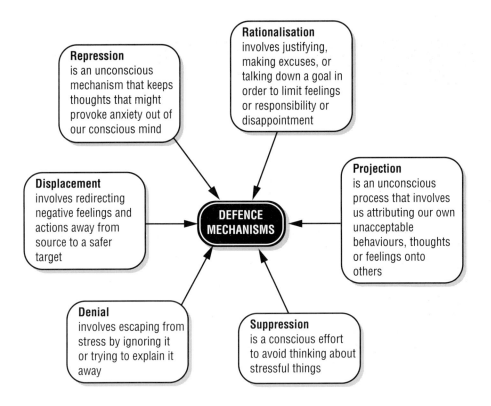

FIGURE 3.1 *Examples of defence mechanisms that are said to protect us from anxiety by distorting or denying reality*

Coping strategies

There are many ways of coping with stressful situations and some methods are more effective than others. This has led psychologists to try and identify the major coping strategies (the ways that we cope) to look for their relative effectiveness in various stressful situations. Coping strategies are often divided into two classes: problem-focused strategies which are directed at changing the situation that is creating the problem; and emotion-focused strategies, which are directed at managing the distress rather than changing the situation. Box 3.1 overleaf lists the coping strategies identified by Folkman et al. (1986) with some examples of each strategy.

Billings and Moos (1981) looked at the various attempts to classify coping, and combined them into one scale. They looked at the way that people avoided stress (the defence mechanisms approach), they also looked at the approach by Folkman and Lazarus (looking at the focus of the coping) and they added a further classification of the method of coping (either cognitive or behavioural). They collected data using a range of measures including

Box 3.1 Coping strategies

PROBLEM-FOCUSED STRATEGIES

Confrontive coping
- I stood my ground and fought for what I wanted
- I expressed anger to the person who caused the problem

Planful problem-solving
- I knew what had to be done so I doubled my efforts to make things work
- I made a plan of action and followed it

EMOTION-FOCUSED STRATEGIES

Distancing
- I made light of the situation and refused to get too serious about it
- I went on as if nothing had happened
- I tried to forget the whole thing

Self-controlling
- I tried to keep my feelings to myself
- I kept others from knowing how bad things were

Seeking social support
- I talked to someone to find out more about the situation
- I asked a respected friend for advice

Accepting responsibility
- I criticised myself
- I made a promise to myself that things would be different next time

Escape-avoidance
- I wished that the situation would go away or somehow be over with
- I hoped a miracle would happen
- I tried to make myself feel better by eating, drinking etc.

Positive reappraisal
- I changed or grew as a person in a good way
- I came out of the experience better than I went in
- I rediscovered what is important in life

their coping responses table (see Table 3.1), where people were asked to think of a recent personal crisis or stressful event and say how they dealt with the event.

Billings and Moos found that it was impossible to identify 'positive' or 'negative' types of coping, because they all seemed to be equally successful or unsuccessful. We have to develop a style of coping that suits us as a person, and also the particular event we are dealing with. They did note, however, that lower levels of stress were associated with active coping strategies (doing something about it) and also with less examples of avoidance responses. However, even this general statement does not apply to all circumstances, as shown below in the work by Cairns and Wilson.

Table 3.1 Coping with a personal crisis

Coping items	Method of coping			Focus of coping	
	Active cognitive	Active behavioural	Avoidance	Problem-focused	Emotion-focused
Tried to see positive side	X				X
Tried to step back from situation and be more objective	X				X
Prayed for guidance and strength	X				X
Took things one step at a time	X			X	
Considered several alternatives for handling the problem	X			X	
Drew on my past experiences: I was in a similar situation before	X			X	
Tried to find out more about the situation		X		X	
Talked with a professional person (e.g. doctor, clergy, etc.)		X		X	
Took some positive action		X		X	
Talked with spouse or another relative about the problem		X		X	
Talked with a friend about the situation		X			
Exercised more		X			X
Prepared for the worst			X		X
Sometimes took it out on other people when I felt angry or depressed			X		X
Tried to reduce the tension by eating more			X		X
Tried to reduce tension by smoking more			X		X
Kept my feelings to myself			X		X
Got busy with other things in order to keep my mind off the problem					X
Didn't worry about it; figured everything would probably work out fine					X

It is possible to observe the effectiveness of various coping strategies in real-life situations. For example, Cairns and Wilson (1984) found that people who lived in areas in Northern Ireland which had a high degree of sectarian violence during the long period of the Troubles tended to have a higher level of psychological disorder than people who lived in more peaceful areas, particularly if they had a realistic appraisal of the amount of violence that was going on. But those who adopted a coping mechanism which the researchers termed *denial*, in which they inaccurately perceived there to be relatively little violence, seemed to have lower levels of disturbance. What this seems to suggest is that if you are in a situation where reality really is threatening, violent and intolerable, then being unrealistic about how dangerous it is may help you to cope!

In a later study, Wilson and Cairns (1992) used an adapted version of the Lazarus and Folkman checklist to explore differences in coping among people in different areas of Northern Ireland. They had found that their denial mechanism linked with the coping strategy of *distancing* identified by the checklist. Residents of the high-violence areas which the researchers had surveyed earlier seemed to be particularly inclined to use this coping strategy. But a comparison with the residents of Enniskillen, after a particularly violent and unexpected bomb explosion that was targeted at civilians, rather than soldiers or property, showed that they did not use distancing to any great extent. Instead, they used the more active styles of coping involving attempts at positive reappraisal of the situation – at the time it seemed as though Enniskillen might provide a turning point leading to a decrease in violence – and seeking social support from others.

PSYCHOLOGICAL CONTRIBUTIONS

Psychological contributions to the issue of coping have looked at the factors that make us more able or less able to cope with stressful events. If we go back to the interactive model of stress described in Chapter 2 (pages 21–24) and add coping to it (see Figure 3.2) then we are interested in the coping strategies that people use and the resources, social support, other stressors and personal qualities that affect these strategies. In this section we will look at resources and social support. The issues around stressors like life events were covered in Chapter 2 (pages 27–30), and some of the issues around personal qualities are covered in the discussions on hardiness (Chapter 2, pages 22–23) and locus of control (Chapter 12, pages 174–176).

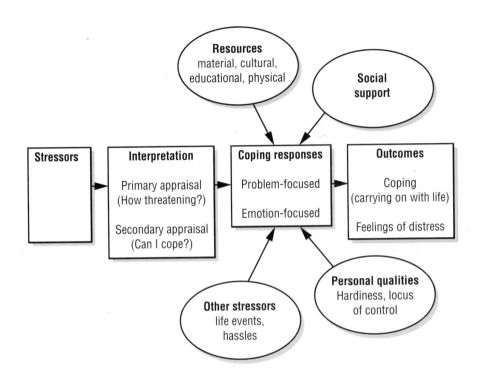

FIGURE 3.2 *Stress and coping*

Resources for coping

There has been a growing interest in the resources that allow us to cope with most of life's stressors. These are summarised in Sheridan and Radmacher (1992) under the following headings:

- **Material resources,** which basically come down to money. Wealth alleviates and helps people to avoid many of the stressors in life. Money buys warmth, food, relaxation, prestige, safety and good health care.
- **Physical resources,** such as strength, health and attractiveness can all help someone cope with stressors.
- **Intra-personal resources** are the inner strengths that help us deal with stressors, for example our self-esteem. In everyday speech we might refer to these qualities as 'character' or 'determination' or 'strength of will'.
- **Educational resources** refer to the value of knowledge. If we know about health risks we are able to moderate our behaviour to reduce the risks and cope with the stress.
- **Cultural resources** are the means by which we give meaning to our lives, by being part of a cultural group that has a history and purpose that goes beyond here and now.

Social support

Social support is something we all want, and when we are in trouble we often experience the feeling that we do not receive enough of it. But what do we mean by social support? Psychologists have a number of definitions, though they all refer to the social, emotional and other supports which are provided by an individual's social contacts. One way of looking at social support is provided by Cohen and Wills (1985), who describe the following features:

1 **Esteem support,** which refers to the effects of other people promoting your self-esteem (making you feel valued)
2 **Informational support,** which refers to the useful information you may get from your social contacts
3 **Instrumental support,** which refers to material support, such as money, which you might get from others
4 **Social companionship,** which refers to the support you get from spending time with other people.

A further distinction is made between perceived support and actual support. The difference between the two is that some people may receive a large amount of instrumental support and esteem support from their friends but think that they are relatively unsupported. It is generally thought that perceived support is a more useful measure for predicting health outcomes or health behaviour than is real support (Johnston, Wright and Weinman, 1995).

The advantage of looking at actual support is that it is relatively easy to assess. The information can be gathered from observations, or from records of behaviour such as membership of organisations etc. Even if it is based on self-report then the information is relatively factual and easy to collect. One of the standard ways of measuring the features of social networks is the Social Network List (Stokes, 1983). Using this list it has been possible to show that low levels of social relationships are associated with an increased risk of mortality. An alternative measure is the Social Support Questionnaire (Sarason et al., 1983), which quantifies both the size of social networks and also the perceived qualities of social relationships.

The value of social support has been found in studies on a range of disorders. Breast cancer is one the leading causes of death in women (see pages 60–61), and it might be that social support has an important role to play. Waxler-Morrison et al. (1991) studied 133 women after they received their diagnosis of breast cancer. They looked at their medical records and also obtained information about their social networks using questionnaires. As you might expect, one of the key factors that predicted how long the women survived was how developed the disease was. Social support, however, also had an effect, and longer survival was connected with women who had more friendships and deeper friendships, and with women who worked outside the home.

Explanations of social support

There are two basic psychological explanations of the role of social support in health. The main effects model suggests that social relationships enhance health and well-being regardless of stress. The way this might work is through promoting healthy behaviours. Social support is likely to provide models of healthy behaviours, it is likely to reinforce healthy behaviours that the person is carrying out and it is likely to provide encouragement. Although the model can explain some of the findings, it is clear that not all social support will enhance health. For example, some health-damaging behaviours such as excessive drinking or smoking occur within a social supportive framework.

The other approach to social support is the stress buffering model. This suggests that the health benefits of social support are evident during periods of high stress but are relatively irrelevant during periods of low stress. According to this approach, social support acts as a reserve and a resource that blunts the effects of stress or enables the person to cope more effectively with high levels of stress.

Social support and ill-health

Whatever the connection is between social support and health, the importance of social support has been shown in a range of disorders, including:

- **Asthma,** where the general finding is that family reactions, particularly those of the parents, can provoke asthmatic symptoms through being over-protective and over-concerned.
- **Coronary heart disease,** where social support has been helpful in encouraging people to adapt their lifestyle.
- **Back pain,** where concerned, supportive family members sometimes reinforce pain behaviour by carrying out tasks for the patients whenever they grimace. The patient is, therefore, reinforced for not getting well and the pain may become chronic.

This short-list highlights the negative as well as positive aspects of social support. (For a larger review of this area see Kaplan et al., 1993, chapter 7.) The psychological research largely looks at the effects of social support on serious disorders though it is clear that social relationships can have an effect on some of the minor irritations of life as well. The survey of German women shown in Figure 3.3 overleaf compares the complaints about their health made by women who were either single or in a long-term relationship. On the whole, the women in relationships had fewer complaints about their health except in the areas of insomnia and backache.

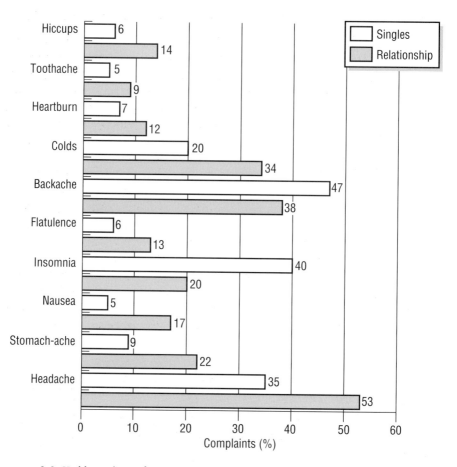

FIGURE 3.3 *Health complaints of women aged 25–50 (single and in a long-term relationship). (Source: New Internationalist, no. 267, May 1995)*

SPECIAL ISSUE:
Coping and bereavement

Sometimes, psychological research contradicts our common-sense understandings of how things are. An example of this comes from the work on how we cope with death and bereavement. In Western society, people often try and avoid issues around this inevitable event and rarely discuss their deepest anxieties and fears. Psychological approaches, however, have traditionally encouraged people to break through their inhibitions and cultural conventions which lead us to hide our feelings and to distort our experience. Kübler-Ross (1969) suggested that dying people and their relatives should be more open about the approach of death. Kübler-Ross suggested that if this taboo is broken, it would become possible to see death more positively, as the final stage of personal growth.

Kübler-Ross (1969) suggested that there were five stages of psychological adjustment to death:

1 Denial (it's a mistaken diagnosis)
2 Anger (why me?)
3 Bargaining (dealing with fate for more time)
4 Depression (sadness and crying)
5 Acceptance

This work has been heavily quoted with the unfortunate consequence that it has been seen as the 'natural' way to approach death. Although these stages are widely accepted, there is little empirical evidence to support their existence (Wortman and Silver, 1987).

There are also a number of assumptions about the responses we make to loss that have been found to be incorrect. For example, it is commonly believed that a common response to loss is to experience an absence, or drastic reduction, of positive emotions. Wortman and Silver (1987) investigated the emotional response of parents following the sudden death of an infant (Sudden Infant Death Syndrome – SIDS). They discovered, in fact, that the parents, on average, still experienced a considerable amount of positive emotion (see Figure 3.4). It would seem that the balance of our emotions is different but that we experience happiness alongside the sadness of a tragic loss.

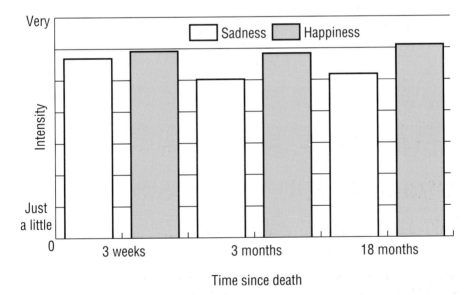

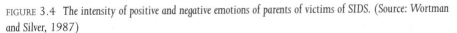

FIGURE 3.4 The intensity of positive and negative emotions of parents of victims of SIDS. (Source: Wortman and Silver, 1987)

Another commonly held belief about bereavement is that it is important to 'work through' grief by talking to people and showing our feelings so that we can achieve an emotional and cognitive resolution. This is based on the idea that unexpressed emotion will have some negative effects on us in the long term. Wortman and Silver (1987) point out that there is also very little evidence to support this idea, and in their study they found evidence for the reverse effect. They found that the parents who had done the most 'working through' of their grief showed the greatest distress at the time of loss and also 18 months after the loss (see Figure 3.5).

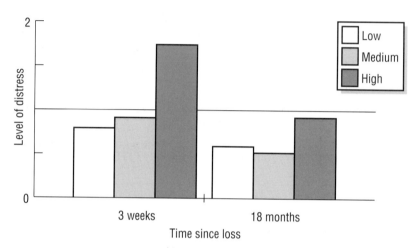

FIGURE 3.5   *The relationship between working through loss and distress for parents of victims of SIDS. (Source: Wortman and Silver, 1987)*

APPLICATIONS: IMPROVING COPING AND REDUCING STRESS

There have been an amazing number of techniques developed to help people reduce their stress or to help them develop their coping skills. These use a variety of psychological concepts and theories, and although they each seem to have their uses, there is not an easy answer to the stresses and strains of everyday living. The following section gives a flavour of the range of these techniques.

Biofeedback

The principle behind biofeedback is that we gain control over bodily functions and actions if we are aware of what is happening. However, with most bodily reactions, such as our blood pressure, we are relatively unaware of what is happening and so are unable to control them. Biofeedback aims to give an individual some direct feedback about bodily responses and so encourage them to take control of that response. Biofeedback concentrates on biological systems that are not under conscious control and that are having an adverse affect on the person.

The sort of information that can be given to a person includes the pattern of their brain activity (using an electroencephalogram), their heart rate, their skin conductance (using a galvanic skin response meter) and their temperature. An example of the application of biofeedback in health was developed by Budzynski, Stoyva and Adler (1970) who used the technique with tension headaches. Budzynski et al. gave their patients biofeedback of the muscle tension in their foreheads. They combined this biofeedback with training in deep muscle relaxation, and were able to provide relief for people with a long history of chronic headaches.

This seems to be a simple solution to the problem of headaches but, sadly, nothing is ever that straightforward. The causes of headaches are far from clear, and there are numerous other factors that affect the onset and development of headaches apart from muscle tension.

Imagery

Techniques for training people to use mental imagery have proved helpful in stress reduction. Bridge et al. (1988) described how imagery was used to help to reduce the unpleasant emotional consequences of radiotherapy for women who had breast cancer. In the study, women who were undertaking this treatment were allocated to one of three groups. Two of the groups were relaxation training groups, one of which just emphasised physical training, particularly control of muscle tension and breathing, while the other used relaxation training along with mental imagery (asking each person to concentrate on a peaceful scene of her own choice). The control group was encouraged to meet and simply talk about themselves for an equal amount of time as the two treatment groups.

Bridge et al. assessed the women's moods, using standard psychometric tests, and found that women in both of the treatment groups were significantly less disturbed than those who were in the control group. However, it was also clear that those women who had been encouraged to use imagery techniques as well were more relaxed than those whose intervention had focused only on physical relaxation. This appears to show the benefits of imagery, although it is not at all clear why or how imagery is effective.

Treating post-traumatic stress disorder

A wide range of psychological interventions have been used on people with post-traumatic stress disorder (for a full summary, see Hodgkinson and Stewart, 1991). These include behavioural treatments, cognitive treatments, psychotherapeutic approaches, group methods, and bereavement counselling and grief therapy. One of the most common treatments for the emotional reactions of post-traumatic stress disorder is *systematic desensitisation*. This treatment is based on the principles of classical conditioning and generally has the following four features:

1 **Training the person in relaxation techniques** in which the person learns how to relax their muscles. As the technique is learned, cue words are often associated with the feelings of relaxation so that they can produce similar feelings without the necessity to go all through the relaxation procedures.
2 **Exposure to the feared stimulus through imagination** during treatment, either in a hierarchical way (imaging the least feared part of the situation and then progressing on to the most feared part) or by flooding (imaging the worst scenario).
3 **Going back to the feared situation.** For example victims of the *Herald of Free Enterprise* disaster (see pages 24–25) were accompanied on ferry trips across the English Channel.
4 **Self-directed treatment,** where the person starts to carry out their own sessions of desensitisation and flooding, and may expose themselves to real-life fearful situations.

Rational emotive therapy

Since the experience of stress is affected by the way we cognitively appraise the situation, it then follows that we can deal with stress through adjusting that appraisal. This is usually referred to as *cognitive restructuring*. One of the best-known examples of this is rational emotive therapy (RET), which was developed by Albert Ellis. According to Ellis, stress often comes from faulty or irrational ways of thinking, for example:

■ awfulising – thinking that it is awful if you get reprimanded at work
■ can't-stand-it's – thinking that you can't stand being late for a meeting.

The therapy looks at a person's thought processes and tries to change those thoughts and beliefs which are irrational and negative. The basic plan for RET is the A-B-C-D-E framework shown in Box 3.2. There is mixed reaction to the therapy, in particular there is disagreement about whether people have any long-term change in their experience of stress.

Box 3.2 The A-B-C-D-E framework for rational emotive therapy

A is the **activating** experience that creates the stress, for example being told by your partner that you are fat lazy slob who has no friends because you prefer to sit in at night and watch *Match of the Day*.

B refers to the thoughts and **beliefs** that go through your mind in response to A. The thoughts might be quite reasonable such as 'I should go out more often' or unnecessarily negative such as 'I am a fat useless slob and I should get a life'.

C refers to the **consequences** of A and B. These might be quite positive like resolving to be more sociable and less tied to the television, or they might be quite inappropriate like feeling useless and even more socially inept than you really are.

D refers to **disputing** irrational beliefs. This forms part of the therapeutic approach and helps the person to distinguish between 'true ideas' such as 'I could behave better' and irrational ideas like 'I am a total loser'.

E refers to the **effect** of the therapy which will hopefully consist of a restructured system of beliefs so that you can sit in and watch *Match of the Day* on Saturday without any guilt or feelings of uselessness.

(Note: I wouldn't want the reader to think that this is any way autobiographical!)

Coping and pain

Basler and Rehfisch (1990) looked at how coping training could be used to help people who were suffering from chronic pain. They developed a 12-week intervention package, which included training patients to reinterpret the pain experience, training in physical relaxation techniques, avoiding negative and catastrophic thinking, and training in how to use distraction at key times. They found that compared with untreated patients on a waiting list (the control group), there were significant improvements for these patients at a six month follow-up. The patients reported fewer general and pain-related symptoms, and a lower level of anxiety and depression. There was also a decline in the number of visits which they made to the doctor.

Stress inoculation

Some medical treatments give people weak versions of a disease in order to encourage the body to develop defences against the full-blown version. This is called inoculation. A form of cognitive therapy uses a similar idea as a preparation for a stressful event and it is called, not surprisingly, stress inoculation. It was developed by Meichenbaum (1977) and it is designed to prepare people for stress and to help them develop skills to cope with that stress. The inoculation programme involves three stages:

1 **Conceptualisation**

The trainer talks with the patient about their stress responses, and during this phase the patient learns to identify and express feelings and fears. The patient is also educated in lay terms about stress and its effect.

2 **Skill acquisition and rehearsal**

The patient learns some basic behavioural and cognitive skills that will be useful for coping with stressful situations. For example, they might be taught how to relax and use self-regulatory skill. The patient then practices these new skills under supervision.

3 **Application and follow-through**

The trainer guides the patient through a series of progressively more threatening situations (a bit like the hierarchy in desensitisation, see above). The patient is given a wide range of possible stressors to prepare them for real-life situations.

As with RET, the jury seems to be out on whether this is an effective intervention or not. It has been used in sports with some effect; for example, Zeigler, Klinzing and Williamson's (1982) study of cross-country runners showed that stress inoculation was useful in reducing stress and improving performance at running.

SUMMARY

There are a range of techniques at our disposal to help people deal with stress and become better at coping. However, it must be said that stress is sometimes there for a reason, and it should not necessarily be coped with. Imagine a stressful work situation where people are given unrealistic work schedules and are given little or no support. Should they be given stress counselling or should they be encouraged to take up trade union activity to negotiate for a better working environment? Psychologists are unfortunately drawn toward the counselling answer because their focus is more on the individual, and they tend to place less emphasis on the social and political world in which that individual is living.

chapter four

PROMOTING HEALTH AND PREVENTING ILLNESS

CHAPTER OVERVIEW

The INTRODUCTION looks at health promotion and how it is defined. It also looks at some early attempts at health education, and considers the range of problems we encounter when trying to devise programmes of illness prevention. These include the barriers to prevention created by the traditional structure of medicine, and the difficulty in getting people to practice effective health behaviours. The PSYCHOLOGICAL CONTRIBUTIONS include the use of fear appeals and the insights offered by the Yale Model of Communication. The SPECIAL ISSUE looks at how the commercial world gets messages across and considers the example of the changing image of Lucozade. APPLICATIONS OF PSYCHOLOGY include attempts to deal with coronary heart disease and excessive drinking, the effect of mass media campaigns in changing health behaviours, the attempt to encourage breast self-examination in women, and some attempts to reduce the number of accidents.

INTRODUCTION

Health promotion

Health promotion is concerned with enhancing good health and preventing illness. It is defined by the World Health Organisation (1984) as 'the process of enabling people to increase control over, and to improve, their health'.

The role of health promotion has changed over the years. Around 100 years ago the poor health of the British working class led to the introduction of physical education, but the main concern was not the health of the people but the availability of fit young men to join the army. Today the aim of health promotion is to improve a person's quality of life and also to reduce the demands on the limited resources of state health care.

The modern concerns of health promotion are listed by Ewles and Simnett

(1992) as:

- **health education programmes,** which are designed to raise awareness of health risk and encourage changes in behaviour
- **primary health education,** which aims to prevent ill-health developing in healthy people. It deals with topics such as hygiene, nutrition, social skills etc.
- **preventive health services,** which refers to services such as family planning, well-person clinics and immunisation
- **community-based work,** which encourages local communities to identify their own health needs and address them
- **organisational development,** which refers to the development of practices that promote the health of workers and customers within organisations
- **healthy public policies,** which encourage policies to promote health in the area of housing, employment, transport etc.
- **environmental health measures,** which are about making the physical environment better for our health at work and at home
- **economic and regulatory activities,** which refer to political activity aimed at politicians and planners, and involve lobbying for such changes such as the labelling of food and increases in tobacco taxation.

Psychology makes a contribution to some of the areas mentioned above, and in particular, health education and primary health care. Psychology can also make contributions to public policy and environmental health by producing research that identifies the policies and environments that can promote health.

Health education

Psychology has most to offer in the attempts to change attitudes and change behaviour. The involvement of psychology in health education goes back to the First World War (1914–1918) when the American military were worried about the spread of venereal disease in its troops. They asked psychologists Karl Lashley and John Watson (1921) to look into the effectiveness of filmed health education messages. Lashley and Watson investigated the impact of two films about venereal disease which were produced in the form of stories and had graphic images of the devastating medical and social effects of having sex with prostitutes and developing venereal disease. They surveyed and interviewed over 1000 people who saw the films and found that 70% had a good knowledge of the points made in the film. Sadly, though, they found no evidence that the films had any effect on behaviour either to avoid sex with prostitutes or to take health precautions.

Watson and Lashley made a number of observations that are relevant today, and remarkably do not seem to have been addressed throughout the 70 years since they were made. They observed that:

- using storyline techniques is risky since viewers follow the action rather than the information
- young people respond with flippancy to sex information, and so the best way to present information is in a frank and serious style
- the use of fear-arousing images does not always have the desired effect. For example, their survey found that 89% of the audience believed that venereal diseases are easily transmitted and they should therefore not touch anything that had ever been touched by a prostitute.

The work of Lashley and Watson was a response to the sexual fears of an earlier generation. More recently there has been a lot of concern about sexual behaviour and the spread of HIV/AIDS. Baggaley (1991) reviewed the media campaigns on HIV/AIDS and concluded that they have not taken the lessons first observed by Lashley and Watson. Baggaley concluded that the various mass media campaigns have often used storylines, created a great sense of fear and also used amusing or dramatic styles to get the message across. But if Watson and Lashley are correct then this type of campaign serves only to please the administrators and politicians and has no effect on the health of the population.

Before we go on to look at the contributions of psychology to promoting health and preventing illness, we will have a look at the issues surrounding prevention.

Prevention

Primary prevention refers to the attempts to combat risk factors before an illness has the chance to develop. *Secondary prevention* refers to the actions which are taken to identify and treat an illness or injury early with the aim of stopping or reversing the problem. *Tertiary prevention* involves actions that contain or slow down the damage of serious injury or disease, and, hopefully, rehabilitate the patient. Secondary and tertiary prevention can also involve attempts to improve the quality of life by, for example, reducing pain and increasing mobility.

Barriers to primary prevention

The main effort in primary prevention is to either develop programmes to encourage people to change their health-threatening behaviours, or prevent people from developing health-threatening behaviours in the first place. There are, however a number of barriers to primary prevention including:

- We have only limited knowledge about what behaviours are threatening to our health. For example, it is only in the last 40 years that we have discovered the very harmful effects of tobacco smoking.

n We have a lack of knowledge about how we develop health-threatening behaviours. Some behaviours to do with diet or exercise, for example, develop over many years from our childhood.

n A number of health behaviours are learnt in the home. For example, the children of smokers are more likely to smoke than the children of non-smokers.

n At the time that health-threatening behaviours develop, people often have little immediate incentive to practice health-enhancing behaviours. For example, the effects of smoking are felt in middle to later life rather than when people start smoking.

n People are unrealistically optimistic about their health (see pages 80–81).

Primary prevention has been largely ignored until very recently, and there are three main reasons for this: firstly the traditional structure of Western medicine; secondly, the difficulty of getting people to practice effective health behaviours; and thirdly, the difficulty in applying methods of attitude and behavioural change to health.

The traditional structure of medicine

The biomedical approach (see Chapter 1, pages 4–5) underestimates the role of behavioural factors in health. This medical approach has historically corrected conditions (made people better) rather than prevented them. So we go to the doctor when we are ill and not when we are well. The doctor has a way of diagnosing illness but no way of diagnosing health. However, if doctors did apply diagnosis to healthy people then they could identify risk behaviours and so prevent the development of illness.

Difficulty of getting people to practice effective health behaviours

There are two main problems with getting people to behave in healthy ways. First, health habits are independent (for example, someone might have a very healthy diet but smoke 40 cigarettes a day), and secondly, health behaviours are unstable over time (for example, someone may start the new year by taking regular exercise, but by the summer they may have reverted to being a couch potato). There are many reasons for this independence and instability including:

n Different health habits are controlled by different factors, for example smoking may be stress-related whereas a lack of exercise may be a response to local facilities.

n The factors affecting a health behaviour may change over the history of that behaviour, for example people might start smoking because of peer pressure, but they continue smoking because of habit and comfort, and they relapse into smoking after an attempt to give up because their budgie died.

- The factors that affect health may change over time, for example, a change of job from something physical to one where you sit in an office all day.

Difficulty in applying the methods of attitude and behavioural change to health

The most effective way of changing attitudes and behaviour is in one-to-one contact. This is the traditional approach of psychological interventions and there are many therapeutic procedures that have good results. The problem is one of resources, and although it is appropriate to have one-to-one therapies for the small number of people who develop serious health problems, it is not practical to have this approach for the whole population. This means that we have to devise methods to reach large numbers of people and change their attitudes and behaviour. Psychology has some research findings that are useful here, but health educators have been slow to react to these findings (see the response to Lashley and Watson, above).

In summary, prevention of illness is the aim of governments and health promotion workers, but there are numerous barriers to prevention not least our traditional way of treating illness rather than encouraging health. It is an important footnote, however, that primary prevention is currently the only way to prevent the spread of AIDS.

PSYCHOLOGICAL CONTRIBUTIONS

Fear appeals

Discussion of the effects of fear appeals usually starts with the study by Janis and Feshbach (1953). For their study, they prepared three 15-minute illustrated lectures on the dangers of tooth decay and the need for good oral hygiene. The main difference between the three recorded talks was the amount of fear they were designed to create. The strong fear appeal emphasised the painful consequences of tooth decay, diseased gums and other dangers such as cancer and blindness that can result from poor oral hygiene. This appeal also included pictures of diseased mouths. The moderate fear appeal described the same dangers but in a less dramatic way, using less disturbing pictures. The minimal fear appeal talked about decayed teeth and cavities but did not refer to the serious consequences mentioned in the other appeals, and used diagrams and X-ray pictures rather than photographs.

The results showed that the strong fear appeal did its job and created most worry in the students who received the talk. Also, the strong fear appeal talk was rated as more interesting than the other two talks, and the pictures for this talk received a higher rating than the pictures in the other two talks. On the other hand, the strong fear appeal talk also received high negative ratings, with a third of the students saying the pictures were too unpleasant. Overall then, the strong fear appeal produced a strong reaction. However, did it also lead to the biggest change in behaviour? Janis and Feshbach interviewed the students to discover their oral hygiene habits and gave them a 'conformity score' to show how much they had changed their behaviour to follow the advice of the talk. The results showed that the minimal fear appeal created the greatest increase in conformity (36%) and the strong fear appeal created the least (8%).

The main conclusion we can draw from this is that people will resist messages with a strong fear appeal. This finding has been supported by subsequent research which shows that fear appeals sometimes lead to:

- no behaviour change
- the avoidance of further health information
- short-term gains only; the behaviour returns to its original pattern when fear subsides.

The attempt to create fear also raises issues of self-efficacy (see pages 176–177), and is currently not regarded as a necessary part of health behaviour programmes. However, this has not stopped its frequent use in health promotion materials.

The Yale Model of Communication

Starting in the 1950s in America a number of psychologists including Carl Hovland investigated the features of a communication that make it persuasive. The work is often summarised as the Yale Model of Communication, named after the university where much of the research was carried out. Figure 4.1 shows a brief outline of the model which identifies the important features to consider when preparing a message. These features are the source of the message (or the persuader), the message, the medium that the message is presented in, the target audience and the situation in which they will receive the message.

The model attracted a considerable amount of research, though much of it was based on political messages rather than health messages. The general findings from the Yale approach to communication and attitude change were summarised by Zimbardo, Ebbesen and Maslach (1977), who identified the following key suggestions for producing persuasive messages.

1 The source should be credible, and the important features of credibility are expertise and trustworthiness. This means that we are more likely to respond to a message from 'a doctor' than we are to a message from 'a local drunk'. An important point to note is that someone who is a credible source for a middle-aged professional worker might have no credibility for a young production worker.

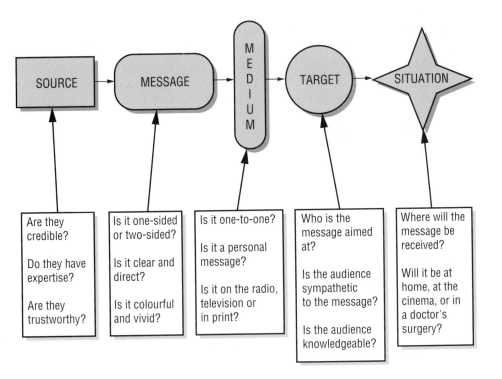

FIGURE 4.1 *The Yale Model of Communication*

2 When an audience is generally positive towards the communicator and the message then it is best to present a one-sided argument. On the other hand, if the audience is not sympathetic to the message or the communicator then a two-sided argument is more effective.

3 There will probably be more opinion change in the direction you want if you explicitly state your conclusions than if you let the audience draw their own. The exception to this rule is with a very informed audience, then it is more effective for them to draw their own conclusions.

4 The message should be short, clear and direct.

5 The communication should be colourful and vivid rather than full of technical terms and statistics.

6 The effects of a persuasive communication tend to wear off over time, though attitude change tends to last longer if the person has actively participated in the communication rather than just passively receiving it.

The work on fear appeals and message design is still relevant today. It is clear that we will respond to some messages and not to others. Advertisements are attempts to influence our behaviour, and the effectiveness of some campaigns shows that it is possible to create persuasive message (see the section below on the Lucozade campaign). It is not clear, however, whether the lessons of psychology are applied to health promotion material, and the reason, as Baggaley (1991) suggests, is that the campaigns are designed to please health administrators and politicians rather than to change the health behaviour of people at risk. You might find it informative to look at some health education material and judge whether it has used any of the psychological findings briefly described above. By way of example, I have included a leaflet on breast feeding (see Figure 4.2).

FIGURE 4.2 *An example of health education material*

The decision to breast feed is not an easy one for a woman to make. There are a number of issues to consider, including embarrassment to expose the breast, discomfort of breast feeding, the need to be available for baby much of the day and the general social disapproval of women breast feeding. There are also a number of cultural and class issues that are important in the decision. My personal feeling about the leaflet is that it is clear, direct and vivid, which are all plus points. However, it has a number of important drawbacks, if our psychological evidence is to be believed. First, it does not appear to be targeted at any particular group of mothers, but at all mothers, as if parenting is the same for people of all classes and all cultures. Secondly, the source seems to be a health professional of some sort, and although this might be credible for the health aspects of breast feeding, it is not credible for the issues around social embarrassment. I might believe a doctor when she says 'You need to take three tablets a day', but I do not believe her at all when she says, 'Bend over, this won't hurt a bit'. My third objection to the leaflet is that it presents a one-sided argument which disregards the research evidence that is important to present both sides of an argument when the audience has mixed feelings toward the message.

Other psychological concepts

There are a number of psychological concepts that are important in the understanding of health behaviour and the development of health promotion campaigns. For example, one of the explanations for the failure of fear appeals is that they create a sense of learned helplessness where people feel unable to do anything about their situation. Another issue is self-efficacy (see pages 176–177) so if people feel that they are able to carry out successful actions then they are more likely to respond to health messages. An example of this is described below concerning chip pan fires, and another example is the 'Back to Sleep' campaign on sudden infant death syndrome in which parents were encouraged to put their babies to sleep on their backs rather than on their fronts. This campaign provided a simple action for parents to carry out, and the campaign coincided with a dramatic fall in the number of sudden infant deaths in the United Kingdom.

Other concepts that help our understanding of health promotion include models of decision-making (see pages 126–128), locus of control (pages 174–176), defence mechanisms (pages 32–33), and the model of behavioural change proposed by Prochaska, DiClemente and Norcross (pages 102–103).

SPECIAL ISSUE:
The changing image of Lucozade

The declining sales of Lucozade

Lucozade is a glucose carbonated drink first made in the 1920s. The drink is a highly concentrated source of energy which is quickly assimilated into the bloodstream. It is easily digested, and its flavour, carbonation and relative sweetness make it easy to take in sickness. During the period 1974–1978, the sales of Lucozade declined consistently. The advertising strategy promoted Lucozade as a unique source of liquid energy that helps the family when they are recovering from illness. In all the advertisements, the emotional way of showing the family was through children. As a result the drink had a very clear market image, but that image was restricted to being a product that was associated with children, illness and occasional use.

Rather surprisingly, the market research showed that only 20% of the sales were for convalescence, and only 30% were being used by children. A substantial volume of the drink was being consumed by healthy adults. Basically, the bottle was being bought when there was a sick child in the house but it was then being drunk by other members of the household. The advertisers summarised the sale position of Lucozade in 1979 as follows:

1 Lucozade is mainly associated with child sickness
2 Child sickness is declining and this means less use of Lucozade by adults since it will not be in the house so often.
3 Advertisements about sick children do not encourage adults to buy or use Lucozade.
4 More Lucozade will be sold if people can be persuaded to buy it for other purposes

than child sickness.
5 The best opportunity for developing sales is to describe the drink as a 'Mother pick-me-up'.

The new advertising strategy

The advertisers developed a strategy with the following features:

- **Advertising objective:** to turn Lucozade from an occasional purchase into a more regular purchase
- **Product positioning:** Lucozade is a unique source of energy in health as well as sickness
- **Target audience:** active women between the ages of 18 and 35 who care about the health and well-being of themselves and their children
- **Proposition:** Lucozade helps the body regain its normal energy level
- **Justification:** refreshing Lucozade is glucose energy in the most natural form the body can use
- **Tone:** contemporary, active, helpful, dependable, optimistic

The campaign

The media campaign set out to create maximum awareness of the 'new Lucozade usage opportunities' as quickly as possible and to maintain this new awareness over a long period. To create the initial impact, a large amount of television advertising was used. At the same time, they placed advertisements in the women's press that carried the traditional message to remind people of the uses

Lucozade
Ups and Downs.

MAN: How often do you start out feeling full of get-up-and-go and then...

after you've been working hard, you start to slow down.

That's the time to sit down and have a glass of Lucozade. Lucozade's not just refreshing...

it provides glucose energy in the most natural form the body can use.

So, before you get up and get going again, have some Lucozade.

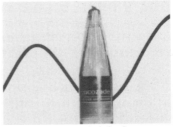

SINGERS: Lucozade refreshes you through the ups and downs of the day.

FIGURE 4.3 The Lucozade campaign. Images from the television campaign

of Lucozade with sick children. A poster campaign was also used to back up the television message. (The images from the television campaign are shown in Figure 4.3.)

The campaign was very successful, so successful that many adults still recognise the tune and message today. Measures at the time showed that in contrast to the previous sales decline, the first year of the campaign showed a 13% increase in volume sales. Market research also showed an increase in the number of people claiming to buy Lucozade 'nowadays', an increase in the num-

ber of people giving 'refreshment' as a reason for purchase and an increase in the recall of Lucozade television advertising.

The campaign changed perceptions of Lucozade so that instead of it being a sickness product it became a health product. Since this campaign, Lucozade has further developed that theme and now markets itself as a sports drink giving high energy. The interesting point for health promotion is the care that went into defining the strategy and the target audience.

APPLICATIONS

In Chapter 1 we looked at the government's strategy for health called *The Health of the Nation* (Department of Health, 1992). This targets five areas for change which are coronary heart disease, cancers, mental illness, HIV/AIDS and sexual health, and accidents. Included in these areas are specific targets about eating habits (which we will look at in Chapter 6, pages 91–93), smoking (which we will look at in Chapter 7, pages 97–98), and the safer use of needles by drug users (which we will look at in Chapter 7, pages 104–105). In this section we will look at how psychology has been, or could be, applied to promoting good health in the areas identified by *The Health of the Nation*. I have not attempted to give a full review of all the psychology that has been applied, but to give some examples of the range of ideas and methods that psychologists can use.

Coronary heart disease and excessive drinking

One of the risk factors for coronary heart disease identified by *The Health of the Nation* is excessive drinking of alcohol. Bennett and Murphy (1994) point out that one of the many problems with attempts to promote 'sensible' drinking is that drinking alcohol is connected with a range of social and cultural norms. For example, they observe that the custom of 'buying rounds' is an important part of belonging to a group of people. It demonstrates that all the people in the group are independent and equal, and it also allows people to give and receive small gifts. This strong social element in drinking alcohol makes it difficult for health educators to reduce the levels of excessive drinking. Bennett and Murphy cite a study (Leather, 1981) of young drinkers in Glasgow. The study investigated the factors that were important in the drinking behaviour of these young people and, as a result, the health promotion campaign based on 'units' of alcohol and recommended limits was abandoned. It was replaced by a campaign that concentrated on the social costs of drinking too much, such as lack of money and losing control in front of your friends.

A different kind of intervention in alcohol drinking was reported by Jeffs and Saunders (1983). They were able to investigate the effectiveness of a community policing strategy which was implemented in an English seaside town in the summer of 1978, and then withdrawn the following year. At the beginning of the summer, two policemen visited the public houses on the harbour area of the town to remind the licensees of their responsibilities especially in the area of under-aged drinking, and serving alcohol to people who were already drunk. During the summer the public houses received regular friendly visits from the local police who conspicuously checked for under-aged drinkers and for people who were already drunk. The effectiveness of this campaign was checked by looking at the crime statistics for the summer of 1978 and comparing them with 1977 and 1979. The figures showed a reduction of crime in 1978 of around 20%, and this reduction was mainly in public order offences and not in crimes that are not associated with alcohol abuse, such as burglary. This minor change in police policy led to 2000 fewer arrests than would be expected.

Coronary heart disease and mass media appeals

It is difficult to evaluate the effect of mass media appeals. In the case of product advertising, the effect can be measured on sales. In the case of health behaviour, it is difficult to come up with appropriate measures since there are so many influences on us every day. One of the most famous studies on the effectiveness of mass media messages is called The Stanford Heart Disease Prevention Programme (see, for example, Farquhar et al., 1977). This research looked at three similar small towns in the USA. Two of the towns received a massive media campaign concerning smoking, diet and exercise over a two-year period. This campaign used television, radio, newspapers, posters and mailshots. The third town had no campaign and so acted as a control.

The researchers interviewed several hundred people in the three towns between the ages of 35 and 60. They were interviewed before the campaign began, after one year, and again after two years when the campaign had ended. The interviews included questions about health behaviours, knowledge about the risks of heart disease, and physical measures such as blood pressure and blood cholesterol levels. In one of the two campaign towns, the researchers used the interview data to identify over 100 people who were at high risk of heart disease and offered them one-to-one counselling.

The people in the control town showed a slight increase in risk factors for heart disease, and the people in the campaign towns showed a moderate decrease. The campaign produced increased awareness of the dangers of heart disease but produced relatively little change in behaviour. The exception to this were the people who had been offered one-to-one counselling; these showed significant changes in behaviour. This study suggests that mass media campaigns by themselves produce only small changes in behaviour, but they can act as a cue to positive action if further encouragement is offered.

Coronary heart disease and health information

It is possible to have an effect on health behaviours with quite small interventions. Lewin et al. (1992), for example, looked at the effectiveness of giving patients an instruction manual when they were discharged from hospital after having a heart attack. The booklet, called *The Heart Manual* dealt with common myths about heart attacks, how to manage anxiety, and information about how much exercise and activity to carry out. Nearly 200 people were involved in the study; the experimental group was given *The Heart Manual* while a control group was not. The patients who received *The Heart Manual* appeared to have better psychological adjustment, visited their general practitioner less, and were less likely to be readmitted to hospital than the control group (less than 10% re-admission compared to 25%).

Cancer and breast self-examination

An important aspect of secondary prevention is to encourage the early identification of serious diseases. Early identification can be obtained through screening people at medical centres (for example, for cervical cancer), or by encouraging people to examine themselves and to contact their doctor if they notice any abnormalities. Breast self-examination (BSE) by women, for example, has been found to be useful in the early detection of breast cancer. Pitts (1991b) suggests that less than 30% of British women carry out breast self-examination despite the health advantages. There are many reasons for this 'non-compliance', and while some are to do with the cognitions and feelings of women, some are also to do with the way women are thought of and dealt with by the medical profession.

One attempt to increase breast self-examination has been to increase the impact of health education messages by emphasising its benefits rather than emphasising the losses of not carrying it out. Meyerowitz and Chaiken (1987) gave health education messages to women students that either emphasised gain or loss (see Box 4.1).

Box 4.1 Messages that emphasise loss and gain in breast self-examination

Gain	Loss
By doing breast self-examinations now, you can learn what your normal healthy breasts feel like so that you will be better prepared to notice any small, abnormal changes that might occur as you get older.	By not doing breast self-examinations, you will not learn what your normal, healthy breasts feel like so you will be ill-prepared to notice any small, abnormal changes that might occur as you get older.
Research shows that women who do breast self-examinations have an increased chance of finding a tumour in the early, more treatable stages of the disease.	Research shows that women who do not do breast self-examinations have a decreased chance of finding a tumour in the early, more treatable stages of the disease.

This simple manipulation in the message had an effect on attitudes to breast self-examination and women's intentions to carry it out, both at the time of the message and also four months later. The results showed that both the gain and loss messages were followed by an immediate intention to carry out breast self-examination. However, this intention was still quite strong for the women who received the gain message, but it decreased in the women who had received the loss message. The gain message also had a positive effect on attitudes towards breast self-examination.

There has recently been a change of emphasis from breast self-examination towards 'breast awareness'. The main reason for this is that women are very reluctant to carry out the relatively complicated processes required for self-examination. The research by Murray and McMillan (1993) described in Chapter 12 (page 175) showed that women were more likely to carry out breast self-examination if they had confidence in their ability to carry it out successfully, so the complicated instructions are one of the likely reasons why many women do not carry it out. Another reason for the move away from breast self-examination is that the medical profession dislikes having to deal with 'false positives' (women who find something in their breast that turns out not to require any treatment). Women are now encouraged to carry out a much simpler procedure which is referred to as breast awareness, and does not seem to carry the same threat as self-examination.

Accidents

Public information films on television often tell us to do very sensible things, like dip our headlights, or fit smoke alarms. They might well affect our attitudes to these procedures and products, but do they affect our behaviour? In the field of accidents, it is possible to estimate changes in behaviour by comparing accident rates before and after an advertising campaign. This discrepancy between attitude (what we think) and behaviour (what we do) is illustrated in a report by Cowpe (1989). This report looked at the effectiveness of a series of advertisements about the dangers of chip pan fires. Before the advertisements, people were asked about this hazard and most of them claimed that they always adopted safe practices. However, the statistics from fire brigades about the frequency of chip pan fires and the descriptions by people of what they should do suggested that their behaviour was not as safe as they thought. A television advertising campaign was developed and broadcast showing dramatic images of exactly how these fires develop, and how people should deal with them. The adverts ended with a simple statement, such as 'Of course, if you don't overfill your chip pan in the first place, you won't have to do any of this.'

By comparing fire brigade statistics for the areas which received the advertisements with those for the areas which did not, the advertisers found that the advertisements produced a 25% reduction in the number of chip pan fires in some areas, with a 12% reduction overall (see Figure 4.4). Surveys taken after the series of advertisements showed that people had more accurate knowledge about what they should do in the event of a chip pan fire than before. The implication from this report is very clear. Public information films and health promotion advertisements are most effective if they contain information about what to do rather than what to think or what to be scared of.

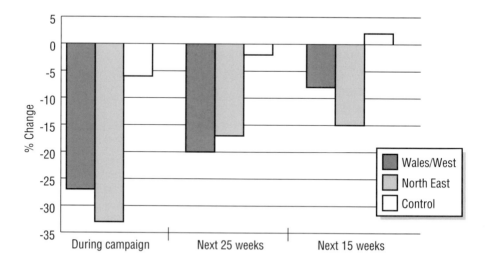

FIGURE 4.4 *Change in the number of chip pan fires during and immediatley after the advertising campaign in two television regions*

SUMMARY

During this century there has been an increasing emphasis on promoting good health in the general population. A range of techniques have been used to encourage people to change their behaviour, though they are notable mostly for their relatively modest success. The reasons for this lack of success involve the complex relationships between habits, attitudes and our decision-making processes.

chapter five

CHAPTER OVERVIEW

The CONTEXT looks at the traditional approaches in social psychology to the issues of obedience and compliance. These approaches suggest that people are very compliant, but the recent evidence shows that our compliance to health requests is very low. The PSYCHOLOGICAL CONTRIBUTIONS include the various methods of measuring compliance that have been devised. Other things that are considered include the health belief model of how we make decisions, and also the explanation for our behaviour suggested by the process of rational non-compliance. The SPECIAL ISSUE considers the difficulties associated with diabetes and compliance, in particular the issues around self-medication and adherence to a strict diet. The final section, INTERVENTIONS: ENHANCING COMPLIANCE, looks at how the presentation of information can be used to encourage compliance and how a range of behavioural methods have been used with varying degrees of success.

CONTEXT

Traditional approaches in social psychology

Compliance to health requests means doing as we are told and being sensible about our health. It means taking our medicine, eating the right foods and putting on a warm vest when we go out in winter. This all seems straightforward enough, especially if we look at the early psychological studies on conformity which show how compliant and malleable people can be.

The research on compliance that is popularly quoted was carried out in the 1950s and 1960s with the aim of explaining why seemingly ordinary people carried out hideous acts against fellow human beings during the Second World War (1939–45). This research gives a picture of people as compliant automatons who readily conform to most social pressures and obey authority without much hesitation. The work of Asch (1955) and Milgram (1963) is used as evidence to support this pessimistic view. In Asch's study, people would agree with the judgement of a group even when it was transparently incorrect. In the Milgram study, individuals were required to give electric shocks to another person in an attempt to improve their recall of a word list. About two thirds of the subjects of this study continued to give shocks up to a lethal level of 450 volts despite the screams of the victim. (For those of you who are unfamiliar with this study, it is important to point out that nobody was actually given electric shocks.)

These studies are interestingly presented and discussed in most introductory psychology texts, and they give us a clear picture of people as being compliant to social demands, and blindly obedient to requests from authority. In the world of health, however, the problem is very different. People are not compliant and obedient to requests from authority figures, far from it. In fact we are more likely to ignore health requests than we are to follow them. So why is there this discrepancy between the studies of Asch and Milgram and our observations of health behaviour?

Types of request

One of the issues to consider with compliance is the type of behaviour we are asking someone to do. In the social psychology studies mentioned above, the person under investigation was usually isolated from their friends and, in the Asch studies, asked to carry out simple and transparently pointless tasks. In the Milgram study, they were asked to carry out something very unusual in a very unusual situation. The requests for health compliance, on the other hand, are usually made in familiar situations and the behaviour can be discussed with friends and family.

The types of health request fall into a number of categories:

- **requests for short-term compliance with simple treatments,** for example, 'take these tablets twice a day for three weeks'
- **requests for positive additions to lifestyle,** for example, 'eat more vegetables and take more exercise'
- **requests to stop certain behaviours,** for example, 'stop smoking'
- **requests for long-term treatment regimes,** for example, sticking to a diabetic diet, or the diet prescribed for people undergoing renal dialysis.

A cursory look at these types of request reveals some striking differences, and suggests that the problems of compliance may be different for the different types of medical request. For example, with the short-term request to take my tablets three times a day, I have to make an effort for only a short time and even then it is unlikely to impose any strain on the way I conduct my life. On the other hand, the dietary requirements for patients undergoing renal dialysis are very severe, difficult to follow, and will continue while the patient has dialysis. The diet requires the patient to severely restrict their fluid intake which not only cuts out a Friday night down the Dog and Partridge, but also leaves them feeling thirsty and uncomfortable for much of the time.

When we talk about compliance to health requests, we need to consider what we are asking people to comply with. It is too much of a simplification to regard all health requests as being the same. The reasons why we do not comply with one type of request might be very different to reasons why we do not comply with another. The space available does not allow us to look at all the possible types of compliance in health but I will try to give a summary that shows the range of psychological approaches and the range of methods used in this area.

How compliant are people to health requests?

Developing an accurate picture of treatment compliance can be tricky, and the estimates of patient compliance vary widely from one study to another. This is partly a matter of definition. Taylor (1990), for example, suggested that 93% of patients fail to adhere to some aspect of their treatment regimes, whereas Sarafino (1994) argued that people adhere 'reasonably closely' to their treatment regimes about 78% of the time for short-term treatments, and about 54% of the time for chronic conditions. In other words, the two researchers were using different definitions. Taylor was talking about precise conformity to every detail of the recommended treatment; Sarafino, on the other hand, was allowing for the way that most people 'customise' their treatments to fit in with their own lifestyles, but recognising that they may still be complying with the general features of the treatment.

Sarafino also found that the average adherence rates for taking medicine to prevent illness is roughly 60% for both long-term and short-term regimes, but compliance with a requirement to change one's lifestyle, such as stopping smoking or altering one's diet, was generally quite variable and often very low. There are limits, it seems, as to how far people will conform to medical demands if they seem to involve too great a change.

Overestimating compliance

When we look at the studies on compliance, there are two reasons for thinking that the estimates of compliance might be a bit optimistic. The first problem is the selection of people to take part in studies. For example, a study by Nessman et al. (1980, cited in Cluss and Epstein, 1985) looked at the effectiveness of group sessions in improving compliance in patients with hypertension. They found that their experimental group improved their compliance from 38% to 88%. The problem with this finding is that researchers were only able to persuade 56 people to take part in the study from a possible number of 500. It is most likely that the volunteers were more motivated than the people who declined to take part, and the positive result could be explained by their motivation rather than the group sessions. The obvious problem is that we can only estimate individuals' compliance if they make themselves available for research even if that just means answering a questionnaire.

The other problem with compliance research is that people will not always tell the truth. One of the reasons for this is to present a good impression to health workers. This can be very important, since the patient might well believe that they will only receive the best treatment if the health staff believe that they are carrying out instructions. The extreme example is of smokers who have been refused treatment if they admitted that they were still smoking.

PSYCHOLOGICAL CONTRIBUTIONS

Measuring compliance

It is important to develop reliable ways of measuring compliance and Cluss and Epstein (1985) suggest that the following methods can be used:

1 **Self-report**
   Ask the patient and they may tell you how compliant they have been. Unfortunately, it is a consistent research finding that patients overestimate their compliance with the treatment programme. Some studies have been able to compare a patient's report of their compliance of taking medication with some blood or urine samples that record the level of medication in the body. These studies show that patients seriously overestimate their compliance.

2 **Therapeutic outcome**
   Is the patient getting better? If, for example, a patient is taking medication for hypertension then we would expect their blood pressure to decrease. However, there are a range of other factors that also affect blood pressure including changes in the environment and the level of stress for the patient.

3 **Health worker estimates**
   Ask the doctor and they should be able to estimate how compliant a patient is being. Once again, this method has been found to be very unreliable.

4 **Pill and bottle counts**
   If we count the number of pills left in the bottle and compare it with the number that ought to be there then we should get a measure of compliance. The drawback to this method is that patients can throw the pills

away, and unless we have random, unexpected raids on bathroom cabinets by crack teams of experimental psychologists, we are not much further forward than the method of self-report.

5 Mechanical methods

A number of devices have been developed to measure how much medicine is dispensed from a bottle. These devices are expensive and they only measure how much medicine goes out of the bottle and not how much goes into the person.

6 Biochemical tests

It is possible to use blood tests or urine tests to estimate how compliant a patient has been with their medication. For example, it is possible to estimate compliance with diet in renal patients by measuring the levels of potassium and urea in their blood when they report for their next session of dialysis.

Overall, we can use a wide variety of methods to investigate patient compliance, but like all methods in psychology, they only produce estimates of behaviour, and they all contain some degree of error.

Attitudes and behaviour

If we are going to examine why people do or do not comply with health requests, we ought to have some idea about how they make decisions about their own health behaviour. The common approach to health promotion outlined in Chapter 4 is based on the idea that if we can change a person's attitudes then we will change their behaviour. This connection between attitudes and behaviour has been investigated by psychologists for the best part of the 20th century with the consistent finding that people often behave in ways that do not correspond to their attitudes. So, for example, many people think that it is a good thing to eat sensibly and look after their health, but still go out on a Friday night and have several pints of beer followed by a high-fat meal.

The health belief model

The ways in which we make decisions about our health behaviour are clearly more complex than just responding to our attitudes. One of the attempts to describe how we make these decisions is the health belief model (Becker and Rosenstock, 1984). According to this model (see Figure 5.1), the likelihood that a person will carry out a behaviour that will protect their health depends on two assessments.

1 Evaluating the threat

When we are confronted with a health risk we evaluate our personal threat by considering how serious the condition is (*perceived seriousness*), and how likely we are to get it (*perceived vulnerability*). For example, if a person is overweight they might be in danger of developing a heart condition. The person would probably recognise this as a serious condition, but they might believe that because they are still quite young they are unlikely to develop this problem just yet. Therefore they might judge the threat as relatively low. Even if we judge the threat to be serious, we are only likely to act if we have some cue to action. This cue might be a physical symptom like developing chest pains, it might be a mass media campaign, or it might be the death of a colleague with heart disease.

2   **Cost–benefit analysis**
The other assessment is a cost–benefit analysis which looks at whether the perceived benefits of changing our behaviour exceed the perceived barriers. The barriers might be financial, situational (difficult to get to a health clinic), or social (don't want to acknowledge getting old). The benefits might be improved health, relief from anxiety, and reducing health risks.

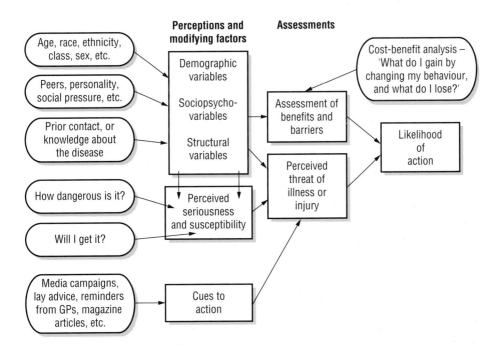

FIGURE 5.1 *The health belief model, (Source: Becker and Rosenstock, 1984)*

Applying the health belief model

One of the big health campaigns of the 1980s attempted to encourage people, especially young people, to use condoms in their sexual behaviour to reduce the threat of HIV and AIDS. In a study of over 300 sexually active Scottish teenagers, Abraham et al. (1992) looked at how the various components of the health belief model related to the intentions and behaviour of the young people. They found that the perceived seriousness of HIV infection, the perceived vulnerability, and the perceived effectiveness of condoms had little effect on their behaviour. The factors that had the greatest effect on their intentions and behaviour were the costs of condom use. These costs included beliefs about pleasure reduction, awkwardness of use and the likely response from their partner if they suggested using a condom.

These findings suggest that the early campaigns which emphasised vulnerability and threat had little effect on the behaviour of sexually active people, and that it would be more effective to concentrate campaigns on the barriers to condom use.

The health belief model has attracted a large amount of research and much of it is supportive of the basic theory. However, there is no standard way of measuring the variables in the model such as perceived susceptibility. Also there are a number of health behaviours that do not fit the model, such as habits (for example, teeth brushing). This means that the model has limited value in predicting whether people will comply with health requests, but it has been useful in trying to understand why people choose the health behaviours that they do.

There are a number of other models of health behaviour, including the theory of reasoned action, protection motivation theory, and subjective expected utility theory. All the theories have some value but none of them provides a comprehensive model of health behaviour. For a review, see Weinstein (1993).

Rational non-adherence

One of the most obvious reasons why patients do not comply to health requests is that they do not believe it is in their best interests to do so. This view sees the patient as making a rational decision not to comply. The patient might not believe that the treatment will help them get better, or they might believe that the treatment will cause more problems than it solves. For example, a study by Bulpitt (1988, cited in Kaplan, Sallis and Patterson, 1993) on the use of treatments for hypertension found that the medication improved the condition by reducing the symptoms of depression and headache, but it also had the side-effects of increased sexual problems such as difficulty with ejaculation and impotence. For some men this would be a price not worth paying. It would therefore be a rational decision to decline to take the medication (see Figure 5.2).

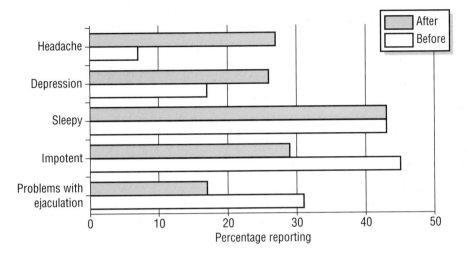

FIGURE 5.2 *Symptoms reported by people with hypertension before and after treatment. Patients are only likely to be compliant if they judge that the changes have an overall benefit*

Studies on compliance rarely consider the negative outcomes of the treatment that the patient is being asked to follow, and the costs of compliance are rarely calculated. Various studies, however, have found that treatment programmes often have serious side-effects. For example, Williamson and Chapin (1980) suggested that 10% of admissions to a geriatric unit were the result of undesirable drug side-effects. So if we are looking at compliance we should also consider the negative effects of the treatment and the preferences of the patient.

Sarafino (1994) summarises the reasons why a rational patient might not adhere to the treatment as follows.

- they have reason to believe that the treatment is not helping
- the side-effects are unpleasant, worrying or reduce their quality of life
- they are confused about when to take the treatment and how much is required
- there are practical barriers to the treatment, such as the cost of the medication
- they may want to check that the illness is still there when the treatment is discontinued.

Therefore, far from being awkward or ignorant, the noncomplying patient is often making the best sense they can of their health problem.

Other useful concepts

There are a number of other concepts in psychology that can be used to help explain the compliance or noncompliance of patients. These include:

- **Behavioural explanations**
  Learning theories offer a number of possible explanations for noncompliance. These include the role of habits, the power of imitation and the effects of reinforcement.
- **Defence mechanisms**
  The psychoanalytic approach suggests that we protect our ego by a variety of means – for example, avoidance (smokers are known to avoid information about the harmful effects of smoking) and denial ('this isn't really happening'). These issues are often described as *coping mechanisms* and they are described more fully in Chapter 3.

Other useful concepts include self-efficacy and locus of control. Both of these concepts are discussed in Chapter 12. *Locus of control* refers to the sense of control a person feels over their situation; whether they have personal choice or whether they can have little influence on what is happening. The more a person feels in control of their health and their treatment, the more likely they are to comply with the treatment programme. The concept of *self-efficacy* refers to the belief that a person will be successful in what they are trying to do. People are unlikely to follow a treatment programme if they doubt their ability to carry it out. For example, most smokers know that smoking is harmful and that quitting will improve their health. However, many smokers believe that they are not able to give up, and so do not try. If we want someone to follow a treatment programme then we need to ensure that the patient believes that they capable of carrying it out.

SPECIAL ISSUE:
Diabetes and compliance

Diabetes is a life-threatening disorder which can be successfully controlled so that diabetics can lead relatively normal lives. It is a disorder of the systems in the body that are responsible for the storage and use of glucose which is the main energy source that we get from food. The regulation of glucose in the body is mainly carried out by the hormone insulin which is produced in the pancreas. There are basically two types of diabetes, referred to as Type I and Type II. Type I diabetes (also called insulin-dependent diabetes) involves a complete failure of the pancreas and requires insulin replacement by injection. Type II diabetes (or noninsulin-dependent diabetes) is far more common, and in this condition individuals retain some endogenous insulin and are able to maintain good health through diet, weight management and oral medication.

Psychology is very important in the successful treatment of diabetes for a number of reasons:

- Diabetes can affect most areas of life, for example schooling and family relationships in children, and mood and interpersonal relationships in adults.
- Management of diabetes requires long-term self-regulation of behaviour, and the necessary behaviour is quite intrusive.
- Some complications might require rehabilitation and counselling.

The management of Type I diabetes

In this brief summary we will look at Type I diabetes and the issue of compliance to health requests. Type I diabetics need to follow a number of important guidelines if they are to remain in reasonable health. The important thing is to give themselves the appropriate amount of insulin in their regular injections so that they maintain a steady glucose level in the blood. If they let the glucose level go too low then they will have a hypoglycaemic attack ('a hypo') which is life-threatening unless dealt with quickly. If, on the other hand, the level is too high, then the immediate health consequences are slight (provided that a very high level is not maintained for several days) but there is likely to

be long-term damage and the diabetic is more likely to have circulation problems, vision problems and heart problems (reviewed in Bradley, 1994). Compliance to the diet and injection regime is therefore important for continued good health (see Table 5.1).

Diabetics have to respond to the following health requests:

- administer regular injections of insulin at the correct dosage and in a hygienic way
- monitor the level of glucose in the blood with regular testing
- take regular meals and monitor the intake of carbohydrates
- attend regular appointments for general health monitoring
- take exercise to maintain a good physical condition
- do not drink much alcohol because it lowers the level of blood sugar.

Compliance and diabetics

Diabetics often report noncompliance to their treatment regimes. For example, a survey of diabetics by Wing et al (1986) reported that 80% of patients administered insulin in an unhygienic manner; 58% of them regularly administered the wrong dose of insulin; 77% tested their urine incorrectly or made incorrect interpretations of the result; 75% did not eat the prescribed foods; and 75% did not eat with sufficient regularity (see Table 5.1)

Table 5.1 The noncompliance of diabetics

Unhygienic injections	80%
Wrong insulin dose	58%
Inappropriate diet	75%
Irregular diet	75%

A study by Glasgow et al. (1987) found that diabetics have more difficulty following the exercise and diet advice than they do with the medical aspects such as glucose testing and insulin injections. However, as mentioned above, self-reports are an unreliable way of collecting information and studies where memory chips were secretly put into the glucose-testing machines found that the diabetic patients kept inaccurate records of their own testing. They recorded some tests that never took place, and failed to record others which did.

Why don't diabetics always follow their treatment programme? There are a number of social variables that have been found to affect compliance in diabetics, including embarrassment of testing and injecting in social situations, and the amount of social support for the diabetic. There are also issues concerning knowledge about food and medical procedures.

FIGURE 5.3 *New methods for injecting insulin, such as the injection pen shown in the photograph, are more convenient and less embarrassing to use in public*

Some diabetics believe that they do not need to test their blood glucose levels because they can tell the level without testing. There is some evidence to support this, and research findings, summarised by Bradley (1994), show the following:

■ some diabetics are very accurate at recognising their blood glucose levels
■ some diabetics think they can tell the level but are not very accurate without training
■ each individual has reliable symptoms (physical changes and mood) associated with high and low glucose levels, but these are unique to the individual
■ most diabetics can learn to recognise their blood glucose levels.

One of the contributions that psychology can make is to develop programmes that help diabetics to learn how to accurately predict their blood-glucose levels.

Self-regulation

The above studies are examples of the general findings that show that diabetic compliance is quite poor. Some psychologists, such as Shillitoe and Miles (1989), however, suggest that there are some problems with using the term 'compliance' to describe the behaviour of diabetics. In the first place, the term implies that the patient has a set of specific guidelines to follow and this is often not the case. Secondly, as shown in the studies above, diabetics are good at following some instructions but poor at following others. Thirdly, the treatment regime varies every day depending on the blood tests, the amount of exercise and the presence of infection or anything else that might affect the level of glucose in the blood. In these circumstances it is virtually impossible to define and measure compliance.

The other problem with the term 'compliance' is that it implies that the diabetic should just do as they are told by the doctor. One of the important things for diabetics, however, is that they take control of their condition and their health and learn to manage it themselves. It is probably better, then, to describe 'levels of self-care behaviour' rather than 'compliance'.

INTERVENTIONS: ENHANCING COMPLIANCE

Psychology can help us understand why people do not comply, or find compliance difficult, and it can help us improve compliance with treatment programmes.

One factor that might improve compliance is designing information sheets and treatment programmes that are easy to understand and carry out. An important aspect of this is to consider the special needs of different client groups. Old people, for example, have different understandings and health beliefs to young people. Kaplan et al. (1993) identify three problems for old people in following treatment programmes.

1 Some old people have difficulty understanding and following complex instructions. Although ageing is not necessarily related to mental decline, some old people develop cognitive problems, such as memory loss, which make it more difficult to follow treatment programmes.
2 Older people sometimes have difficulty with medicine containers because they lack the manual dexterity to deal with child-proof caps. It has been noted that older people sometimes get over this problem by transferring the tablets to other containers which can lead to confusion about which tablet is which.
3 Older people are sometimes on a range of medications for different conditions and these might be prescribed by different doctors. This increases the risks of unpleasant side-effects, and so increases the chances that the patient will decide to discontinue with the treatment.

Looking at the above, it would appear that treatment programmes for the older patient need to take special consideration of this client group in order to improve compliance.

Presentation of the information

People will be more likely to follow the instructions for their treatment if they understand what they have to do and why they have to do it. One of the important factors here is the quality of the communication between health worker and patient (see Chapter 9 for further discussion of this). A range of training programmes for health workers have been used to improve this communication and Sarafino (1994) summarises the general findings from these studies as follows:

■ make verbal instructions as simple as possible and use straightforward language
■ give instructions that are specific rather than general
■ break down complicated treatment programmes into a series of smaller ones
■ emphasise key information
■ use simple written instructions
■ get the patient to repeat the instructions in their own words.

The health worker is very important in encouraging compliance. Taylor (1986) suggests that the health worker is a very credible source who can tailor the health message to the individual needs of the patient. The face-to-face nature of the interaction between patient and health worker tends to hold the attention of the patient and allows the health worker to check that the patient understands what they've got to do. The health worker can also enlist the support of other family members and increase the level of social support available to the patient. (Social support is further discussed in Chapter 3.) Finally, the health worker has the patient under partial supervision and so they can monitor their progress and encourage them to continue with the treatment.

Our concerns about compliance are usually directed at the patient. Researchers look for reasons why the patient does not follow the treatment programme and suggest what might be done about it. The above summaries, however, suggest that one of the best ways to improve compliance is to change the behaviour of the health worker who gives the treatment instructions. If the interaction between the patient and the health worker is improved then we might see dramatic improvements in compliance rates.

Behavioural methods

There are a number of effective behavioural approaches to compliance including:

- **feedback:** where the patient gets regular reports of the state of their health, and so is reinforced for their compliant behaviour
- **self-monitoring:** where the patient is encouraged to keep a written record of their treatment, such as their diet or their blood glucose levels (diabetics)
- **tailoring the regime:** where the treatment is customised to fit in with the habits and lifestyle of the patient
- **prompts and reminders:** something that helps the patient to remember the treatment at the appropriate time, for example, setting an alarm timer on a watch or receiving a reminder phone call
- **contingency contract:** where the patient negotiates a contract with the health worker concerning their treatment goals and the rewards they should receive for achieving those goals
- **modelling:** where the patient sees someone else successfully following the treatment programme and imitates that behaviour.

SUMMARY

Health professionals show considerable concern about people's failure to follow their instructions. There are, however, a number of good reasons for this reluctance to comply including the costs of compliance such as painful procedures and side-effects. Psychological models of health behaviour have been useful in our understanding of these processes, and might lead to helpful interventions in the future.

chapter six

LIFESTYLE AND HEALTH

CHAPTER OVERVIEW

The INTRODUCTION considers what we mean by the term lifestyle, and looks at the issue of health and poverty. It also considers the changing diet of the British and looks at how optimism can be damaging to our health. The PSYCHOLOGICAL CONTRIBUTIONS include a look at research into the Type A behaviour pattern and also consider biological factors and psychological factors in healthy lifestyles. The SPECIAL ISSUE looks at the eating disorders of anorexia nervosa and bulimia nervosa and considers a number of psychological concepts that have been used in an attempt to understand these conditions. The INTERVENTIONS include attempts to change Type A behaviour, and some attempts to encourage a healthy diet.

INTRODUCTION

What is a lifestyle?

How does the way we live affect our health? Psychologists and health workers refer to lifestyle as a risk factor in health, but what is the difference between a health behaviour and a lifestyle? The distinction is that when we talk about behaviour then we are referring to something that a person does, such as deciding to go to the doctor. A lifestyle, on the other hand, is a pattern of behaviours that are often tied into the type of job an individual has, the culture and sub-culture they feel part of, and the people they live with. In this chapter we will look at measurable behaviour patterns (such as the Type A behaviour pattern) and health habits (for example, our eating habits).

Health and poverty

It is important to point out that the most damaging lifestyles for our health are those associated with low incomes. Throughout the Western world, the most consistent predictor of illness and early death is income. People who are unemployed, homeless, or on low incomes have higher rates of all the major causes of premature death (Carroll, Davey Smith and Bennett, 1994). The reasons for this are not clear though there are two main lines of argument. First, it is possible that people with low incomes engage in risky behaviours more frequently, so they might smoke more cigarettes and drink more alcohol. This argument probably owes more to negative stereotypes of working-class people than it does to any systematic research. A study cited by Carroll et al. (1994) excluded smokers from the statistics and still found that income had a considerable effect on health. This suggests that smoking and drinking are not the cause of the poor health of working-class people.

The second line of argument is that poor people are exposed to greater health risks in the environment in the form of hazardous jobs and poor living accommodation. Also, people on low incomes will probably buy cheaper foods which have a higher content of fat (currently regarded as a risk factor for coronary heart disease). All this means that psychological interventions on behaviour can only have a limited effect since it is changes in economic circumstances that will do most to improve the health of the nation.

The changing diet of the British

The last 30 years have seen a fairly consistent trend in the changing diets of the British (see Figure 6.1). Even those of us who thought 'Saturated Fats' was an alcoholic blues singer from the Deep South of America have changed our basic diet. There is a clear message that we should reduce the level of fat in our food, and although many people might not know why this is so, they are still major purchasers of low-fat food products. This change conforms to one of the risk factor targets in the British Government's Health of the Nation strategy: 'To reduce the average percentage of food energy derived by the population from saturated fatty acids by at 35% by 2005 [The baseline measure is consumption in 1990].' (page 20).

The charts in Figure 6.1 overleaf show how much the diet of British people has changed in the last 30 years. Our consumption of butter (high in fats) is under a third of what it was in 1961, our consumption of full-fat milk has fallen dramatically, and we have changed our meat-eating from red (beef and lamb) to white (poultry). Total meat consumption is also down by about one fifth. These are major changes in our eating habits and they have taken place in one generation. If the health professionals are correct, then this change in diet should lead to improved life expectancy of the British population.

One of the factors that affects our eating habits is the image we have of the 'perfect body'. This image of what a person should look like varies from culture to culture, and is also affected by trends in fashion. Over the past 30 years, as Western society has become more affluent, we have developed an

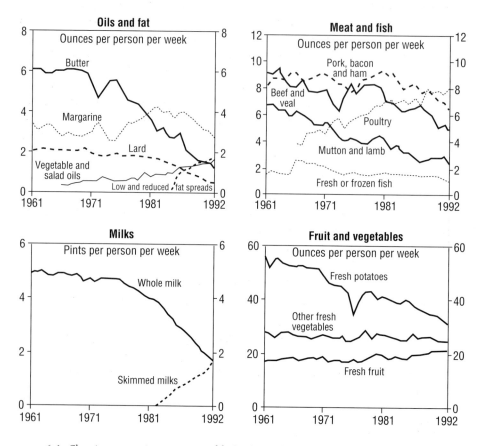

FIGURE 6.1 *Changing patterns in consumption of food at home.* (Source: *Social Trends* 1994. Crown copyright (1994)/Office for National Statistics)

increasing concern with being slim. This is not necessarily associated with good health, since although it is not healthy to be obese, neither is it healthy to be very slim. This increasing concern with slimness is illustrated by Wade and Tavris (1990), who looked at the body weights of female beauty contest winners. They report that Miss Sweden of 1951, who was judged to be the 'most glamorous' woman in the competition, was 5'7" tall and weighed 151 pounds. However, Miss Sweden of 1983 was 5'9" tall and weighed only 109 pounds. Other studies have found similar results in America and Britain, and this is at a time when the average weight of British and American women was increasing. Body image is thought to be one of the factors in eating disorders such as anorexia (see below).

Optimism

One of the problems that health educators have to deal with when they are trying to change an individual's behaviour is our unrealistic optimism about our health. A number of studies, for example, Weinstein (1987), have asked people to rate their personal risk of developing various disorders compared with the risk of people like them. Individuals usually rate their chances of illness as less than that of other people. The problems with this optimism are illustrated in a study by Turner et al. (1988) of students at Oxford University who judged that their own risk of contracting AIDS was less than that of their fellow students. This was even true of students who were taking part in high-risk behaviours such as unprotected penetrative sex, and sex with bisexual partners, intravenous drug users, or prostitutes. So, why are we so optimistic about our health? Weinstein suggested four cognitive factors that affect this optimism:

1 People tend to believe that if a problem has not appeared yet, then it is unlikely to develop in the future.
2 People tend to think that personal action can prevent the problem.
3 People believe that the problem is rare.
4 People have little or no experience of the problem.

These cognitive factors do not provide a logical framework for making judgements about personal risk, but people do not operate on the basis of logic (see the section on bias in judgement, page 00). On the whole, this optimism is no bad thing since it prevents us from developing a maudlin preoccupation with illness, but it does mean that we are resistant to health messages about the dangers of our lifestyle.

Nutrition and health

Every generation and every culture has stories it tells about the value of foods. For example, as a child I was told that carrots are good for your eyesight and fish is good for your brain. In Britain today we talk about calories and fats, but is there really a connection between these concepts and good health?

One of the villains of modern stories is *cholesterol*. This is a fatty substance that builds up in patches on the walls of our arteries and, over time, narrows those arteries, creating circulation problems and heart problems. Most of the cholesterol is made in our own bodies but some of it comes from the food we eat. As we get older, these fatty deposits harden and we can develop arteriosclerosis. Various studies have found that people with high levels of cholesterol in the blood are much more at risk of heart disease or a stroke than are people with low levels.

(Note: as ever, the above is a very simplified version of a very complex process. One of the complicating factors is that there is more than one type of cholesterol, and not all of them are damaging to your health.)

Another serious condition associated with diet is *hypertension* (consistently high blood pressure). People can reduce the risk of hypertension by reducing their intake of sodium, which is mainly found in salt (though how you can ask anyone to eat a boiled egg without lashings of salt, I don't know.) It is thought that reducing sodium has a positive effect on the blood pressure of healthy people as well as people with hypertension. The same is true for caffeine (found in coffee, tea and cola). However, the connection between caffeine and heart disease is much more controversial than the salt connection, and some studies have found that regular coffee drinkers have lower blood pressure than non coffee drinkers. This highlights the dangers of 'sound-bite' health messages that tell us to eat this, or not to eat that. The best defence against ill-health is a balanced lifestyle that includes exercise as well as a healthy diet.

Psychological Contributions

The contributions of psychology to lifestyle that we are going to consider in this chapter look at two different topics. First, there are the patterns of behaviour that might make us prone to particular diseases, and the example we will look at is the Type A behaviour pattern. Secondly, there are the habits of daily living that might affect our health, and the example we will look at is eating. There are a number of other psychological factors discussed elsewhere in this text that are important in discussions about lifestyle. These factors include self-efficacy (see pages 176–177), locus of control (see pages 174–176) and models of health decision-making such as the health belief model (see pages 68–70).

The Type A behaviour pattern

Do some lifestyles make people more vulnerable to disease? Are we justified, for example, in associating high-stress behaviour with certain health problems such as heart disease? Friedman and Rosenman (1959) investigated this and created a description of behaviour patterns that has generated a large amount of research and also become part of the general discussions on health in popular magazines.

Before we look at the work of Friedman and Rosenman, it is worth making a psychological distinction between behaviour patterns and personality. Text books and articles often refer to the Type A *personality*, though, at least in the original paper, the authors describe a *behaviour pattern* rather than a personality type. The difference between these two things is that a personality type is what you *are*, whereas a behaviour pattern is what you *do*. The importance of this distinction comes in our analysis of why we behave in a particular way ('I was made this way', or 'I learnt to be this way'), and what can be done about it. It is easier to change a person's pattern of learnt behaviour than it is to change their nature.

Friedman and Rosenman devised a description of Pattern A behaviour that they expected to be associated with high levels of blood cholesterol and hence coronary heart disease. This description was based on their previous research and their clinical experience with patients, and a summary is given below.

Pattern A behaviour

- An intense, sustained drive to achieve your personal (and often poorly defined) goals.
- A profound tendency and eagerness to compete in all situations.
- A persistent desire for recognition and advancement.
- Continuous involvement in several activities at the same time that are constantly subject to deadlines.
- An habitual tendency to rush to finish activities.
- Extraordinary mental and physical alertness.

Pattern B behaviour, on the other hand is the opposite of Pattern A, characterised by the relative absence of drive, ambition, urgency, desire to compete, or involvement in deadlines.

Research into Type A

The classic study of Type A and Type B behaviour patterns was a 12-year longitudinal study of over 3,500 healthy middle-aged men reported by Friedman and Rosenman in 1974. They found that, compared to people with the Type B behaviour pattern, people with the Type A behaviour pattern were twice as likely to develop coronary heart disease. Other researchers found that differences in the kinds of Type A behaviour correlated with different kinds of heart disease: angina sufferers tended to be impatient and intolerant with others, while those with heart failure tended to be hurried and rushed, inflicting the pressures on themselves.

The Type A behaviour pattern has stimulated a vast amount of research. Some of this research has supported the connection between the behaviour and coronary heart disease, and some of it has not. The reason for the differences in the research findings can be partly explained by the different methods used by the researchers, but the area remains controversial. The idea continues to be researched but it is clear that the relationship between behaviour and coronary heart disease is not as straightforward as was originally suggested.

A study by Ragland and Brand (1988) illustrates how complex the relationship is between behaviour and coronary heart disease. In their original study, they found that measures of Type A behaviour were useful in predicting the development of coronary heart disease. However, in the follow-up study conducted 22 years later, the initial behaviour pattern of the men was compared with their subsequent mortality rates. Ragland and Brand found that among the 231 men who survived the first coronary event for 24 hours or more, those who had initially displayed a Type A behaviour pattern died at a rate much lower than the men who displayed a Type B behaviour pattern (19.1 versus 31.7 per 1000 person-years). This finding was rather unexpected and seems to contradict the general view about Type A behaviour. One explanation is that people who display the Type A behaviour pattern may respond differently to a heart attack than do people who display the Type B behaviour pattern. Alternatively, Type A behaviour patterns may cease to be a risk factor after such an event. People may take the warning and change their lifestyle.

The lasting appeal of the Type A behaviour pattern is its simplicity and plausibility (an example of the types of question used to judge the behaviour pattern are given in Box 6.1). Unfortunately, health is rarely that simple and the interaction of stress with physiological, psychological, social and cultural factors cannot be reduced to two simple behaviour patterns. However, the work has focused attention on the role of lifestyle in health, and provided a stimulus for a range of research projects and therapeutic interventions with coronary-prone patients.

Box 6.1   Type A and Type B behaviour patterns

Classifying behaviour into Type A or Type B is usually done by interview or by questionnaire. Examples of questions are:

1 **'Has your partner or friend ever told you that you eat too fast?'**
   Type A's are likely to say, 'Yes, often'.
   Type B's are likely to say, 'Yes, once or twice' or 'No'.
2 **'How would your partner, or best friend, rate your general level of activity?'**
   Type A's are likely to say, 'Too active, need to slow down'.
   Type B's are likely to say, 'Too slow, need to be more active'.
3 **'Do you ever set deadlines or quotas for yourself at work or at home?'**
   Type A's are likely to say, 'Yes, once a week or more often'.
   Type B's are likely to say, 'Only occasionally'.
4 **'When you are in the middle of a job and someone (not your boss) interrupts you, how do you feel inside?'**
   Type A's are likely to say, 'I feel irritated because most interruptions are unnecessary'.
   Type B's are likely to say, 'I feel O.K. because I work better after an occasional break'.

Nutrition

How do we develop our eating habits? And why do we choose the foods that we do? Around the world, many people have a restricted choice of food, and it is only in very recent years that people in wealthy countries have been able to choose theirs. Throughout the development of human societies, people ate the food that was available, and that meant the food that was grown or caught in the local area. Until Walter Raleigh brought the potato to this country, no one in Blackpool had ever had a bag of chips. In today's shops, however, it is possible to buy food from all parts of the world due to the advances of food preservation. The factors that influence our choices of food can be categorised into three: biological, cultural and psychological.

Biological factors

A common experience we have is of an empty stomach, and one of our lay beliefs about hunger is that it comes from this empty stomach. However, people who have their stomachs removed or bypassed by surgery still report feelings of hunger and are able to maintain their body weight by eating smaller and more frequent meals. Various theories have tried to explain why we feel hungry, including the glucostatic theory (looking at levels of sugar in the blood), the lipostatic theory (looking at levels of body fat) and the set-point theory. The set-point theory proposed that the body had a set-point weight (or target weight) and it was maintained by homeostatic mechanisms in the hypothalamus (part of the brain). Homeostatic mechanisms are thought to operate like a thermostat on a central heating boiler. When the boiler gets hot, the thermostat cuts off the power, and when it cools down, the thermostat switches the power back on. So, if we apply this to hunger, then we feel hungry when our body's food resources are depleted, and we lose this hunger when we have replenished those resources. This model is shown in a simplified form in Figure 6.2 overleaf.

This approach is very plausible and still appears in some textbooks, but as Pinel (1993) points out, the theory can not explain a number of everyday experiences in our eating habits. For example, if we only eat when our energy reserves are low, how is it that after a big meal we are still able to eat 'Death by Chocolate' and cover it with lashings of whipped cream?

Current theories on eating look at the role of incentives, such as taste. They also look at learning and habit formation. A development of the set-point Theory is the idea of *settling points*. The distinction is that a set-point is an innate level for our body weight, but a settling point is a point that we develop and maintain. We find our own settling point, and this can change as our circumstances change and our behaviour changes. This view suggests that we are not fully dependent on our in-built hunger mechanisms to regulate our eating.

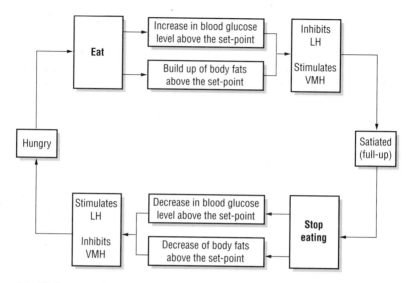

FIGURE 6.2 *The homeostatic set-point model of eating*

Cultural factors

The family is our main source of information about food, and we are likely to eat a similar diet to that of our parents. One of the important features of family approaches to food is the use of certain foods as rewards. For example, we might say, 'You can have a sweet if you eat up your cabbage.' A study by Birch, Zimmerman and Hind (1980) found that children preferred foods that were associated with praise and reward. They claim that children began to like carrots more when they were given as a reward, though I think that saying something like, 'If you don't eat your chocolate, you won't have a carrot', is unlikely to be very effective.

Another medium for transmitting culture is television, and there are numerous advertisements for food. A study on advertisements in the United States of America found that the average American child watched 10,000 commercials for food every year. Of these commercial, 51% were for cereals, and 33% were for sweets and biscuits. Less than 5% of the adverts were for products without sugar and there were no adverts at all for vegetables (Wadden and Brownell, 1984). As part of the same study, 75% of mothers said they were influenced in their food choices by the requests of their children. So, a major issue in the promotion of healthy lifestyles is the commercial pressure applied to children through advertisements. It would be possible to make significant progress towards the targets in *The Health of the Nation* (see pages 8–10) if the government took action to regulate commercials aimed at children. They are unlikely to do this.

Psychological factors

One of the important factors in weight gain is alcohol. People who regularly drink a lot of alcohol tend to gain weight because of the calories in alcoholic drinks and also because alcohol reduces the body's disposal of fat. Watching television also has an effect, since it decreases the amount of physical activity a person does and it also decreases the rate at which the body burns calories. Another factor that affects our intake of food is how sensitive we are to food cues in the environment. Research suggests that people who are very over-weight are more sensitive to food cues than people who have an average body weight. For example, Herman, Olmstead and Polivy (1983) found that descriptions of desserts in a restaurant had more influence on the choices made by overweight people than average weight people.

There are various theories about why people eat too much or eat too little, and some of these are described in the section about eating disorders below.

SPECIAL ISSUE:
Eating disorders

Eating is an important part of social activity as well as being essential for life. It is also tied up with a range of issues to do with our perceptions of ourselves and our general mood. Sometimes people have unusual eating patterns that can be damaging to their general health, in some cases to the point of being life-threatening. Concerns about weight and appearance are not new and can be seen in the customs of ancient civilisations. For example, the Roman civilisation invented the 'vomitorium' over 2000 years ago where people could go and vomit after a big meal. This allowed them to eat and drink to excess without getting any fatter.

In wealthy societies where plenty of food is available, people have used various means to control their weight, and sometimes these means are taken to excess. The first clinical descriptions of excessive self-induced weight loss were made in 1694 (see Cooper, 1995), though the term 'anorexia nervosa' was first introduced in 1874.

Anorexia nervosa and bulimia nervosa

There are various approaches to the eating disorders known as anorexia nervosa and bulimia nervosa (see Box 6.2), though there is no common agreement on the causes or the treatment. Anorexia nervosa is 15 times more prevalent in women than men (Abraham and Llewellyn-Jones, 1987), it starts between adolescence and the age of 25, and it is esti-mated to affect as many as 1 in 100 people (Matlin, 1987), though estimates of young women with mild versions of the disorder are as high as 10% (Brownell and Foreyt, 1986). Around 15% of women who are diagnosed as having anorexia nervosa die from the disor-der, and under half regain a reasonable adjustment to eating.

Box 6.2 Proposed criteria in DSM-IV for anorexia nervosa and bulimia nervosa (American Psychiatric Association, 1991)

Anorexia nervosa

A Refusal to maintain body weight over a minimal normal weight for age and height (e.g., weight loss leading to maintenance of body weight 15% below that expected; or failure to make expected weight gain during period of growth leading to body weight 15% below that expected.)

B Intense fear of gaining weight or becoming fat, even though underweight.

C Disturbance in the way in which one's body weight or shape is experienced, undue influence of body shape and weight on self-evaluation, or denial of the seriousness of current low body weight.

D In females, absence of at least three consecutive menstrual cycles when otherwise expected to occur (primary or secondary amenorrhea).

Specific types

- **Bulimic type:** During the episode of anorexia nervosa, the person engages in recurrent episodes of binge eating.
- **Non-bulimic type:** During the episode of anorexia nervosa, the person does not engage in recurrent episodes of binge eating.

Bulimia nervosa

A Recurrent episodes of binge eating. An episode of binge eating is characterised by both of the following:

  1 Eating, in a discrete period of time (e.g. within any two-hour period), an amount of food that is definitely larger than most people would eat during a similar period of time.

  2 A sense of lack of control over eating during the episode (i.e. a feeling that one cannot stop eating or control what or how one is eating).

B Recurrent inappropriate compensatory behaviour in order to prevent weight gain, such as: self-induced vomiting; misuse of laxatives, diuretics or other medication; fasting; or excessive exercise.

C A minimum average of two binge eating episodes a week for at least three months.

D Self-evaluation is unduly influenced by body shape and weight.

E The disturbance does not occur exclusively during episodes of anorexia nervosa.

Specific types

- **Purging type:** Regularly engages in self-induced vomiting or the use of laxatives or diuretics.
- **Non-purging type:** Use of strict dieting, fasting or vigorous exercise, but does not regularly engage in purging.

Bulimia nervosa is also predominantly observed in women, with most known cases being in their 20s. Bulimia is not life-threatening; however, it can lead to disorders of the kidney and intestines, and can also cause throat and dental problems due to the acid in vomited material. Its prevalence is not known, though there are some indications that self-induced vomiting as a means of weight control is quite common in young women. In 1980, *Cosmopolitan* magazine published a small advertisement inviting letters from its female readers who used self-induced vomiting as a method of weight control. The response was so large that the researchers chose to follow up only the first 800 replies. These women were sent a questionnaire about their behaviour, and the returns indicated that 83% fulfilled the diagnostic criteria for bulimia. Community surveys, for example by Cooper and Fairburn (1983, cited in Colman, 1987), have suggested that as many as 2 in 100 people have the clinical symptoms of this disorder. The incidence of both anorexia nervosa and bulimia nervosa is more common in women from the more wealthy socio-economic classes.

Psychological explanations

There are number of concepts that psychologists introduce into discussion about eating disorders including the following.

Eating habits

From an early age we are encouraged to make an association between eating and being loved. A chubby baby is seen as a healthy and well cared-for baby. This connection between love and eating stays with us throughout life. Some psychologists suggest this connection between comfort and eating is a major factor in anorexia nervosa, and also in over-eating and obesity.

As we grow up, we eat more food. In particular, during our adolescent growth spurt we dramatically increase our food intake. When boys have completed their growth spurt, they continue to increase their muscle mass and so need to maintain their habits of increased eating. However, when girls complete their growth spurt their energy needs decrease because they do not develop their muscle mass in the same way as boys. According to Abraham and Llewellyn-Jones (1987) 'If the girl continues to eat the quantity of food she ate in early adolescence obesity is inevitable' (page 23). This means that girls must change their eating habits at this age and learn to control their weight by dieting or some other means. This suggests that dieting is an important part of healthy development for young women. The problem, then, is not dieting *per se*, but dieting to excess.

Body image

There is some controversy over whether people with anorexia nervosa have an unusual self-image. There have been a number of studies (for a brief review, see Colman, 1987) where people have been asked to estimate their body shape. This can be achieved by asking them to use callipers to show their perceived width, or beams of light to produce a silhouette most like themselves. Recent studies have used video images which can be adjusted using a distorted lens. The findings from these studies are not consistent so although many anorexics overestimate their body size, the error is often quite small. Colman (1987) concludes that about one third of women with anorexia nervosa overestimate the size of their body by over 10%, though this level of overestimation can also be found in women without an eating disorder. Colman goes on to suggest that the women who do make the gross overestimates of body size are those women who are less likely to improve.

A further aspect of this work concerns how

satisfied we are with our body shape. We might, for example, overestimate our body size but be perfectly relaxed about it. This issue was investigated by Fallon and Rozin (1985) who asked men and women to identify their ideal body and their current body shape on a linear scale. A summary of the results are shown in Figure 6.3, and they indicate that, on average, women are less satisfied with their body shape than men.

Socio-cultural influences

Psychological approaches to health behaviours emphasise the role of cues to action (for example see the health belief model, pages 68–70). Among the cues to action are the media messages we receive about attractiveness and eating, for example, the changing image of glamour (see the description of 'beauty' contestants above). This change in our stereotype of the ideal female body has increased the strength of the message to women about controlling their weight.

Another source of cues are advertisements, and the contradictory cues we receive through these advertisements are that to be attractive means to be slim and active, but on the other hand, to enjoy yourself means to consume. Food advertising is mostly concentrated on fattening foods such as sweets, cakes and biscuits, so our cues to action are largely to consume food which will increase our weight (Wadden and Brownell, 1984, see above).

The incidence of both anorexia nervosa and bulimia nervosa appears to be increasing in Western societies (Fallon and Rozin, 1985), and this increase might be well be the result of the increasing strength of the cues to action.

Eating disorders are a serious health threat to a significant minority of young women. Although they have been heavily researched it is not clear whether they represent a pathological response to food, or just the extremes of regular eating behaviour.

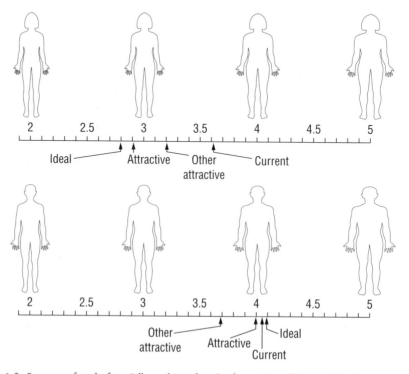

FIGURE 6.3 *Summary of results from Fallon and Rozin's study of perceptions of desirable body shape*

INTERVENTIONS

Changing Type A behaviour

There have been a number of attempts to reduce the chances of illness by changing the frequency of risk behaviours. For example, Friedman et al. (1986) studied over 1000 people who had suffered a heart attack. The patients were allocated into three groups:

1 **The control group,** who received no intervention from the psychologists.
2 **The cardiac counselling group,** who received frequent counselling about the causes of heart attack and the importance of altering standard coronary risk factors such as smoking and excessive exercise.
3 **The Type A/cardiac group,** who received the cardiac counselling and also took part in a programme designed to reduce Type A behaviour. This programme included relaxation techniques and exercises in cognitive restructuring.

Not surprisingly, the people in the Type A/cardiac group showed a greater reduction in Type A behaviours than people in the other two groups. They also showed less problems with heart disease and also a lower mortality rate.

Dietary change programmes

One of the most commonly cited attempts to change diet is the Multiple Risk Factor Intervention Trial carried out in the USA and reported by Dolecek et al. (1986). This six-year study looked at over 12,000 men who showed risk factors for heart disease. Half of the men were assigned to the usual care condition, and the other half were assigned to the special intervention condition, which focused on dietary change, smoking, and the treatment of hypertension with medication, and used group work and individual counselling. The results of the study are shown in Table 6.1.

Table 6.1 Summary of results from the Multiple Risk Factor Intervention Trial

	Baseline	Change scores	
		Special intervention group	**Usual care group**
Calories	2433	−532 (22%)	−277 (11%)
Total fat (% of total food intake)	38.2	−4.4 (12%)	−0.2 (0.5%)
Cholesterol (mg)	451	−186 (41%)	−22 (5%)

These results are interesting for a number of reasons. First, the group who had no treatment (the usual care condition) showed a significant drop in calorie intake and cholesterol level. There is not an obvious reason for this unless it indicates a general change in men's diets. The special intervention group showed dramatic changes in their intake of calories (11% reduction) and their cholesterol levels (41% reduction). However, at the end of the study there was no difference in the mortality rates for the two groups, though it might be that the effects of the programme will be seen as the men get older. It is clear that the programme helped the men change their diet, but it is not clear whether this had any long-term health benefits.

Dieting

We can control our diet for health reasons and we can control our diet for cosmetic reasons such as the desire to fit into fashionable clothes. Many people in Western society who diet are not overweight in any medical sense, but judge themselves to be overweight because of their desire to look very slim. The effects of the various commercial diet plans and products are reviewed by Sarafino (1994), who comments that there is very little evidence for their success. Crash dieting is not a substitute for taking on a healthy lifestyle of exercise, drinking alcohol in moderation (if at all) and eating moderately-sized meals with a balance of natural food.

A small minority of people become very overweight (obese) and this can become a serious health hazard. The reasons that people become overweight are varied and complex. It can be a biological condition, and it can be affected by a number of psychological factors and cultural expectations. Preventing overweight can begin in childhood, since 70% of children who are obese between the ages of 10 and 13 grow up to be obese adults (Sarafino, 1994). Since children get most of their food from parents, there are a number of ways that parents can help in the prevention of obesity. Nutritionists make the following recommendations:

- encourage physical activity rather than television watching
- avoid using unhealthy food as a reward
- reduce the amount of food available with a high fat content and with a high sugar content
- encourage the consumption of fruit and nuts
- encourage the child to have a healthy breakfast, and avoid high-calorie, late-night snacks
- make regular checks on the child's weight
- encourage the child to take regular exercise.

Other techniques to control weight

One of the more successful psychological interventions is the use of behavioural techniques to change eating habits. These techniques tend to have a low drop-out rate and relatively high success rates. In particular, they show sustained weight loss over a twelve month period. The techniques that are most effective include:

- **self-monitoring,** where people keep an accurate record of their eating
- **stimulus control,** where you try and control your exposure to the cues that encourage you to eat; for example you might store food out of sight, or only eat in one room
- **change eating habits,** for example put your knife and fork down between mouthfuls
- **contract and rewards** – making a contract with yourself so that if you keep to your diet you can have a reward, though it is better if the reward does not involve 'Death by Chocolate' and three pints of lager.

END NOTE: BLAMING THE PATIENT

One of the objections to looking at lifestyles as an explanation of ill-health is that it tends to blame the ill person for their illness: 'So you put salt on your chips do you? Well, you can expect to get high blood pressure.' People get ill for all manner of reasons, and we have only a dim understanding of the range of factors that prevent illness and enhance health. The focus on lifestyle suggests that the most important factors are those that people have responsibility for, and control over. However, as mentioned in the introduction to this chapter, the greatest risk factor in health is poverty, and this is a factor that most people are unable to control. With regard to other factors like smoking and diet, there are huge commercial pressures to consume unhealthy substances and some of these pressures are directed at children. The regulation of commercial messages to encourage good health, or the requirement for manufacturers to be responsible for the effects of their products and commercial messages, might well have a dramatic effect on our lifestyles and our health (see the section on smoking, pages 97–98). The government is unlikely to enforce this action.

SUMMARY

The way we live has a large effect on our general level of health. Good health is protected through regular exercise, a healthy diet, a regular work pattern and moderation in risk behaviours and alcohol and drug use. This relatively simple message is not followed by most people in the population for various personal, social and cultural reasons. These reasons are only partially understood by psychologists and health workers, who usually discuss the issue over a cigarette when they are down the pub.

chapter seven

ADDICTIVE BEHAVIOURS AND SMOKING

CHAPTER OVERVIEW

The INTRODUCTION looks at the medical approach to addiction and compares it with the psychological description of addictive behaviours. It also considers the social value of substances and looks at some of the different cultural responses to substances. The SPECIAL ISSUE looks at the issue of smoking and considers the development and the dangers of this habit. The PSYCHOLOGICAL CONTRIBUTIONS include the biological explanations of addictive behaviours, and a consideration of the effects of availability on the development of addictive behaviours. There is also a description of the spiral model of behavioural change proposed by Prochaska, DiClemente and Norcross (1992). Psychologists have suggested a number of APPLICATIONS to help reduce the damage of addictive behaviours including the use of reinforcement, harm minimisation campaigns and a number of quit smoking campaigns.

INTRODUCTION

The medical approach to addiction

One approach to addictive behaviours is to see them as a medical problem. This approach concentrates on the excessive use of various substances and commonly defines addiction as 'dependence on a drug, resulting in tolerance and withdrawal symptoms when the addict is deprived of the drug' (Rosenhan and Seligman, 1989).

This view of addictive behaviours starts with a social problem, such as alcoholism or opiate addiction, and then looks for a psychological explanation of these behaviours. By taking this approach, health workers have generally looked at alcoholism and drug addiction in isolation from other behaviours. Alcoholism and drug addiction have generally been seen as diseases, probably because the alternative to this was to see them as 'crimes' or 'sins'. However, although they are described as diseases, there are underlying themes about the social crime of abusing drugs or alcohol and the moral wickedness of trying to obtain pleasure through chemical means.

Addictive behaviours

An alternative approach sees drug addiction, for instance, as just one example of a wider set of addictive behaviours. In our everyday speech, the term 'addiction' is used as a metaphor for other activities, for example in the song 'Addicted to Love' by Robert Palmer. But can we be addicted to love in the same way as we can be addicted to alcohol? Yes we can, says a psychological approach to addictive behaviours put forward by, for example, Orford (1985) and Griffiths (1995a).

This approach suggests that people can develop addictive behaviours for a wide range of activities including drug use, alcohol use, gambling, game playing, eating and sex. Although these behaviours appear to be very different, they also involve a number of similar components. Griffiths (1995a) suggests that addictive behaviours have six components:

1 **Salience**
   This refers to how important the behaviour becomes to the individual. Addictive behaviours become the most important activity for a person so that even when they are not doing it, they are thinking about it.
2 **Euphoria**
   This is the experience people report when they carrying out their addictive behaviour. People with addictive behaviour patterns commonly report a 'rush', a 'buzz' or a 'high', when they are taking their drugs or when they are gambling, for example.
3 **Tolerance**
   This refers to the increasing amount of activity that is required to achieve the same effect. A drug addict might have to increase the intake of drugs and a gambler might have to increase the stakes.
4 **Withdrawal symptoms**
   These are the unpleasant feelings and physical effects which occur when the addictive behaviour is suddenly discontinued or reduced. This can include 'the shakes', moodiness and irritability. These symptoms are commonly believed to be a response to the removal of a chemical that the person has developed a tolerance to. However, they can also be experienced by gamblers (see Orford, 1985), so the effects might be due to withdrawal from the behaviour as well as the substance.
5 **Conflict**
   People with addictive behaviours develop conflicts with the people around them, often causing great social misery, and also develop conflicts within themselves.
6 **Relapse**
   Although people sometimes manage to shake off their addictive behav-

iour, the chances of relapse are very high. Even when the person has been 'dry' for a considerable time, they can quickly develop the same high levels of addictive behaviour.

This psychological approach to addictive behaviours highlights the many similarities within a wide range of damaging behaviour patterns, and indicates that the disease model of addiction is quite limited.

A further similarity between a number of addictive behaviours can be found in the groups that support people who want to change their behaviour, such as Alcoholics Anonymous, or Gamblers Anonymous, and even Weight Watchers. Orford (1985) suggests that when people change their addictive behaviour it might involve them reinventing themselves, which means they take on a new identity and change their attitudes and values on a wide range of issues. The organisations that support this change often have a religious approach to the problem. They frequently require the person to give personal testimony ('I was a sinner', 'I was a drunk', 'I was a gambler') and accept the authority of the group or a 'higher power'. They usually emphasise that the person should change from being self-centred (egocentric) and pleasure-seeking (hedonistic), to being humble and ascetic. All this suggests that the person is undertaking a moral (or spiritual) change rather than a medical change. Perhaps it is not surprising, then, that the expert treatments offered by psychologists and health workers only have a small role to play in helping people change their addictive behaviour.

The approach suggested by Griffiths allows us to see addictive behaviours within a psychological context rather than a medical one. It also allows us to consider them within a much wider range of behaviours. In this chapter, however, we will concentrate on the areas of alcohol consumption and smoking, which are the two addictive behaviours that are currently seen as the major concerns in health.

The social value of substances

One of the complicating factors in any discussion of addiction and substance misuse is the different social value that various substances have. This social value can change over time, for example, the opiates (such as opium, morphine and heroin) currently generate a lot of moral concern but this was not always the case. Opium was used for hundreds of years to relieve pain, to induce sleep and to control common ailments like coughs and colds. The common way it was taken was in laudanum which was a mixture of opium and alcohol. Opium was seen as an acceptable medication and it was only during the 19th century that concerns began to develop when the use of the drug increased, and people started using it for recreational as well as medical purposes. Orford (1985) reports that up the middle of the 19th century it was accepted that many people living in the fens (of Lincolnshire, Cambridgeshire and Norfolk) were regular users of opium. In fact, the *Morning Chronicle* of 1850 described the fenland town of Ely as the 'opium-eating city'. This heavy use was attributed to the damp conditions of fenland and the rheumatism and neuralgia that many people developed.

The history of opium use could fill a book, but the point to be made here is that in different cultures and in different times, a substance can have a very different social significance and a very different social use. What this means is that the substances that health workers currently choose to look at and create the maximum social concern about are not necessarily the most threatening substances for our health. They are, however, the substances that we are currently most concerned about for all manner of health, financial, moral and political reasons. Also, as we will see below, the methods that are most commonly used to reduce substance abuse are not necessarily the most effective for reducing health risks. These methods are also affected by the political and moral responses from the rest of the community (for example, see Mestel and Concar's report on treatment for cocaine abusers later in this chapter).

There is currently a lot of concern about the social use of opiates, though the behaviour that is thought to have the most damaging effect on the nation's health is smoking. This behaviour is singled out for particular attention in *The Health of the Nation* (Department of Health, 1992; see pages 8–10), so this chapter takes a special look at the issues surrounding smoking and how it might be discouraged.

SPECIAL ISSUE:
Smoking

Smoking tobacco is a strange thing to do. We pick some leaves off a bush, dry them out, roll them up and surround them with paper, set fire to them and then suck. Tobacco came to Europe from South America during the 16th century and its danger to health was recognised as early as 1604 by King James I, who imposed a heavy import duty to reduce consumption and protect the health of the nation. During the 20th century, the consumption of cigarettes in Britain and the USA increased dramatically until the 1960s, when a growing awareness about the links between smoking and lung cancer led to a decline in smoking. Currently there is a slow but steady decline in the number of people who are smokers in Britain (Central Statistical Office, 1994), though just under one third of adults still describe themselves as smokers. (In case you are worried that the tobacco companies might be going out of business, you will heartened to hear that they have transferred their business to underdeveloped countries where their glossy advertising is not contradicted by health education messages.)

The active ingredient in tobacco is nicotine, but this is only one of the health-damaging components of tobacco smoke, the other two being tar and carbon monoxide. The general findings about the health risks of these components are summarised in Kaplan, Sallis and Patterson (1993) and Parrott (1991).

Nicotine

Nicotine has an addictive effect and also increases the risk of heart disease by:

- stimulating the release of noradrenaline (norepinephrine) which increases heart rate and blood pressure
- disturbing heart rhythms
- increasing the amount of free fatty acid in the blood
- making the blood more likely to clot.

Tar

Cigarette smoke contains gases and solids, many of which are harmful. The solid parts of smoke are called tars, because that is what they look like if you collect them. These tars include chemicals such as benzene (a known carcinogen), arsenic, nickel and pesticides. Needless to say, this cocktail of poisons does not do the lungs any good at all. Tar is associated with cancer of the lung, cancer of the mouth, lung disease such as bronchitis, and an increase in colds and coughs.

Carbon monoxide

Among the many gases in tobacco smoke are ammonia, hydrogen cyanide and formaldehyde. The gas that gets the most attention, however, is carbon monoxide which has been identified as particularly damaging to health.

- Carbon monoxide reduces the amount of oxygen circulating in the blood.
- The reduced circulation of blood leads to tissue death, gangrene and amputation.
- It narrows the arteries increasing the risk of stroke.

Smoking is generally regarded today as being incredibly harmful to health. According to *The Health of the Nation* (Department of Health, 1992), smoking is associated with:

- at least 80% of lung cancer
- up to 18% of deaths due to coronary heart disease
- about 11% of stroke deaths
- increased risk of other cancers, such as of the larynx, oesophagus and bladder
- increased risk of lung disease
- increased risk of infant mortality for women smoking during pregnancy
- increased risk of asthma and glue ear in the children of smokers.

The above information paints a dramatic picture about the health risks of smoking and makes the reader question why anyone would smoke. It is fair to note, however, that many people enjoy smoking and find it a relaxing social activity. It is also fair to note that there is a moral panic about smoking which goes way beyond its health risk. People are exposed to a range of other health risks such as food additives, and air pollution, neither of which generate the moral outrage that smoking seems to produce. Likewise, it could be argued that alcohol is an even greater threat to general health with over a million people believed to be alcoholic in this country and many more consuming way over the suggested healthy limits. Alcohol is believed to be the most common factor in road traffic accidents, and it is also linked with domestic violence. Smoking, however, has attracted particular attention because it is something we can see, something we can measure and something we can 'tut-tut' about.

PSYCHOLOGICAL CONTRIBUTIONS

Biological explanations of addictive behaviour

The medical approach to addiction looks for biological explanations for these behaviours. One of the key questions is, why do people do something that appears to be harmful to their health? A possible answer to this comes from the discovery of 'pleasure centres' in the brain. Olds and Milner (1954) found that rats would press a lever for the reward of mild electrical stimulation in particular areas of the brain. The rats would continue to press the lever in preference to other possible rewards such as food, drink or sexual activity. The researchers did not record whether the animals had silly smiles on their faces, but they did name the areas of the brain 'pleasure centres'.

The experience of pleasure is very important for our healthy development. If, for example, we found food or sex boring, then our species would probably starve to death or fail to breed. The feelings of pleasure associated with these activities act as a reinforcement. If we associate these pleasure feelings with other activities, then they too will be reinforced. So, the pleasure that encourages essential behaviours is also the pleasure that can encourage damaging behaviour. Could it be that the threat of addiction is the price we pay for pleasure?

Biological explanations of addiction currently centre on some pathways in the brain mediated by the neural transmitter dopamine (see Pinel, 1993). The problem with this approach, as Concar (1994) points out, is that pleasure is a very personal experience, and it does not make sense to try and reduce it to the actions of neural pathways and neural transmitters. Also, this biological approach is unlikely to offer us any suggestions for treatment of people with addictive behaviours. A more fruitful approach comes from social psychology with its models of behavioural change for example – see 'the spiral model of behavioural change' below.

Availability

There are a number of factors that affect the incidence of addictive behaviours in a society. One factor that affects the level of alcoholism in a society is the availability of alcohol and the average consumption of alcohol by the general population. Comparison studies have found near-perfect correlations between the number of deaths through liver cirrhosis (generally attributed to alcohol abuse) and the average consumption of alcohol in different countries (for a discussion, see Orford, 1985). The availability factor also affects the consumption of cigarettes as shown in the study below.

If we examine the pattern of cigarette consumption compared with the retail price of cigarettes in this country, we can observe a remarkable relationship. Figure 7.1 shows how the curve for consumption is the mirror image of the curve for retail price (Townsend, 1993). Since 1970, any increase in price has brought about a decrease in smoking. At the time of writing, there is a trend for a decrease in the price of cigarettes (figures are adjusted to take account of inflation) and a corresponding rise in smoking. This rise in smoking is particularly noticeable in young people, and according to Townsend (1993), regular smoking by 15-year-old boys has increased from 20% to 25% and by 16 to 19-year-old girls from 28% to 32%. This connection between price and consumption suggests an obvious policy for governments that want to reduce smoking.

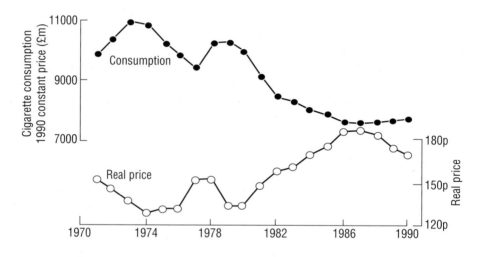

FIGURE 7.1 *The relationship between the price of cigarettes and consumption 1971–1990 (both variables are adjusted for inflation)*

National Lottery

The evidence about availability suggests that if the opportunity for a potentially addictive behaviour increases then, in the long term, there will be a rise in people who are addicted to that behaviour. As Griffiths (1995b) points out, this suggests that the National Lottery and, in particular, scratch cards will lead to a dramatic increase in gambling addiction. Evidence suggests that the number of regular gamblers in this country has dramatically increased since the start of the National Lottery. The evidence also suggests that many children are using scratch cards and being introduced to a socially acceptable form of gambling. This behaviour is further condoned though the connection between the National Lottery and charities. It would seem likely that we will see a large rise in gambling addiction in future years.

Tobacco advertising

In their response to the *Health of the Nation* strategy (see pages 8–10), the British Psychological Society (1993) called for a ban on the advertising of all tobacco products. This call was backed up by the government's own research (Department of Health, 1993), which suggested a relationship between advertising and sales. Also, in four countries that have banned advertising (New Zealand, Canada, Finland and Norway) there has been a significant drop in consumption.

Public policy, however, is not always driven by research findings, and the powerful commercial lobby for tobacco has considerable influence. In her reply to the British Psychological Society, the Secretary of State for Health (at that time Virginia Bottomley) rejected a ban saying that the evidence was unclear on this issue and efforts should be concentrated elsewhere. This response highlights how issues of addictive behaviours cannot be discussed just within the context of health. There are a range of political, economic, social and moral contexts to consider as well.

Changing behaviour

There are a number of issues to consider when we are trying to change our own or other people's behaviour. With regard to smoking, we might want to know why people choose to start smoking, why they continue to smoke, why they choose to give up, and why they choose to start smoking again. If we explore any one of these questions we find another five questions waiting behind it. One group of factors that attracts a lot of attention is the cues that encourage health behaviour. For example, media campaigns provide cues for smokers to continue, or for nonsmokers to start. Cues that might encourage people to stop include personal ill-health, the ill-health of a relative, pregnancy, smoking policy at work, and lack of money. The health belief model (see pages 68–70) is quite useful in our discussion of this issue, though it does not provide us with any predictions about which cues will stimulate health behaviour and which will not. One practical model of behaviour change that has attracted a lot of interest in psychologists and health workers alike is the spiral model described below.

The spiral model of behavioural change

People sometimes give up addictive behaviours after seeking professional help, and sometimes they give up these behaviours through their own efforts. When people manage to change themselves without professional help it is sometimes referred to as 'spontaneous remission'. This is a patronising description which implies that the change just happened to the person and required no effort or decision from them. It also implies that the only meaningful change in behaviour is one that is brought about through professional guidance. Prochaska et al. (1992) looked at both professionally initiated and self-motivated changes in behaviour to see if there were any common features. Their paper 'In search of how people change' reviews the evidence and puts forward a five-stage model of behavioural change.

1 **Precontemplation**

   In this stage, the person has no intention of changing their behaviour and probably does not even perceive that they have a problem. The problem might be obvious to the person's family and friends, but the person might well respond to these concerns by saying, 'I know I have some faults but there is nothing I really need to change.'

2 **Contemplation**

   In this stage, the person is aware that they have a problem and they are thinking that they should do something about it. However, they have not yet made a commitment to take action. People can stay in this stage indefinitely, and Prochaska et al. quote some of their own research that observed some smokers who were stuck in the contemplation stage for the full two years of the study.

3 **Preparation**

   In this stage, the person is intending to take action in the near future and may well have already started to do something. Most commonly they will have reduced the number of cigarettes they smoke, or delayed the time of the first cigarette each day. If this was a race then people in this stage are at the 'get set' point, just before they start to run.

4 **Action**

   In this stage, people change their behaviour, their experience, or their environment so that they can overcome their problem. A person is said to be in the action stage if they have successfully altered their behaviour for a period of between one day and six months. In the case of smoking, the change must involve not smoking at all. People often incorrectly see the action stage as the main part of change and overlook the importance of the preliminary stages that prepare the person for change, and the efforts that are required to maintain the change.

5 Maintenance

In this stage the person works to prevent a relapse and to consolidate the changes they have made. Someone is said to be in the maintenance stage if they are able to remain free from the problem behaviour for more than six months.

The model shown in Figure 7.2 presents change as a spiral. This takes account of the observation that most people who take action to change a habit are not successful at the first attempt. Prochaska et al. (1992) suggest that smokers commonly make three or four action attempts before they reach the maintenance stage.

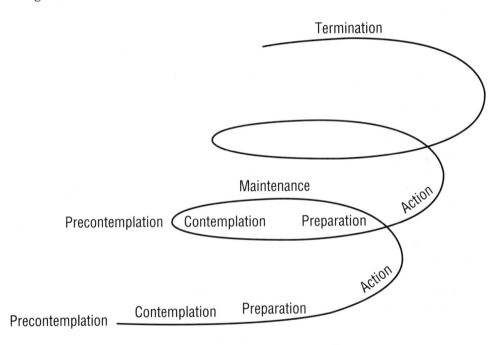

FIGURE 7.2 *The spiral model of change proposed by Prochaska et al. (1992)*

APPLICATIONS

Reinforcement

One way to reduce substance abuse is to give people rewards for not taking the substance. There are two psychological ways of looking at this, one is to see it as reinforcement for a behaviour, and the other is to see it as a distracter from the pleasurable reinforcement of the substance. A programme in the USA reported by Mestel and Concar (1994) tried to change the behaviour of people with a serious cocaine problem. The subjects of the programme had their urine tested several times a week for traces of cocaine, and every time it was clear of any cocaine they were given vouchers. The vouchers started with a value of $2.50, but every time they were clear of cocaine the value went up by $1.50, so that if they had ten consecutive clear tests they would receive $17.50 for the next clear test. If they had one test that showed traces of cocaine then the payments went back to $2.50 again. The best way to cash in on this programme, then, was to stay clear of cocaine for as long as possible.

The vouchers were backed up with counselling on how best to spend the money, so they were encouraged to spend it on, for example, sports equipment to take up a hobby, or a family meal in a restaurant to help build up relationships which might have been damaged by the substance use. The voucher therapy approach was reported to have good results. The norm for drug treatment programmes is a drop-out rate of 70% within six weeks. On this programme, however, around 85% stayed in the programme for 12 weeks and around two thirds stayed in for six months.

The problem with this approach does not concern its success rate but the reaction of other people to the idea of giving drug users money not to take drugs. It is not difficult to imagine the hostile reaction of politicians and the general public to this sort of programme. It is the same hostile reaction that is met by harm-minimisation programmes which seek to reduce the dangers to health in people carrying out risky behaviours.

Harm minimisation

Health education programmes that encourage people to stop taking drugs are remarkably unsuccessful. The message 'Hey kids, just say "No!"' does not produce much reduction in substance use. An alternative approach is to encourage harm minimisation. These controversial campaigns accept that people will engage in risky behaviour and try to reduce the health risks by encouraging users to take the drug safely. One way of reducing the health risks for intravenous drug users is to provide needle exchanges so that they do not share injecting equipment. Using sterile equipment dramatically reduces the risk of getting blood infections such as hepatitis or HIV and AIDS.

Safer drug use can be encouraged by messages for harm minimisation which involve a hierarchy of behavioural changes such as:

- do not use drugs
- if you must use drugs, do not inject
- if you must inject, do not share equipment
- if you must share, sterilise the injecting equipment before each injection.

The harm minimisation programmes also give information on how to sterilise injecting equipment easily and effectively (see the example in Figure 7.3). Instead of treating drug dependency by trying to achieve abstinence, this approach tries to educate drug users about safe practices they can adopt to minimise the risks to themselves and others. Another way of reducing the potential harm to intravenous drug users is to provide medically controlled drugs as a substitute for street drugs. These drugs, such as methadone, are less harmful than street heroin, partly because they are free from impurities. Harm minimisation programmes can improve the health of drug users, but they attract a lot of criticism because they appear to condone drug use.

FIGURE 7.3 *An eight-foot-tall 'Bleachman' distributes packets of bleach to intravenous drugs users on the streets of San Francisco. An extensive advertising campaign backs up the scheme with instructions for users on how to sterilize their needles with bleach. The move is to counter the growing threat of HIV/AIDS among intravenous drug users who acquire the virus through sharing infected needles.*

The public resistance to the above approaches for dealing with excessive drug use suggests that concerns about personal health are not the only ones we have to take into account when designing health programmes. It appears that health workers have to take account of the moral concerns of their society as well as the health needs of their clients.

Anti-smoking campaigns

The two approaches described above are not very appropriate for anti-smoking campaigns. It is impractical to offer financial inducements to all smokers so that they will stop, and it is difficult to reduce the harm in cigarette smoking. Even the low-tar cigarettes contain a damaging amount of tar and most of the poisonous gases that are present in full-strength cigarettes. So, the only way to improve health is to stop smoking completely. A large number of methods have been used to help people stop smoking and some of these are identified below.

Campaigns for adolescents

Health messages for young people are notoriously ineffective. One of the many problems is that risk-taking is part of being adolescent, so messages that encourage people to behave in a sensible way are unlikely to have much impact. Flora and Thoresen (1988) suggest that some anti-smoking programmes are successful with young people and that the most successful campaigns have the following features:

- peer-pressure resistance training through role playing and behaviour skills training
- information on the immediate physiological effects of smoking
- making a public commitment to behave in particular ways
- altering misperceptions about how many people actually smoke
- discussing family influences
- inoculation against mass media on smoking (see the section on stress inoculation, pages 45–46)
- use of high-status peer leaders.

In the most effective programmes, the information is accompanied by group discussions, role plays of difficult situations and active participation in the programme.

QUIT

The British charity QUIT produces materials and campaigns to help people stop smoking. Their approach is largely based on the model of Prochaska et al. (1992) described above. They produce materials for smokers and also for health workers to use with their clients. An example of their approach is shown in Figure 7.4.

A quick survival guide

Cravings

Most cravings last about 3 minutes; plan to distract yourself for the full 3 minutes.

Suggestions:
- Talk to a workmate or friend.
- Suck mints; chew gum – the low-sugar variety.
- Brush your teeth.
- Make a 'phone call (remember freephone QUITLINE on 0800 - 002200).
- Eat an apple.
- Take a shower.

Cravings will become less frequent after the first few days.

Irritability and nervousness

It is natural when you stop smoking to feel moody or irritable. Plan some new distraction.

Suggestions:
- Take up a new hobby.
- Try some activities such as walking, or doing the weeding.
- Join an evening class.
- Remember exercise reduces stress.
- Try some simple breathing exercises.

Poor concentration

Losing your ability to concentrate is not permanent but it may cause a few problems during the first few weeks, particularly at work.

Suggestions:
- At work, take frequent short breaks.
- Try some simple relaxation exercises – shrug your shoulders, rotate your head and neck.
- Pop out into the fresh air briefly if you can.

Sleep disturbance

When you quit you may find your sleep patterns change; don't lie in bed thinking about smoking.

Suggestions:
- Have a warm bath.
- Try a warm milky drink.
- Read a book.

Digestive disturbance

Some people suffer from indigestion and constipation when they quit.

Suggestions:
- Reduce your tea and coffee intake.
- Avoid indigestible foods such as chips.
- Your pharmacist will be able to recommend treatments for constipation and diarrhoea.

FIGURE 7.4 *A Quick Survival Guide*, © QUIT, 1994

Nicotine substitution

There are various ways of allowing people to get their dose of nicotine without the dangerous activity of smoking. The idea behind this is that smokers will be able to change their habits of smoking without suffering the cravings associated with nicotine withdrawal. However, if we follow the model of addictive behaviours proposed by Griffiths (described above) then we might expect some smokers to have withdrawals from the habits of smoking as much as they would from the nicotine itself. The ways of substituting nicotine include nasal droplets (a bit embarrassing to use in public), chewing gum, and skin plasters (patches). All of these methods have been useful in helping some smokers, though as in all treatments, the relapse rate is quite high.

Skills training

Programmes have been developed in *coping skills* (to remind people of the negative consequences of smoking and positive consequences of quitting); *social skills* (helping people to reject cigarettes that are offered to them); and *relaxation skills* (for example, learning alternative ways to deal with stress).

Other behavioural methods

The behavioural method of *aversive conditioning* attempts to associate smoking with unpleasant sensations. One way of doing this is by rapid smoking. The smoker is asked to inhale deeply and frequently (every six seconds instead of the average 90 seconds) until they begin to feel ill and stop. The smoker eventually starts to associate smoking with feeling sick, and so becomes aversive to cigarettes. An alternative method based on *operant conditioning* requires the smoker to pledge money to a disliked organisation to be paid if the person starts to smoke again. The idea behind this method is that a person will find the thought of giving money to such an organisation so unpleasant that they will feel it is not worth starting to smoke again.

SUMMARY

Some people engage in habitual behaviours that can become damaging to their health and well-being. These behaviours have commonly been seen in a medical context and described as a disease. An alternative approach sees them as being a relatively common feature of human behaviour which can be influenced by various cues in the environment. The approach that a society takes to these behaviours is affected by its norms of acceptable social behaviour and its values about such things as the pursuit of pleasure. There are various methods that health workers use to help people reduce the harm of these behaviours or to abstain from them altogether. On the whole, these methods have only limited success.

CHAPTER OVERVIEW

Our health is affected by the culture we live in, but this is not often acknowledged in discussions about health. The CONTEXT for this chapter, then, looks at the issues of ethnocentrism and how health services are relatively blind to people from minority cultural groups. It also looks at the differences that exist between cultures and identifies some of the health needs of minorities. The PSYCHOLOGICAL CONTRIBUTIONS to this discussion include a consideration of the way that language can affect our view of health. They also include a look at traditional societies and health, and how some customs such as those associated with death and rites of passage are not common to all members of our society. The SPECIAL ISSUE looks at the diagnosis of mental disorders and illustrates how ignorance of cultural traditions can lead to the incorrect diagnosis of people from minority groups. The APPLICATIONS are limited since there is little written about the relationship between health psychology and the health needs of minority groups. This section considers some cultural differences in risk factors for common illnesses and looks at the issue of child survival.

CONTEXT

This chapter is about the cultural differences in health. It is very easy to ignore the many differences that exist between individuals and between groups of people. The government strategy document The Health of the Nation makes no mention of the different risk factors for people from various cultural groups, and its targets for change are therefore inappropriate for some of these groups of people. In the field of psychology, there is also a tendency to ignore cultural differences and talk about people as if we are all the same. In this chapter we will look at the effect of ethnocentrism on health judgements, the health needs of minority groups in Britain, cultural differences in the experience and explanations of ill-health, and some attempts by psychologists to address issues of diversity in health.

Ethnocentrism

In our everyday lives we are asked to make judgements about people and events. In our judgements we are often inclined to show a little egocentrism (seeing things from our own particular viewpoint to the exclusion of others). Another bias that can be identified in our judgements is ethnocentrism (seeing things from the point of view of our group). This bias means that we tend to believe that the things that happen to us are the things that happen to all people, and we tend to ignore the experiences of people who are not like us.

In a society like Britain that is predominantly white but has substantial ethnic minority groups, then the particular health needs of these groups tend go unnoticed by health professionals. This can have tragic consequences. Torkington (1991) describes a number of cases where people received psychiatric treatment, not because they were psychiatrically disturbed but because they were black. In one case a 51-year-old black man was rushed to hospital in Merseyside with convulsions and severe leg pains. The doctors said there was nothing wrong and the staff called in a psychologist. The man was put in an acute psychiatric ward where he died unattended one hour later. The symptoms were not recognised by the health workers and the man's behaviour was not seen as a sign of physical distress but of mental disturbance. The problem is that health workers are not familiar with the way the people behave who are not like them, and are therefore likely to misinterpret that behaviour.

Ethnocentrism, then, can make us blind to the experience of people who are not like ourselves. Another side of ethnocentrism is the actions that people take to help members of their own community, and in some cases to actively disadvantage people in other communities. Racism is a feature of everyday life in Britain, and the experience of being racially abused or attacked, and the fear of these events is a major stress factor in the lives of many people from minority cultures in this country (see below).

Different types of culture

We often make the assumption that the way we do things in our society is *the* way to do things, and anything else is odd. Cultures vary quite a lot, however, and Hofstede (1980) identified four basic dimensions which can be used to compare them:

1 **Power-distance:** how far people in authority are expected to exercise their power. For example, do you consider your boss to be a colleague, or does he or she seem to be much more powerful than you?
2 **Uncertainty avoidance:** how far people like things to be clear and orderly, with everyone knowing their place. People in some cultures (though not British culture) can tolerate a high level of change and uncertainty, and do

not experience anxiety and stress as a result.

3 **Individualism:** how far the culture encourages personal (or individualistic) ambitions and concerns, and how far people are seen as members of a collective group.

4 **Masculinity–femininity:** Hofstede suggested that masculine cultures emphasise performance and money above all else, whereas feminine cultures value the quality of life, and consider environmental issues to be important.

The differences of cultural groups on these dimensions will have an effect on the health of the group members. If the culture has a high degree of power-distance then it is likely that people will not be able to assert themselves with their doctor very easily, and will defer to their authority. The amount that we are able to tolerate uncertainty and change (see the section on coping with HIV and AIDS in Chapter 12, pages 172–174) will have an affect on our level of stress and our adjustment to illness. One of the central features of Western culture is the importance placed on individualism. Western peoples tend to value the individual rather than the group, whereas many other cultures place more emphasis on community and co-operation (for example, see Nobles, 1976). Hofstede's final point about masculine societies will affect our judgements – for example, about whether to put our quality of life before our achievement at work.

Health psychology

It is clear that a number of risk factors for health are associated with lifestyle, and these lifestyles vary from one cultural group to another. Health psychologists have started to investigate these factors to estimate the impact of culture on health, and also to design health programmes that are aimed at particular cultural groups. For example, one of the factors that might affect our response to illness is religion. This is not often researched in this country, probably because the majority of the white population does not actively take part in religion. It is, however, a much more important part in the lives of many black people. An American study by Krause (1992) looked at how religious beliefs and social support affected stress in elderly black Americans. The research found that religious commitment was an important coping resource, especially when dealing with bereavement.

This research suggests that the beliefs we hold, and the social and religious groups to which we belong, will have an effect on our health. The question then arises about how much we know of the religious and social support that people receive who are not in our own social group. In our diverse society do we know how people behave who are not in the same cultural group as us?

Minority groups in Britain

Table 8.1 shows the population of ethnic groups in Britain. The relatively low total percentage disguises an uneven distribution of people around the country; for example, 60% of all black people live in Greater London.

Table 8.1 The population of Britain by ethnic group in 1991

	Number of people (thousands)	% of population
Black Caribbean	500	
Black African	212	
Black other	178	
Indian	840	
Pakistani	477	
Bangladeshi	163	
Chinese	157	
Other Asian	198	
All ethnic minority groups	3,015	5.5
White	51,874	94.5
Total British Population	54,899	

Source: Social Trends (1994). Crown copyright (1994)/Office for National Statistics

The health needs of minorities

Very little has been written about the health needs of minority groups or their experience in making use of the health service, and we have very little information about the risk factors associated with culture. As a result, the health of ethnic minorities has been largely ignored or unrecognised. There are two main reasons why this state of affairs has developed in this country:

1 When mass immigration from the Caribbean and Asia to this country started after the Second World War (1939–45), concerns were expressed that 'new' immigrants brought disease into the country and created the risk of epidemics. Research, however, failed to support this and so the health service lost interest in ethnic health.
2 There was a change in the view of ethnic minorities. As the ethnic groups became established in Britain, they were no longer seen as newcomers or classic immigrants. Instead they were viewed as just another part of the community without any specific needs.

What this means is that, as far as health is concerned, black people are invisible. The health service is relatively unaware of their health needs and their lifestyles, and is unable to deal with many specific problems that they might have. McNaught (1987) argues, however, that people from ethnic minorities

Box 8.1   Awareness of black needs checklist

Look at the questions below and tick the response you think is most appropriate.

1   The statement 'I and I' made by a black person should be interpreted as
   A   Speech disorder   ☐
   B   Thought disorder   ☐
   C   Schizophrenia   ☐
   D   Culturally specific language   ☐
   E   Collective identity   ☐

2   An Iranian woman gives her religion as Muslim. Her diet will therefore be
   A   Vegetarian diet   ☐
   B   Non-vegetarian diet   ☐
   C   Halal meat   ☐
   D   None of these necessarily   ☐
   E   Vegan diet   ☐

3   To die in dignity a practising Muslim patient would want to
   A   Sit or lie facing the sun   ☐
   B   Sit or lie with their back to the sun   ☐
   C   Not be touched by a non-Muslim   ☐
   D   Sit or lie facing Mecca   ☐
   E   Prepare by eating fish   ☐

4   The term 'soul food' refers to
   A   Traditional Asian foods   ☐
   B   Meals with lots of spices   ☐
   C   Traditional black foods   ☐
   D   Special religious meals   ☐
   E   Fruit from the Caribbean   ☐

5   Hair care of a white person is
   A   Similar to the hair care for a black person   ☐
   B   Different to the hair care for a black person   ☐

6   When a black person gets chicken pox they have
   A   No noticeable symptoms   ☐
   B   Black spots   ☐
   C   Red spots   ☐

7   When a black African woman claims that she is sometimes able to hear
   voices even though no one is actually talking, the most likely explanation is
   A   She is schizophrenic   ☐
   B   She is taking some form of psychoactive drug   ☐
   C   She is talking about a religious or spiritual experience   ☐

The answers and notes for these questions can be found in Appendix 2.

Adapted from Hylton (1994), used with permission.

do have specific needs, and we will look at these needs and problems in the next section. First, though, look at the questions in Box 8.1 and see how many you can answer. They all have considerable importance for the way people from ethnic minority groups experience the health service, and you might be surprised how many you find difficult to answer (see Appendix 2 for correct answers).

PSYCHOLOGICAL CONTRIBUTIONS

There are a number of contributions from psychology that can help us understand the cultural differences in health. We can only look at a few of them and the ones I have chosen include language, traditional explanations of health, bereavement and the study of culture-based disorders.

Language, culture and health

In Western societies we have a particular language for talking about health. We tend to talk about health in rather mechanical terms as if we are made up of separate bits and that each bit can be dealt with independently, much the way we deal with a car engine. This is the basis of the biomedical model of health (see Chapter 1, pages 4–5). Other cultures talk about health in different ways and so have different concepts of health. In the West we tend to be suspicious of traditional medicines and any view of illness that does not involve the biomedical model.

In the study of linguistics, the Sapir–Whorf hypothesis suggests that the structure of our language affects the structure of our thinking. There are some powerful examples of this in the area of health. For example, Warner (1976) looked at the relationship between the structure of language and the concepts of disease held by different cultures. In traditional Chinese medicine, the crucial issue is balance. The two universal forces of yin and yang regulate the universe and must be balanced to achieve harmony within the body and within nature. In particular, Chinese medicine sees the organs of the body as being in a co-operative balance, promoting health and harmony. This is very different from the biomedical view of the organs as being individual bits to be replaced when they become faulty.

In Western language we often describe our experiences by using spatial metaphors. For example, we talk about 'falling' in love or 'getting carried away' by the music, or 'grasping' an argument. Warner suggests that this language bias encourages us to see the experience of illness in spatial terms ('I feel under the weather'), and to see illness itself as an object ('Our Gavin has caught the measles'). These physical explanations of health and ill-health encourage us to use physical treatments. So we are likely to use excessive surgery to remove things, and ignore the social and cultural features of ill-health.

Traditional societies and health

Horton (1967) describes how traditional medical treatments in Africa focus on social factors even when diagnosing infectious diseases. They look for the person who has fallen out with the patient, and who might therefore have 'cast a spell' on them. This seems bizarre to Western minds, yet actually makes perfect sense when the person is seen in a more holistic context.

In a traditional society, with a relatively high rate of infant mortality, those who grow to adulthood tend to have a high natural immunity to disease. So if someone falls sick, the question is not where the germ came from, but how their immune system has been weakened to the extent that the illness can take hold. Research suggests that one of the consequences of prolonged stress is to reduce the effectiveness of the immune system. In traditional communities the primary sources of stress comes from disturbed interactions with other people. So when the traditional medicine practitioner tries to find out who the person has quarrelled with lately, and to solve their dispute and so lift the spell, this is actually an extremely practical method of treatment. If the stress can be removed, then the natural recovery process will be able to fight the illness.

If we applied this approach in a Western setting then we might look for the person at work who is giving you a hard time, or the neighbour who is irritating you beyond belief. However, it is more likely that any medical discussion would involve individual medication rather than social healing.

Co-operative and individualistic societies

One of the differences between cultures is how individualistic they are (see Hofstede's (1980) cultural dimensions described on pages 110–111). The Western societies are very individualistic and emphasise personal enrichment and personal responsibility. Other societies put greater emphasis on co-operative activity and the enrichment of the group. In Western societies, people see illness as a personal event. Herzlich (1973) describes how, in France, people view illness as:

- destructive of your usual activities
- a liberation from your usual obligations
- an 'occupation' or pastime.

When people from an individualistic society consult a doctor they often talk about their feelings such as anxiety or depression. In co-operative cultures, however, it is more likely that the patient will talk about their physical symptoms rather than their personal feelings. Draguns (1990, cited in Smith and Harris Bond, 1993) suggests that if you are going to describe your feelings as a problem or an illness then you need to have a self-concept that views yourself as being apart from other people and relatively independent.

All this suggests that people from ethnic minority groups within Britain might well view their illness in terms different from white peoples and describe it using different concepts. This is clearly a problem for any diagnosis which relies on the self-report of patients.

Childbirth pain and culture

A further example of the different descriptions of experience and symptoms comes from cross-cultural studies of childbirth. Taylor (1986) gives a brief summary of these differences and describes how in some cultures women have an expectation that childbirth will be painful. For example the Mexican word for 'labour' (*dolor*) means 'sorrow' or 'pain', in contrast to the English word which means 'work'. Taylor suggests that this fearful expectation is followed by painful deliveries with many complications. In contrast, Taylor cites the culture of Yap in the South Pacific where childbirth is treated as an everyday occurrence. Yap women are reported to carry out their normal tasks until they begin labour, at which point they go to a childbirth hut and give birth with the assistance of one or two other women. After the birth, there is a relatively brief rest period before the woman resumes her regular tasks. In this community, complications are reported to be rare. Taylor suggests that expectations are an important factor in the experience of childbirth, and these expectations come from cultural stories and customs. (I hasten to add that this does not mean that we can reduce the problems and pains of childbirth just by pretending they do not exist.)

Death and rites of passage

One of the big distinctions between cultures is the way we view dying and death, and the ceremonies we carry out before and after someone has died. Some religions, for example Hinduism (the main religion of India) believes in reincarnation, believes that birth is followed by death, and believes that death is followed by re-birth. Therefore, death is another transition in life and should be met with tranquillity and meditation (Kübler-Ross, 1975, see Figure 8.1).

In traditional Japanese culture, the purpose of the rites of passage is to help the spirit of the dead person make the journey to another world. The funeral events begin with a bedside service in which the minister consoles the family. Following this, the body is ceremonially bathed, and then there is the funeral. When the period of mourning is over there is a party for friends and relatives,

(a) Kathmandu, Nepal — an untouchable lighting a funeral pyre

(b) A British funeral ceremony

(c) Bali, Indonesia — pagoda carrying dead body on the way to a cremation

(d) Funeral ceremony for Indian Sadu (Holy Man). His disciples are about to release him onto the sacred waters of the River Ganges

FIGURE 8.1 The contrasting approaches to death in different cultures

which helps the mourners adjust back into everyday life (Kübler-Ross, 1975).

By far the strangest rituals are those of white British people. Death often takes place in hospital, with the dying person alone except for the medical staff. The body is promptly removed without the help of the bereaved family, who will probably not see it until it has been made to look more acceptable. Sometimes the body is never seen by the relatives. The funeral director who does not know the family or the deceased takes over control of the viewing and the funeral rituals. A brief service is carried out, usually in a Christian style, even though many people are not practising Christians and know little of the rituals involved. The mourners are expected to show as little emotion as possible, and after the funeral there might be a brief get-together of the mourners and friends.

SPECIAL ISSUE:
The diagnosis of mental disorders

Who is normal and who is abnormal, and how can we judge this? Judgements about abnormality can be affected by a number of factors, including the ethnocentric bias (see above). In her paper 'Black women and mental health', Anuradha Sayal (1990) reminds us that there has been a historical tendency to view black people as 'sick'. Sometimes they were seen to have a physical sickness (for example, black skin was said to be a form of leprosy) and sometimes they were seen to have a mental sickness (for example, runaway slaves were diagnosed as having a mental disease, 'drapetomania' – an incurable urge to run away).

In Britain, the proportion of black people in the population is 5%, yet 25% of patients on psychiatric wards are black. The chart in Figure 8.2 shows the admission rates of people from different countries into British psychiatric hospitals. These data give an interesting picture of the differences in admissions but they do not include, of course, black people who are born in this country. Black patients in psychiatric hospital are more likely than white patients to see a junior rather than a senior doctor, they are more likely to receive major tranquillisers, and more likely to receive electroconvulsive therapy (Littlewood and Lipsedge, 1989). So, we have a picture of different diagnoses for black people, and different treatments. This leads us to two questions.

1 Do different ethnic groups display different levels of psychotic behaviour, and if so, why?
2 Are psychiatrists more likely to diagnose people from minority ethnic groups as psychotic, and if so, why?

Playing dominoes

One explanation for the high incidence of schizophrenia diagnoses for black people is

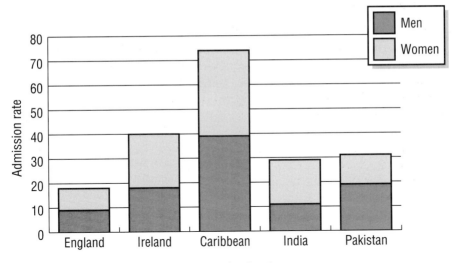

FIGURE 8.2 *Country of birth and hospital admissions for schizophrenia*

that the people who make the diagnoses have little experience of black people and so do not understand their behaviour and conversation. Horsford (1990) discussed how a white middle-class psychiatrist can often misinterpret behaviour, which is perfectly ordinary within an Afro-Caribbean culture, as being abnormal, simply because it is not the sort of behaviour shown by white professional people. An example of this is the way Caribbean men play dominoes. If you are used to the sedate way that white people play bridge, for example, then watching the dominoes game might be quite startling, and you may think that it is aggressive and threatening.

'West Indian Psychosis'

One of the major stressors for black people in this society is racism. Tewfik and Okasha, (1965, cited in Rack, 1982) studied patients from Caribbean backgrounds, who had been admitted to British hospitals and diagnosed as schizophrenic. They found that only 15% of the patients showed the classic symptoms of either schizophrenic or manic depressive psychosis. The remaining 85% had a distinctive

pattern of symptoms which some psychiatrists referred to as 'West Indian Psychosis'. Littlewood and Lipsedge (1989) suggest that this so-called 'West Indian Psychosis' is actually an acute psychotic stress reaction which ought not to be confused with schizophrenia and which does not require the same treatment. They point out that mental illnesses of people in minority groups often involve feelings of being persecuted, which reflect the disadvantaged social conditions of many of these people.

Littlewood and Lipsedge describe how paranoid reactions of this type have been noted in many minority groups, including West Indians in Britain, German-speaking servants in England in the 1920s, Arab immigrants in France, Turkish migrant workers in Germany, Eastern European immigrants in Australia, and so on. In short, these reactions can be found in any disadvantaged minority group in society. In the Caribbean, delusions of persecution are not common in most of the community, the exception being the white minority. Littlewood and Lipsedge suggest that these delusions of persecution are a response to the experience of discrimination, not a characteristic of the cultural group itself.

Adaptive paranoid responses

One of the symptoms of schizophrenia is delusions of persecution, which have been defined as 'fears that individuals, groups or the government have malevolent intentions and are "out to get me"' (Rosenhan and Seligman, 1989).

Of course, if individuals, groups and the government *are* out to get you, then this is not a symptom of mental disorder but an accurate perception of the world you are living in. Grier and Cobbs (1968), writing about the experience of black people in the USA, use the term *adaptive paranoid response* to describe a mental disorder brought about by a hostile environment. They write:

> For a black man, survival in America depends in large measure on the development of a 'healthy' cultural paranoia. He must maintain a high degree of suspicion toward the motives of every white man and at the same time never allow this suspicion to impair his grasp of reality. It is a demanding requirement and not everyone can manage it with grace.

Although Grier and Cobbs are writing about America in the 1960s, the point is still relevant for Britain today. It is fair to say that awareness of hostility in others is an important coping mechanism for black people as they learn to deal with the discrimination they experience in Britain.

Good health

A final thought concerns the way psychologists describe good mental health. Psychologists such as Maslow (1968), for example, describe the healthy individual as one who is a 'self-actualiser' – that is, someone who is fulfilling their unique human potential. In a similar way, Jahoda (1958) suggests there are six themes of positive mental health:

1 Positive attitudes towards self
2 Growth and self-actualisation
3 Accurate perception of reality
4 Environmental competence
5 Autonomy
6 Positive interpersonal relations

This list describes the features of positive health in Western societies but in other societies these features might not describe good health. For example, self-actualisation and autonomy are only signs of good mental health in societies that believe the individual is more important than the family and the groups the individual belongs to (Ramseur, 1991).

APPLICATIONS

In the other chapters of this book, this final section has looked at how psychology has been applied. This is difficult to do in the area of culture and health since I am not aware of many interventions made by psychologists. This might be a feature of my limited knowledge as much as of the practice of health professionals, but a search of the literature revealed very few reports of interventions. There is, however, a growing amount of research on the health needs of people from a variety of cultural groups.

The health needs of ethnic minorities

McNaught (1987) suggests that ethnic minorities have a number of special health needs and also problems of access to health care. The health needs can be divided into genetic health issues and the incidence of common illness. This distinction is not clear-cut since it is difficult to estimate the role of genetics in some disorders.

Two genetic disorders which are relatively common in ethnic minorities but rare in Northern Europeans are sickle cell disease and thalassaemia, both of which are disorders of the blood. The group of conditions collectively known as sickle cell disease is most commonly found in people of African or Caribbean descent. Thalassaemia, on the other hand, is most common in people from the Indian subcontinent and from the Eastern Mediterranean. The issue for health workers in this country is that the disorders are very rare in white people, and so health campaigns for the whole population are relatively useless. It is important, therefore, to provide campaigns targeted at the people who are most at risk. The issues for the health service include the availability of screening, genetic counselling for people who are considering having a family, and outreach work into the minority communities.

The interaction of genetics with lifestyle

Type II diabetes (see page 00 for a brief description) is a disorder which appears to have a genetic component, but is also influenced by environmental factors like lifestyle and, in particular, diet. In the USA there are about 1.5 million people of native American heritage. One of the dramatic changes in the health of this group of people has been the increase of diabetes, which was relatively unheard of before 1930 but has now reached almost epidemic proportions. In the Pima tribe, for example, it is estimated that half of the people over the age of 35 have diabetes. According to Kaplan, Sallis and Patterson (1993), the development of diabetes in these people is related to obesity. As people increase their weight so they increase their risk of developing Type II diabetes. It is possible that this group of people is genetically predisposed towards diabetes, but it only develops if the people become overweight. If these people maintain their traditional lifestyle then the diabetes does not develop. However, their lifestyle has changed due to the unemployment imposed on them by industrial society and, as a result, the diabetes comes out.

Common illnesses

Some cultural groups appear to have a higher than average risk of developing some disorders. The problem for health workers and psychologists is that we know very little about these risks. One of the problems is the lack of data, which until very recently have not been collected in this country. One source of available data is death certificates which include the country of origin and the cause of death. The problem with these data, of course, is that they do not include black people born in this country. According to McNaught (1987), these data suggest that people from Africa and the Caribbean are particularly at risk from hypertension, strokes and liver cancer, and people from Asia are particularly at risk from heart disease, diabetes and liver cancer.

Risk factors for common illnesses; John Henryism

There are a number of possible causes for the higher frequency of these disorders, though it is difficult to come to any firm conclusions because of the confounding factor of income. The average income of people from ethnic minorities is below the national average, and unemployment is also higher in these groups. These economic factors greatly increase the risk of poor health (see pages 78–79) and might provide the main explanation for the health data. An alternative explanation considers the role of diet and other lifestyle factors, though there is relatively little British research on these issues.

There is some American research that has some relevance for our understanding of the health of ethnic minority groups. A study on hypertension found that black men living in high-stress environments (high unemployment, high crime, low incomes) had higher blood pressure than those living in low-stress environments (James et al., 1987). This relationship between environmental stress and blood pressure was not found in white men. James et al. suggest that the high blood pressure was a response to an active coping style used by some black men who tried to change their environment. He developed a psychometric scale to measure this active coping style and named it the John Henry Scale, after a legendary black worker who had battled against the odds to win a physical contest but then dropped dead from physical and mental fatigue. James found that black men who scored high on his scale of John Henryism were three times more likely to have hypertension.

The coping strategy that is measured in this scale concerns gaining control over your life and changing your circumstances. For many people this is a sign of good health, and for the white men in the study, a high score on the John Henryism scale did not coincide with hypertension. The black men with the high score, in fact, tended to be satisfied with their lives and perceived their own health to be good. James et al. suggest that the attempt to heroically change your circumstances when you have very little power to make any real difference can have a damaging effect on your health. This makes an interesting addition to the discussion about locus of control (see pages 174–176).

Child survival

One of the applications of psychology outside the Western world has been in the UNICEF strategy to improve the rates of child survival. The strategy is called GOBI after the first words of the four points listed below (Harkness, Wyon and Super, et al. 1988).

1 **G**rowth monitoring to identify early cases of malnutrition and failure to grow.
2 **O**ral rehydration therapy for infants and children with severe diarrhoea (a major cause of death in poor countries, and in fact the major cause of infant death in British cities until the turn of this century). The therapy reduces the high rate of death from fluid loss.
3 **B**reast feeding promotion, because breast milk is high in nutrition, and it also helps to immunise the baby from some common diseases. Breast feeding also reduces the chances of infection from unsterilised bottles.
4 **I**mmunisation against the major childhood infectious diseases.

Psychology can make a major contribution to this programme, especially in the promotion of breast feeding. This behaviour is full of social meanings and it is not enough to present a direct message in the terminology of Western medicine. Fernandez and Guthrie (1983, cited in Berry et al., 1992) suggest that it is important to take account of lay beliefs about health when education programmes are designed. If the programme describes traditional behaviours and beliefs as harmful, then it is unlikely that people will respond to the message. There is also the counter pressure from multinational companies which encourage women to buy their baby milk despite the lack of available money and the health risks of bottle feeding in poor communities. Fernandez et al. (1983, cited in Berry et al., 1992) were able to make a successful intervention to encourage breast feeding in the Philippines. Their success was based on the behavioural idea of rewards, and they offered women praise, health coupons and lottery tickets as incentives to breast feed, plant leafy vegetables and visit the health centre every month.

The issues around the choice to breast feed are very complex and health workers in this country find a great reluctance in mothers to breast feed for more than a few days, because of, among other things, the need for the mother to be available, the social stigma of revealing her breasts in public, the connection in the public imagination of breasts with sex, and cultural taboos about the body. There are also psychological issues such as self-efficacy, learned helplessness and locus of control.

SUMMARY

Cultural differences in health have largely been ignored for a variety of political and economic reasons. It is clear, however, that different groups within any society have particular health needs as well as the general health needs they share with all other people. There is a need for health workers to consider the needs of people from ethnic minorities, and there is also a lot to be gained from considering approaches to health in other societies.

chapter nine

THE DOCTOR AND THE PATIENT

CHAPTER OVERVIEW

The INTRODUCTION looks at some of the basic issues in the interactions between health workers and patients. These include the non-verbal communication between people, and the process of making judgements and decisions. Two factors that have an effect on these judgements are the way we make base rate errors, and the influence of linguistic relativity. PSYCHOLOGICAL CONTRIBUTIONS include a look at our decision to go to the doctor, and the way we respond to such things as the technical terms that are used during a consultation. They also include a consideration of the process of making a diagnosis, and how we make judgements of risk. The SPECIAL ISSUE concerns the relationship between male doctors and female patients, and illustrates the problems women can have when they seek help from health workers. The APPLICATIONS include techniques for improving communication, improving understanding, and improving memory.

INTRODUCTION

This chapter will look at some of the issues around why we choose to visit the doctor, what happens when we get there and how the doctor makes a diagnosis. These events are not as well understood as you might imagine and there are a number of questions that psychologists need to consider. For example:

- how well do health workers and patients communicate?
- how do people make the decision to seek medical help?
- how do health workers decide what help to give?

These questions are important to our understanding of health, and psychology has something to offer on all of them.

Communication

Communicating is one of the basic features of being alive. We communicate all the time, often without meaning to and sometimes without knowing it. We can no more stop communicating than we can stop breathing. Even just standing still and saying nothing communicates something about our attitude and mood. If we look at the communication between two people then we can see three elements: the message sender, the message itself, and the message receiver. The interesting thing for psychologists is the different understanding that the sender and the receiver have of the same message.

Non-verbal communication

One area of communication that has attracted the attention of psychologists is non-verbal behaviour. This is very important in any social interaction and some psychologists (for example, Argyle, 1975) suggest that it is four times as powerful and effective as verbal communication. This suggests that if we are with someone who is saying one thing, but their words do not match their facial expression or body posture, then we are more likely to believe our intuitions about their posture than we are to believe their words (for example, we might say, 'Gavin told me that he likes my work, but I know he really thinks it's duff'). The power of non-verbal communication has been recognised for years, and skilled users such as advertisers, politicians and con-artists have been able to make their words appear more convincing through their gestures and mannerisms.

Non-verbal communication is a general term used to describe communication without the use of words. Argyle (1975) suggests that non-verbal behaviours have four major uses:

1 **to assist speech:** they help to regulate conversation by showing when you want to say something, and they emphasise meaning
2 **as replacements for speech:** for example, a gesture such as a raised eyebrow might make a verbal question unnecessary
3 **to signal attitudes:** for example we might try to look cool and unworried by taking up a relaxed standing position
4 **to signal emotional states:** we can usually tell when someone is happy or sad or tense by the way they are sitting or standing.

Non-verbal communication is an important part of the interactions between health workers and patients but it would be untrue to suggest that we can define what all the different gestures mean and give people simple ways to change their behaviour and so change the message. The various magazine articles and books that attempt to say what gestures mean are very misleading because there are variations in non-verbal behaviour in different cultural groups, different age groups and between men and women. Take, for example, what it means if we touch someone. If you touch someone on the arm it might be felt as aggressive, intrusive, supportive, or even romantic. The meaning of the touch will be affected by who is doing the touching and who is being touched. Figure 9.1 illustrates how different body areas are touched or not by different members of your family and friends.

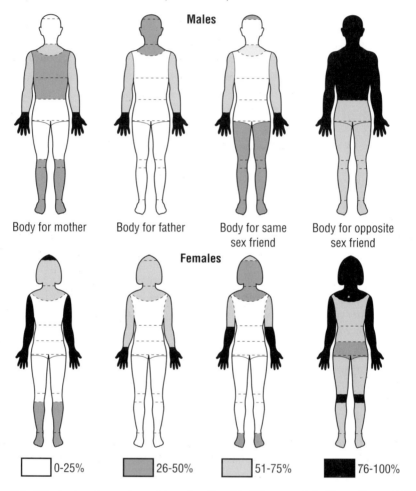

FIGURE 9.1 *Who touches whom, where and how often (for white Western peoples). (Source: Knapp, 1978)*

In the interactions between health workers and patients, non-verbal behaviour will affect how the patients respond to the health messages they are given. Also, as we shall see below, the effectiveness of these messages is affected by the language that is used to describe the illness and the treatment.

Making judgements and decisions

Psychologists have carried out a lot of research into the way we make judgements and decisions. It is often discussed under the heading of 'human

reasoning' but this is misleading because it implies that we think in very logical ways. The reality is that we have a number of influences on the way we
think and make judgements, and it is these influences and biases that are of
most use in the study of health decisions.

Every day we make judgements about probabilities. For example, we might
decide not to put on a coat when we go out because we don't think it is very
likely to rain. People appear to use rules for working out these probabilities
and these rules are called *heuristics*. One of these rules is the *availability heuristic*,
which involves judging the probability that something will happen, based on
the availability or prominence of the information about it. In the area of
health, we tend to overestimate our chances of getting a serious disease.
Serious diseases come quickly to mind because they are more frightening and
also because they form a regular part of television drama. As a result of this
prominence, we overestimate our chances of getting these diseases. The bias
that comes from the availability heuristic might affect our judgements about
how risky certain behaviours are, and it might affect the diagnosis decision
that health professionals make.

Another heuristic that can have an affect on health decisions is the *representative
heuristic*. We make judgements about individuals and events based on what we
think is typical for that group of people or that class of events. For example, if
you are a smoker and you develop a medical problem, it is likely that your
friends and your doctor will be inclined to see your medical problems as
being a result of your smoking. However, even though your smoking will
affect some aspects of your health, it will not be responsible for every possible medical condition that you develop. This is an example of how the representative heuristic can affect medical judgement.

Base rate errors

When we are making judgements, one error we make is to neglect how common an event is in the general population. Look at the example below which
is adapted from Bourne et al. (1986, cited in Sheridan and Radmacher,
1992).

> There is a disease called 'Binky's Disease' [made-up name] which affects
> 5% of the population. A test has been developed to spot 'Binky's Disease'
> at an early stage. This test is rather good and if someone has this disease,
> the test gives a positive result 95% of the time. On the other hand, if
> someone does not have 'Binky's Disease', then the test only gives a positive
> result 10% of the time. The question is this – if I get a positive result on
> the test, what are the chances that I have contracted 'Binky's Disease'?

People usually think that there is a very high chance that the positive result
indicates the presence of 'Binky's Disease'. However, this is incorrect, and it is
incorrect because they have ignored the base rate. For the mathematically-

minded, imagine that you are testing 100 people. 5% have 'Binky's Disease' and of these 5%, 95% will test positive (which in this example probably means all five of them). However, the test also gives a positive result to 10% of the remaining 95 people who do not have the disease (in this case, let's say that is 10 of them). So, for our 100 people we have 15 testing positive on the test and only 5 of them have got 'Binky's Disease'. So if we receive a positive test result there is only a 1 in 3 chance of us developing this disease.

There are a number of other factors which affect judgement including our ethnocentric bias which is discussed in Chapter 8 (page 110)

Linguistic relativity

One other aspect of communication that affects our approach to health is the language that we use. The Linguistic Relativity Hypothesis (also referred to as the Sapir–Whorf Hypothesis, after the two people who developed the idea) suggests that the structure of our language will affect the way we think. One consequence of this is suggested by Slobin (1971), who points out how often European languages use object words (nouns) to describe processes. For example, English might describe the process of flaming using a noun, and referring to 'the flame'. Slobin argues that this tendency to see processes as objects exerted a powerful effect on Western science, because it led directly to the process of *reification* – seeing a process as an object. In modern psychology a lot of time has been spent trying to find and describe processes, as if they were really objects – for example, memory. It is clear that we remember things but it is not clear that we have a box in the head that we can call a memory. Most of the evidence suggests that there is not 'a memory' in the brain, but that memorising is a process that occurs throughout the brain. Just because we have a word for it, it does not mean to say that it exists.

In the area of health, the Western tendency to describe processes as objects means that diseases are described as things rather than processes. I might describe how 'I caught measles' as if they were objects to catch. This leads us towards physical explanations of health and ill-health, and towards medically based treatments. So we are likely to use excessive surgery to remove things and ignore the social and cultural features of ill-health. (The cultural differences in the use of language in health are covered in Chapter 8, on page 114.)

PSYCHOLOGICAL CONTRIBUTIONS

Going to the doctor

We do not go to the doctor every time we feel ill. Research suggests that on the vast majority of occasions that we experience a symptom of illness, we do not report it to a health worker. We usually ask other people, most likely our family and friends, for advice before we decide to go to the doctor. These 'lay consultations' are very common and Scambler and Scambler (1984) estimate that we make 11 lay consultations for every medical consultation. We receive advice such as, 'I went to the doctor with that and she just told me to rest', or more worryingly, 'Our Gladys had symptoms like that just before she died.' So what are the factors that encourage us to go beyond the lay consultations and go to the doctor? Pitts (1991a) suggests the following key features:

- **persistence of symptoms:** we are likely to take a 'wait and see' approach if we get ill and only seek medical advice if the symptoms last longer than we expect
- **critical incident:** a sudden change in the symptom or the amount of pain can encourage us to seek medical advice
- **expectation of treatment:** we are only likely to seek medical advice if we think it will do any good. If we have had the same symptoms before and not received any useful treatment then we are unlikely to bother making an appointment.

On the whole, we do not go to the doctor unless we feel it is important because we think we 'should not waste their valuable time'. This perception means that many people do not seek advice even when they have developed serious symptoms, and if the lay consultations do not encourage them to seek medical advice, their reluctance to go to the doctor can have serious consequences.

NVC in the consultation

It is important in a medical consultation that there should be a good rapport between the health worker and the patient. One of the first things that we notice and make judgements about in any social situation is what people look like, so it is probably important to take account of these first impressions. McKinstry and Wang (1991) showed pictures of doctors to patients attending surgeries. The pictures were of the same male or female doctor, dressed either very formally (white coat over suit or skirt) or very informally (jeans and open-necked, short-sleeved shirt, or pink trousers, jumper and gold earrings). The patients were asked to rate how happy they would be to see the doctor in the picture, and how much confidence they would have in the doctor's ability. The traditionally dressed images received higher preference ratings than the casually attired ones, particularly on the part of older and professional-class patients (see Figure 9.2).

Male doctor wearing:
1 White coat   3.7
2 Suit   4.0
3 Tweed jacket 3.8
4 Cardigan   2.7

Female doctor wearing:
1 White coat   4.2
2 Skirt   4.3
3 Trousers   3.2

Patients who responded that a
male doctor *should usually wear:*
1 White coat   15%
2 Suit   44%
3 Tie   67%

And would *object* to a male doctor:
1 Wearing jeans   59%
2 Wearing an earring   55%
3 Having long hair   46%

Patients who responded that a
female doctor *should usually wear:*
1 White coat   34%
2 Skirt   57%

And would *object* to a female doctor:
1 Wearing jeans   63%
2 Wearing lots of jewellery 60%

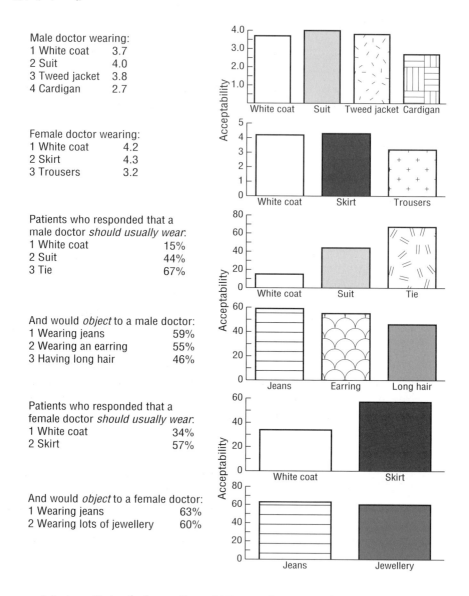

FIGURE 9.2 *Acceptable dress for doctors. (Source: McKinstry and Wang, 1991)*

Appearance, though, isn't the only source of non-verbal communication. Argyle (1975) emphasised that all the various types of non-verbal communication interact with each other, so dress alone will not be enough to create a good communication between doctor and patient. A formally dressed doctor who avoids eye contact and doesn't use appropriate facial expressions is likely to come across as aloof or distant, and this in itself is likely to be a barrier to effective patient–doctor interaction for most people.

Technical terms

People are easily baffled and intimidated by technical terms. This is particularly true in the area of health where are there numerous big words for relatively simple procedures. If you look at the following commonly used medical terms, are you confident you know what they refer to?

- protein
- haemorrhoid
- antibiotic
- virus
- anti-emetic
- insulin
- enema.

'Virus' is a term we might use in everyday conversation. 'I'm not going to work today, I've got a bit of a virus'. What does it mean to 'have a virus' and do we know what a virus is and how we should treat it?

McKinlay (1975) carried out an investigation into the understanding that women had of the information given to them by health workers in a maternity ward. The researchers recorded the terms that were used in conversations with the women and then asked them what they understood by 13 of these terms, including breech, purgative, mucus, glucose and antibiotic. On average, each of the terms was understood by less than 40% of the women. Even more remarkable were the expectations of the health workers who used the terms. When they were asked whether they expected their patients to understand these terms their estimates were even lower than 40%.

It seems that the health workers did not expect their patients to understand what they were being told, so why did they use the difficult terms? The likely answer is that medical language probably makes the health worker appear more knowledgeable and more important, and it might also make the conversation brief because the patient will not be able to ask any questions without the fear of appearing stupid.

Computer doctors

The knowledge of the doctor and health worker can appear intimidating to the patient and make them reluctant to disclose symptoms. A study by Robinson and West (1992) illustrates this point. They were interested in the amount of self-disclosure people make when they attend a genito-urinary clinic (a clinic which specialises in venereal disease). Before they saw the doctor, patients were asked to record the intimate details of their symptoms, previous attendances and sexual behaviour on a questionnaire administered either in a written version or by computer.

The results of the study showed that people were prepared to reveal significantly more symptoms to the computer than they would put on paper or tell the doctor (see Figure 9.3). Also, they made more disclosures about previous attendances to the computer than to the doctor. This result seems a little strange since the information you give to the doctor is personal and private, but when you are responding to a computer you have no idea how many people have access to this information. It might be that the impersonal nature of the computer allows us to come out with information of a highly personal nature. Alternatively, it might be that when we communicate with a machine we are less worried about social judgement of our sexual behaviour.

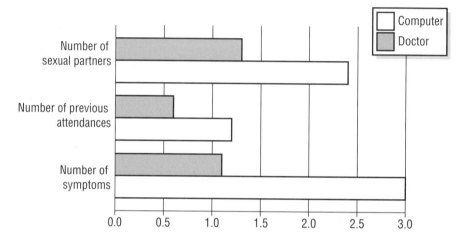

FIGURE 9.3 *Disclosing information to doctors and computers. (Source: Robinson and West, 1992)*

The McDoctors

Our relationship with health workers is affected by the general changes within our society. Ritzer (1993) suggests that all parts of society, even the health services, are affected by the McDonalds culture. Medicine is becoming an assembly line process, and patients are now called customers or consumers. We don't *receive treatment* any more, we *consume* the services of health workers. The management of the health service is concerned with efficiency, numbers of units, and through-put. They are starting to develop 'walk-in-doctors', where the patient will go to an emergency room and receive fairly speedy treatment. The emergency room will deal with a limited range of disorders but will be able to deal with a lot of them and very quickly. This is like a fast food restaurant, such as McDonalds, where the diners have a limited menu choice but know exactly what they will be getting, and know they will get it quickly.

If you walk into a modern British hospital you can see this changing style of health. The Queens Medical Centre in Nottingham, for example, has an international reputation and contains a number of high-profile specialist services as well as medical and nursing schools. As you walk through the front door, the impression is of a shopping mall, with small shops where you can buy anything from fast food to books. There is even a travel agent ('Only got one month to live, madam? I've got a late availability bargain break just for you!'). Health is becoming just another part of our consumer behaviour, and in the process it is becoming dehumanised. This will inevitably change our relationship with health workers – or to use Ritzer's term, our relationship with the McDoctors. Have a nice day!

Making a diagnosis

The doctor (or other health worker) has to discover what signs and symptoms the patient has and make a diagnosis of the problem, and then suggest the best treatment. This is not as easy as it sounds because it is not always obvious which are the most important signs and symptoms, and which are the irrelevant ones. One of the problems that might affect diagnosis is the *primacy effect*. This effect is recognised in a number of areas of psychology and refers to the tendency to remember and give extra importance to the first piece of information you hear. So the first thing you tell the doctor might have an a bigger effect on the diagnosis than information that comes out later in the consultation. Wallston (1978, cited in Pitts, 1991a) found that doctors distorted the information that was given later in the consultation so that it fitted in with the diagnosis they made in the earlier part.

When they are examining and interviewing a patient, doctors have a limited time to obtain the information and make a diagnosis. This is made more difficult by our reluctance to tell the doctor what is wrong with us. A study by Korsch, Gozzi and Francis (1968) found that as many as a quarter of the mothers attending a paediatric (child) out-patient clinic failed to tell the doctor their major concern. This point is also emphasised by the effectiveness of the 'computer doctors' (see above).

The doctor has to come up with a number of possible hypotheses about the condition of the patient, and, according to Weinman (1981), the choice of these hypotheses will be affected by:

1 The doctor's approach to health – for example, the importance they give to psychological explanations, biological explanations, or social explanations of the condition
2 The probability of having a certain disease, and this is affected by the various heuristics mentioned above
3 The seriousness of the disease and its treatability; for example, if a disease is easily treated, and the consequences of not treating it are life-threatening, then it would be a good choice to treat it even if you are not positive about the diagnosis

4 Knowledge of the patient – for example, their medical history and their pattern of visits to the doctor; a person who frequently consults their doctor is likely to be judged differently to someone who rarely consults.

Judgements of risk

One of the factors that will affect the final choice of treatment is the judgement of risk by the patient and by the doctor. This judgement can be influenced by a number of features, including how the information is presented. An example of how the presentation of the message can affect judgement was provided by Marteau (1990b). In this study, a group of medical students was asked whether they would undergo, or whether they would advise patients to undergo, a number of medical procedures such as surgery for terminal liver disease, or termination of pregnancy if the child would have haemophilia. When the risks of the procedures were presented to the medical students, they were framed in either a positive or negative way. For example, the researcher might describe the risk of undergoing an essential operation as being that the person had a 10% chance of surviving surgery (positive frame) or a 90% chance of dying (negative frame).

Marteau found that the way in which the information was presented affected the decisions which people made, even though logically, the chances were identical. If the procedure was phrased in an optimistic way, then the medical students were likely to make a more optimistic judgement. For example, they were more likely to choose an option which gave a 10% chance of surviving, than one which gave a 90% chance of dying, even though logically the two are identical (see Figure 9.4).

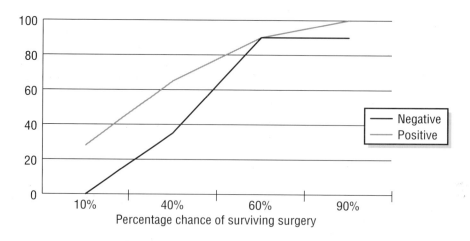

FIGURE 9.4 *Opting for medical procedures. (Source: Marteau, 1990b)*

SPECIAL ISSUE:
Doctor knows best

The medical profession is still largely male in outlook and this makes the interaction between women and doctors quite problematic. Ann Oakley (1984) writes about this and, in particular, the experience of having a baby. She quotes from a 1977 leaflet from the British Medical Association designed for pregnant women:

> You decide when to see your doctor and let him confirm the fact of your pregnancy. From then onwards you are going to have to answer a lot of questions and be the subject of a lot of examinations. Never worry about any of these. They are necessary, they are in the interests of your baby and yourself, and none of them will ever hurt you. (page 170)

The message in this paragraph is relatively clear. Doctors know more about having babies than women do, and women should not worry about the clever and technical things that these doctors do because they probably wouldn't understand it. It seems quite remarkable that having babies has come under the control of men, and the way that this has happened makes a remarkable story, but this is not our concern in this chapter. Our interest in Oakley's account is her description of the consultations between women and male doctors about pregnancy. She records a number of conversations that highlight the difficult relationship between patient and doctor. These include the expert status of the doctor, the tendency to ignore certain symptoms, and the use of technical terms to intimidate the patient.

The doctor as an expert

MALE DOCTOR: *Will you keep a note in your diary when you first feel the baby move?*

PATIENT: *Do you know – well, of course you would know – what it feels like?*

MALE DOCTOR: *It feels like wind pains – something moving in your tummy.* (page 172)

The doctor, of course, does not know what it feels like to have a baby move inside him, but both he and the patient discuss the experience as if he does.

Ignoring symptoms

In the study by Oakley, 12% of the statements made by patients concerned symptoms of pain or discomfort which were dismissed or ignored by the doctor. Two examples are given below.

PATIENT: *I've got a pain in my shoulder.*

DOCTOR: *Well, that's your shopping bag hand, isn't it?* (page 173)

PATIENT: *I get pains in my groin down here, why is that?*

DOCTOR: *Well, it's some time since your last pregnancy, and also your centre of gravity is changing.*

PATIENT: *I see.*

DOCTOR: *That's okay.* [Pats her on the back] (page 173)

What is this 'centre of gravity' and how does it affect pain in the groin? This 'commonsense' explanation just deflects the question rather than answering it.

Technical terms

In the example below, the patient resists the doctor's suggestion that she enter hospital in preparation for giving birth. To start with he tries to ridicule her and her knowledge and then, when she continues to resist, he resorts to a string of big words.

DOCTOR: *I think what we have to do is assess you – see how near you are to having it.* [Does an internal examination]. *Right – you'll go like a bomb, and I've given you a good stirring up. So what I think you should do, is I think you should come in.*

PATIENT: *Is it possible to wait another week, and see what happens?*

DOCTOR: *You've been reading the* Sunday Times.

PATIENT: *No, I haven't. I'm married to a doctor.*

DOCTOR: *Well, you've ripened up since last week and I've given the membranes a good sweep over.*

PATIENT: *What does that mean?*

DOCTOR: *I've swept them – not with a brush, with my finger* [Writes on notes 'give date for induction']

PATIENT: *I'd still rather wait a week.*

DOCTOR: *Well, we know the baby's mature now, and there's no sense in waiting. The perinatal morbidity and mortality increase rapidly after forty-two weeks. They didn't say that in the* Sunday Times, *did they?* (page 173)

It is experiences like these that makes people reluctant to seek medical advice.

APPLICATIONS

Improving communication

The area in which psychology should be most able to provide some help is the communication between doctor and patient – in particular, encouraging health workers to communicate effectively and to be attentive to the needs of their patients. Taylor (1986) suggests that this has not been dealt with in the training of doctors for three main reasons. Firstly, there is no general agreement on what the main features of a good consultation are. The same doctor can appear remote and distant to one patient, yet another patient will describe her as 'someone I can talk to'. Secondly, there is a belief within the medical profession that good communication will make the doctor too sensitive and therefore not tough enough to deal with the difficult daily decisions of being a doctor. Thirdly, there is the argument that it is difficult enough for doctors to stay on top of all the medical information they need without complicating their lives with having to be nice to patients. However, as DiMatteo and DiNicola (1982) point out, many of the failures in medical communications stem from a lack of basic courtesy. Simple things like addressing people by their name, saying hello and goodbye and telling them where to hang their coat will only add a few moments to a consultation but will appear warm and supportive to the patient.

Health workers often have to explain medical conditions to people who have very little medical knowledge. In their explanations they might use visual materials of some sort. Tapper-Jones et al. (1988) investigated how general practitioners use visual material during consultations with their patients. They found that the majority of these doctors used free-hand drawings to illustrate points. The only prepared materials that they used came from drug companies, and very few of the doctors realised that educational materials are available from health education units. The introduction of prepared educational material might help the understanding of patients about their condition.

Improving understanding

A major problem in the communication between patient and doctor is the different understandings and expectations they have about health and illness. In a review of this area, Ley (1989) found that a substantial proportion of patients are dissatisfied with the information they are given by health workers. In 21 surveys of hospital patients the average proportion of dissatisfied patients was 41%, and for general practice patients the average proportion dissatisfied was 28%. Ley attributes much of this dissatisfaction to patients not understanding and forgetting what they are told, and also to their reluctance to ask questions of health workers.

Studies on the understandings of patients often show a discrepancy between patient understandings and the current view of the medical profession. For example, people with peptic ulcers knew that acid caused ulcers but only 10% were able to correctly identify that this acid is secreted by the stomach. Also, many patients with hypertension believed, incorrectly, that they could be cured by short-term treatment (for a review, see Ley, 1989). Other studies have investigated patients' knowledge about the organs of the body, and Boyle (1970) found that only 42% could identify the location of the heart, 20% the stomach and 49% the liver. This means that over half the population are unsure where their major organs are. If people do not know where things are or what they do, it is easy to see how they can be baffled by medical explanations.

Memory

One of the problems for patients in a medical consultation is remembering what they are told by the health worker. We are not very good at remembering detail at the best of times and it is even more difficult when we are trying to remember material that we do not understand or material that is new to us. Ley et al. (1973) investigated how accurately people remember medical statements. Patients attending a general practice surgery were given a list of medical statements and were then asked to recall them. The same list was also given to a group of students. The statements were either given in an unstructured way, or were preceded by information about how they would be organised. For example, a structured presentation might involve the researcher saying something like 'I'm going to tell you three things: firstly, what is wrong with you; secondly, what tests we will be doing, and thirdly, what is likely to happen to you'.

When they were tested to see how much they remembered, Ley et al. found that structuring the information made a very clear difference. The patients who received the information in a clearly categorised form remembered about 25% more than those who received the same information in an unstructured way. The students, who were more used to learning information, were about 50% better if they received categorised information than if it were unstructured. There is clear message in these results for how information can be given to patients so that they will remember it. This has some significance in our discussion on compliance to health requests (see Chapter 5), since if you cannot remember the instructions then you cannot comply with them.

The study above is about list learning, but what do people remember of real consultations? Ley (1988) investigated this by speaking to people after they had visited the doctor. They were asked to say what the doctor had told them to do and this was compared with a record of what had actually been said to them. Ley found that people were quite poor in remembering medical information. In general, patients remembered about 55% of what their doctor had said to them, but the inaccuracies were not random ones. Ley found the following patterns in the errors made by the patients:

- they had good recall of the first thing they were told (the primacy effect)
- they did not improve their recall as a result of repetition – it did not matter how often the doctor repeated the information
- they remembered information which had been categorised (say, which tablets they should be taking) better than information which was more general
- they remembered more than other patients if they already had some medical knowledge.

In a follow-up to the study, Ley prepared a small booklet giving advice to doctors on how to communicate more clearly with their patients. Patients whose doctors had read the booklet recalled on average 70% of what they had been told, which was a significant increase on the previous figure.

SUMMARY

The relationship between health worker and patient has an important part to play in encouraging healthy behaviours. This relationship is affected by a number of factors including communication and judgement. A poor relationship between health worker and patient can lead to poor levels of adherence to treatment programmes.

chapter ten

HEALTH AND ORGANISATIONS

CHAPTER OVERVIEW

Psychologists have carried out a number of studies on THE WORK ENVIRON-MENT to look at how it affects us. One affect of a poor working environ-ment is sick building syndrome, in which our place of work contributes to our ill-health. Other factors causing health problems include the popula-tion density in the building, and the amount of noise we have to put up with. Much is written about STRESS AT WORK and psychologists look at factors that are part of the job as well as personal factors such as relationships and burn-out. The SPECIAL ISSUE: ACCIDENTS AT WORK looks at the various personal and design features that lead to accidents. These can include human error, though, more commonly, the major cause of an accident is poor manage-ment. The APPLICATIONS: IMPROVING HEALTH IN ORGANISATIONS include a number of work-based programmes to improve the health of staff, including health haz-ard appraisal, and also attempts to facilitate accident reduction at work.

THE WORK ENVIRONMENT

We spend a lot of time in large organisations. As children we spend what seems like a life sentence at school, and as adults many of us work for large organisations. There has been a growing concern about how organisations can affect our health, and how they could be used to promote our health. In this chapter we will look at some of issues that affect our health at the work place.

Sick building syndrome

Offices can seriously damage your health. So says the British Health and Safety Executive (Oliphant, 1995) in its report on sick building syndrome. They suggest that a building can be diagnosed as 'sick' when staff complain of illness more commonly than you would reasonably expect. The most com-mon symptoms are:

- lethargy and tiredness
- dry throat
- runny nose or blocked nose
- difficulty in breathing
- tight feelings in the chest
- dry, itchy or watery eyes
- headaches
- coughs
- nausea
- mental fatigue.

The most likely causes of these symptoms are poor air conditioning, low humidity and a high level of dust in the air. Other features such as poor temperature control can add to the generally poor environment of office space.

The Health and Safety Executive recommend a number of things that can be done to reduce the problems of sick buildings. These include ensuring good air flow and appropriate humidity, reducing static electricity in carpets, dampening noise, and maintaining an ambient temperature. Interestingly, they also recommend that workers should be allowed to adjust the light level by the use of dimmers or table lamps. This suggests that control of the environment might be an important factor in individual health (see also the section on locus of control in Chapter 12).

Sick building syndrome is still quite controversial despite the increasing number of reports of the problem. The controversy surrounds whether the syndrome is due to the environment of the building, or whether it is due to some psychological factors. For example, Czander (1994) suggested that sick building syndrome is caused by the social dynamics of the workplace that increase the susceptibility of the workers to illness. On the other hand, Bauer et al. (1992) carried out a range of psychological measures on workers in sick buildings and found very few differences between workers with symptoms of the disorder and workers without the symptoms. This suggests that the illness comes from the building rather from psychologically vulnerable people.

Social factors in buildings

One social factor that appears to affect illness within a building is status. At one building of the financial services company Sun Alliance, natural daylight has become a status symbol, according to Pilkington (1995). The managers have their rooms on the outside edge of the building on the top floor where they can control their environment by opening windows. In contrast, the mainly female clerical staff are corralled in large open-plan rooms with no natural light or ventilation. The problem with this company is not their building but the way they treat their staff.

The report of the Health and Safety Executive notes that some workers are more at risk of sick building syndrome than others. The workers at risk include the low-paid, low-status workers doing sedentary repetitive jobs, clerical staff, public sector workers, people with allergies, and women rather than men. This list further supports the idea that the effects of the sick building are made worse by other factors such as status, personal control and management style. So far, no one has suggested that illness at work could be due to 'sick management syndrome', though this might be a reasonable explanation of the evidence.

Population density

Another feature of the work environment that can affect us is the number of people that we have to work with in a limited space. Being in a crowd does not always make us feel bad, and, in fact we often prefer to be a crowd for some social events such as live music or sports events. The basic physiological effect of crowding is to increase our level of arousal (increased blood pressure and heart rate), but although this is pleasant at leisure events, it becomes increasingly uncomfortable in other circumstances.

It is difficult to measure these effects at work because of the problems in assessing the level of crowding and the level of arousal. The work on population density that is most commonly quoted is a study on the effects of changes in jail population densities on crowding. Wener and Keys (1988) looked at the amount of sickness amongst the prisoners. The researchers collected data before and after a court order that led to a reduction in the population levels in one unit, which was already overcrowded, and an increase in another prison unit. Eventually the final population density in both units became the same. Wener and Keys found that when the population levels were equal in the two units, the perceived crowding and sickness rate was higher in the unit which had become more full than in the unit which had its population reduced. This shows how you cannot measure crowding by just counting the number of people in the space. You also have to consider how the people perceive the level of crowding.

More dramatically, a study by Paulus, McCain and Cox (1978) showed that prisoners living in settings with greater space and less social density had less sickness than prisoners in high-density settings. In fact, as we can see from Figure. 10.1, population density has been found to be closely related to the death rate in prison.

Noise

One of the stressors at work or school that has an effect on our health is noise. For example, a study by Cohen et al. (1980) looked at children from four schools which were under a flight path near Los Angeles airport. The

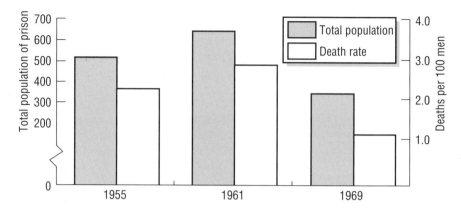

FIGURE 10.1 *Death rate and population size in prison*

children in these schools experienced frequent episodes of uncontrollable, unpredictable and very loud noise. They were compared with children from three matched schools in quiet areas, using physiological and behavioural measures of stress. The researchers found that the children from noisy areas showed some cognitive impairment in that they were more likely to give up on a puzzle-solving task. They also had significantly higher blood pressure.

Studies of industrial workers show that high levels of noise are associated with cardiovascular disorders, sore throats and digestive disorders (for a summary, see Bell et al., 1990). It also appears that noise interacts with other stress-related behaviours to enhance the dangers of ill-health. For example, smokers tend to increase their rate of smoking in noisy conditions. In a study by Cherek (1985), smokers were subjected to 90 decibels of taped industrial noise (the sound of pneumatic drills about 20 metres away). When they were in the noisy conditions they increased their number of cigarettes by about 15% and increased the number of inhalations by about 30%.

Noise also has an affect on mental health, and various studies (reported in Bell et al., 1990) have found that industrial noise is associated with headaches, nausea, instability, argumentativeness, mood changes and sexual impotence. However, it is difficult to make a direct link between noise and ill-health since there are always many other variables to take into account. For example, workers with the worst noise conditions at work are often the workers with the lowest status and the least pay. They may also have more exposure to other health risks such as toxic materials or poor housing conditions, so their poor health may be due to their poor general environment rather than to the specific problem of noise.

STRESS AT WORK

The psychological models of stress are described in Chapter 2. In this section, we are going to look at some of particular stresses that are associated with work. Stress at work is being taken increasingly seriously by employers. This is for three reasons.

1 Stress is now believed to be one of the major causes of absenteeism at work, and the cost to employers is substantial.
2 Stress is also believed to be the cause of increased staff turnover, which also is costly for employers.
3 There is growing fear of litigation for employers if they can be held responsible for the stress of their employees.

In a model of stress at work (see Figure 10.2), Cooper, Cooper and Eaker (1988) identify five major categories of work stress:

■ factors that are part of the job
■ the role of the individual in the organisation
■ relationships at work
■ the opportunities for career development
■ organisational structure and climate.

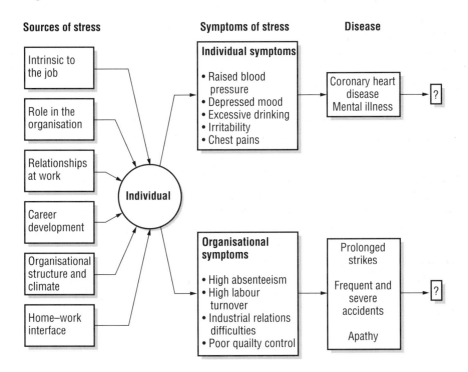

FIGURE 10.2 *Model of stress at work. Source: Cooper, Cooper and Eaker (1988)*

Factors that are part of the job

One of the factors affecting stress at work is the shift pattern that a worker is required to follow. It is a consistent research finding that changing shifts patterns are disruptive to physical and psychological well-being. For example, a study by Sutherland and Cooper (1987) on off-shore oil rig workers found that shift work was an important source of stress. In particular, they found that the longer the work shift – for example, 28 days on followed by 28 days off, rather than 14 days on followed by 14 days off – the greater the stress.

There is a growing trend in British hospitals for nurses to be asked to work rotating shifts. This means that they have to work some morning shifts, some afternoon shifts and some night shifts in every month. This is despite the evidence that shift rotation has an adverse effect on the physical and mental well-being of nurses. A study by Tasto, Colligan, Skjei and Polly (1978, cited in Arnold, Robertson and Cooper, 1991) found that nurses on shift rotation showed increased levels of alcohol use, more health problems, less satisfaction in their personal life, more depression and more anxiety than nurses on fixed shifts. These findings make the forced introduction of shift rotation all the more remarkable, though it is usually enforced by administrators who work fixed day shifts.

Working conditions also affect work stress. Factors such as noise (see above), temperature, pollution or social isolation can all create stress. Health workers often work in very stressful environments. The lighting in hospitals is often bright, the wards are often very noisy and the ventilation systems often inadequate.

Other factors of the job associated with stress include (a) excessively long hours at work required, for example, of junior hospital doctors in Britain; (b) the level of risk and danger; (c) the introduction of new technology; (d) work overload; and (e) work underload.

The role of the individual in the organisation

The sources of role stress at work can be roughly divided into two categories: stress due to role ambiguity and stress due to role conflict (Arnold et al., 1991).

Role ambiguity develops when workers are unclear about what they should be doing and what is expected of them. This can lead to low job satisfaction, physiological strain, lowered self-confidence, greater depression, lowered motivation and a greater intention to leave the job.

Role conflict, on the other hand, might involve conflicting demands from different groups of colleagues. For example, middle managers are often caught between the needs of their staff for better working conditions and the demands of their senior managers for greater output. Conflict can also occur when workers are required to carry out tasks which they dislike or which they believe are outside their job description. Role conflict is associated with physiological strain, low job satisfaction and job-related tension.

Relationships at work

Nobody would claim that living with people is easy, and the relationships we have at work can be among the most stressful experiences in our daily lives. The types of relationships are:

- **Relationships with superiors**
  Workers who felt under pressure reported that their boss gave them unhelpful criticism, took advantage of them, and showed favouritism to certain staff (Arnold et al., 1991).
- **Relationships with subordinates**
  Some people are promoted to management roles because of their expertise in non-management tasks. This means that the manager is being required to carry out new tasks which may not suit their particular skills and inclinations. This is inevitably stressful.
- **Relationships with colleagues**
  Positive social support (see Chapter 3) can help people at work, but a poor social environment, which is often described as 'office politics', can have stressful consequences.

Career development

The stressful aspects of career development can come from a sense of job insecurity, or impending retirement, or job appraisal.

Organisational structure and climate

Being part of an organisation can threaten a person's sense of freedom. The structure of an organisation can either make a person feel as if they belong and can make a positive contribution, or it can increase a sense of personal alienation. The topics of climate and structure are extensively discussed in occupational psychology; for example, see Deal and Kennedy (1988).

Burn-out

Long-term stress at work can sometimes result in burn-out. The term burn-out refers to a syndrome of emotional exhaustion, depersonalisation, and reduced personal effectiveness at work. It is experienced by some people at work, especially when their job requires intense contact with people, usually clients or patients. Maslach (1982) observed that professional health workers who become burnt-out start to lose their caring and concern for patients and clients, and also start to feel bad about themselves. Burn-out is associated with higher rates of absenteeism, poorer job performance, worsening relationships with colleagues, poor personal health, and problems with personal relationships. Harris (1984) points out that the general lower level of working performance associated with burn-out leads to an increased probability of accidents.

Research suggests that a number of the causes of burn-out are due to the structure of the organisation. For example, burn-out is more likely to occur when workers have a large number of patients they are responsible for, or when they are working long hours with a large amount of direct contact with patients. The suggested answer for organisations to prevent burn-out is to adjust work schedules so that workers have enough break from the demands of patient contact.

Unemployment

An important footnote to any discussion of work and stress is the issue of unemployment and stress. If we return to our model in Figure 10.3, then we can see that unemployment brings its own stresses. Being unemployed means being poor, and low income is a major risk factor in health. Unemployed people have a very ambiguous role, and they do not get the support from relationships at work. Their prospects for career development are nil, and the social climate in Britain still stigmatises the unemployed, even though there are very few jobs available.

A review of this topic by Fryer and Payne (1986, cited in Arnold et al., 1991) suggests that the unemployed generally have lower levels of personal happiness, self-esteem and psychological well-being. Interestingly, and most alarmingly, this group of people does not appear in government health statistics such as those presented in *Social Trends* (Central Statistical Office, 1994) or *The Health of the Nation* (Department of Health, 1992). These documents give breakdowns of health by social class, but do not give figures for the health risks of being unemployed.

SPECIAL ISSUE:
Accidents at work

When we think of accidents, we usually imagine the role of health workers is to pick up the pieces after the accident has occurred. Recently, however, there has been a growing awareness that something can be done to reduce accidents, and that accident reduction is an important part of health promotion. Accident reduction is one of the five key areas of *The Health of the Nation* strategy (see Chapter 1), so we will have a brief look at some of the issues around accidents at work.

The first issue to consider is what we mean by the term *accident*. A dictionary defines an accident as:

- an event without apparent cause
- an unexpected event
- an unintentional act
- a mishap.

The definition seems quite clear, but there is the little matter of interpretation. One of the problems here concerns the explanations we give for different events. Imagine that you are the holding a dinner plate in the kitchen and somehow it ends up smashed on the floor. Your explanation is likely to be, 'It slipped out of my hand', in other words, it was an accident and you could not help it. On the other hand, the explanation of your mother, whose best plate it was, is likely to be, 'You dropped it', meaning that it was your fault because of your carelessness, and not an accident at all. You attribute your behaviour to bad luck, and your mother attributes your behaviour to some personal failing.

Psychologists have studied the ways that we make attributions like these and have noticed some systematic biases in the way we explain behaviour. For example, we tend to overestimate the amount of control that someone has over their own behaviour and ignore the way that the situation is affecting them (this is called the *fundamental attribution error*). We tend to blame people, rather than circumstance, when misfortune occurs near to them. So, is the broken plate the result of an accident or not? Perhaps it's just a matter of interpretation. This digression into the kitchen leaves us with the unresolved question of what an accident is. Instead of trying to resolve it, we will look at the more fruitful area of describing the errors that might lead to accidents.

Human error

A way of categorising errors is suggested by Riggio (1990) who identified four types of error that can lead to accidents:

1 **Errors of omission:** failing to carry out a task; for example, not closing the bow doors on the ferry in Zeebrugge harbour (see Appendix 1)

2 **Errors of commission:** making an incorrect action; for example, a health worker giving someone the wrong medicine

3 **Timing errors:** working too quickly, working too slowly

4 **Sequence errors:** doing things in the wrong order.

Not all errors lead to accidents and we often make minor errors of judgement without any unfortunate consequences. Sometimes, however, these errors do lead to an event that we call an accident. If we want to reduce accidents, the obvious thing to do is to examine the errors that people most commonly make, and then change the working practices so that the chance of error is reduced. The problem with this is that most workers are reluctant to report errors because of the consequences for them.

The negative consequences to an individual of reporting a personal error or accident include:

■ time lost
■ feeling guilty
■ admitting mistakes
■ possible disciplinary action
■ possible lost confidence of colleagues
■ making a mountain out of molehill.

Another reason why errors and accidents are under-reported is that management often does not want to know about them. The problems for management of receiving an accident report include:

■ having a written record of the event which increases the danger of litigation
■ increased need for action by management
■ increased need for investment in people or equipment
■ responsibility is shifted from the worker to the organisation.

What this means is that bad procedures and common errors often go unreported. And if they go unreported and unnoticed, then remedial action cannot be taken.

Causes of accidents

Most accidents have multiple causes, though we can divide many of them into two basic categories: individual errors and organisational errors. Reason (1990), in his discussion of human error, presented a series of case studies of major disasters. In each disaster, a situation was created over a number of months or years, where the systems introduced or neglected by management finally produced a major incident. The incident itself was triggered by the action of one or two individuals and it was these individuals who inevitably got the public blame while the organisation remained relatively unscathed. In his description of the *Herald of Free Enterprise* ferry disaster (see Appendix 1 and Figure 10.3), Reason (1990) identified ten factors that contributed to the sinking of the ship. He attributed all of them to bad management decisions and design problems, yet it was three sailors who were punished while the management of the ferry owners (P&O) avoided any sanctions. (Note: you could describe this apportionment of blame as another example of the fundamental attribution error, though a more cynical interpretation might note the contributions made by P&O to the ruling political party of the day).

FIGURE 10.3 *The Herald of Free Enterprise — a disaster caused by management error rather than individual failings of the crew*

Factors affecting individual error

There are a number of factors that increase the chances of error at work, including:

1 **Substance and alcohol abuse**
   This is the most commonly cited cause in the literature for accidents, though it is very difficult to get accurate figures because workers are unlikely to admit to having a lunch time drink, for example, if there is an accident in the afternoon.
2 **Lack of sleep**
   Research (for example, Asken and Raham, 1983) shows that (a) errors are more likely in sleep-deprived people and (b) sleep-deprived people need longer to complete tasks.
3 **Accident proneness**
   This is controversial, since it stigmatises some individuals, though there is some research that suggests accident proneness can be identified. Jones and Wuebker (1988) describe how a personnel inventory can be used to predict a number of accident-related events. Using the questionnaire they were able to identify high-risk individuals on the basis of their attitudes and personality, and to place them in less hazardous positions, or place them on special safety training programmes.

Other factors that might affect accidents include recent stressful life events (see the Social Readjustment Rating Scale, page 28), burn-out (see above), and fear of mistakes.

Factors affecting organisational error

The ways that an organisation can increase the chances of an accident include:

- the selection of inappropriate staff
- poor working procedure
- duty rotas that lead to fatigue
- an organisational climate that creates poor morale
- inadequate equipment for the task
- inadequate levels of training.

APPLICATIONS: IMPROVING HEALTH IN ORGANISATIONS

Work-based programmes

There is a growing awareness that one of the best ways to encourage healthy behaviour is to have health promotion activities at a person's place of work. It is part of The Health of the Nation strategy to encourage a partnership between health services and industry so that healthy workplaces can be developed. This approach has been endorsed by the Confederation of British Industry which acknowledges the benefits of such programmes (Department of Health, 1995).

There are a number of reasons to believe that health programmes at the workplace might be successful:

1 Many workers have a regular pattern of work and so they are able to participate in the programme on a regular basis.
2 Colleagues will also be in the health programme and be able to provide social support.
3 It requires less effort for the worker to take part in the health programme at work than it would be, for example, to attend a clinic or support group after work.
4 The workplace can encourage healthy behaviour through, for example, menu choices at vending machines and snack bars, and through smoking policies.

Among the potential advantages of health programmes for the employer is reduced staff sickness, the cost of which alone might pay for the health programme. Large businesses in the USA have already developed a number of programmes like this and there are two examples given below.

Health hazard appraisal

One example of a work-based health programme was introduced at a glass product company in Santa Rosa, California (Rodnick, 1982, cited in Feuerstein, Labbe and Kuczmierczyk, 1986). A 'health hazard appraisal' counselling session was carried out with nearly 300 employees at the company. As part of the programme, full-time staff were offered a comprehensive health examination which included:

- health history
- weight and height measurement
- blood pressure measurement
- range of blood tests, including cholesterol, liver enzyme level, calcium, protein etc.
- TB skin test
- stool test
- physical examination.

This information was used to provide feedback on the risks of contracting various diseases including specific cancers and cardiovascular disease. About two weeks after the tests, the workers attended a group session where they received feedback about their health-risk profiles. They were also given information about hypertension, heart disease and cancer.

One year later the workers were tested again and the following improvements in their general health were observed:

- decrease in blood pressure (particularly in individuals with mild hypertension)
- reduction in cholesterol levels in men
- decrease in cigarette smoking
- increase in exercise

- increase in breast self-examination
- decline in alcohol consumption in men
- increase in seat belt use by men.

'Stay Well' programme

A similar programme was also developed by a large computer manufacturer in the USA (the Control Data Corporation). This company introduced its 'Stay Well' programme in 1979 and offered it to its thousands of employees in various cities in the USA (described in Sarafino, 1994). As in the programme described above, the workers were given individual screening and feedback. They were then offered courses in physical fitness, nutrition, weight control, how to stop smoking, and stress management. They could also join work-based action teams that either tried to create a healthier work environment or tried to create support groups for changing health behaviours.

The company was able to evaluate the programme by comparing the behaviour of workers at workplaces that offered the programme and workplaces that did not offer the programme. The evaluations suggested that the programme was successful in improving levels of exercise, smoking, weight control and stress. The company also recorded less absenteeism and fewer health insurance claims.

Accident reduction at work

Health promotion can also be used at work to reduce accidents. The most cited methods for reducing accidents are stress reduction programmes. For example, Kunz (1987) describes how a stress intervention programme reduced medical costs and accident claims in a hospital. The programme more than paid for itself with the savings from reduction in accidents. Stress-reduction programmes have also been shown to reduce absenteeism (Murphy and Sorenson, 1988).

Another way of reducing accidents is through incentive programmes. Fox, Hopkins and Anger (1987) looked at the effects of a token economy programme at open-cast pits. Employees earned stamps for working without time lost for injuries, for being in work groups in which all other workers had not time lost through injury, for not being involved in equipment damaging accidents, for making safety suggestions and for behaviour that prevented an injury or accident. They lost stamps for equipment damage, injuries to their work group, and failure to report accidents and injuries. The token economy produced a dramatic reduction in days lost through injury and reduced the costs of accidents and injuries. These improvements were maintained over a number of years.

Other methods of reducing accidents include *poster campaigns* to raise awareness of hazards and to encourage a realistic assessment of risk, *staff training and* organisational review. *Media campaigns* can also be used to reduce accidents, for example, the campaign on chip pan fires (see pages 61–62).

SUMMARY

Organisations are a major part of our lives and so have a large effect on our health. Psychologists have identified a number of features that contribute to ill-health within organisations. They have also identified ways that organisations can enhance the health of their employees through positive action. Work-based health programmes are among the most effective ways of improving the health of the general population.

chapter eleven

CHAPTER OVERVIEW

The CONTEXT explores the puzzle of pain and looks at the relationship between tissue damage and the experience of pain. It looks at examples of injury without pain (for example, episodic analgesia), and it also looks at examples of pain without injury. The SPECIAL ISSUE: PHANTOM LIMB PAIN looks at the strange phenomena of experiencing pain in parts of the body that have been removed. Explanations of phantom limbs give us further insights in the way we feel pain. The PSYCHOLOGICAL CONTRIBUTIONS include theories of pain and, in particular, the gate control theory. Another contribution concerns the various attempts at measuring pain that are important for research and treatment. The INTERVENTIONS: CONTROLLING PAIN include a discussion of the effects of chemicals and surgery as well as the use of a number of psychological treatments of pain including operant techniques and coping training.

CONTEXT: THE PUZZLE OF PAIN

It seems obvious that pain is connected with injury. I touch a hot oven, I injure my hand, and it hurts. So does our experience of pain occur as a consequence of damage to body tissue? The answer is both yes and no. The study of pain presents a number of puzzles that challenge the link between tissue damage and feelings of pain. These puzzles include the experience of injury with pain, the experience of pain without injury and the poor relationship between the size of the injury and the size of the pain. We will look at each of these in turn to illustrate the complexities of pain.

Injury without pain

We can divide the examples of injury without pain into congenital analgesia (a very rare condition where people are born with an inability to feel pain) and episodic analgesia (where people do not feel pain for some minutes or hours after an injury).

Pain is an important part of healthy living and we can see this in the problems experienced by people who do not feel pain. When they are children, they get burns and bruises and cuts, and frequently bite their tongues while eating. The most commonly quoted case is of a Canadian woman referred to in the literature as Miss C. (reported in Melzack and Wall, 1988). She felt no pain when she was given electric shocks, or made contact with hot water or even with an ice bath. When these unpleasant stimuli were being presented to her, she did not show any change in heart rate, blood pressure or respiration. In short, there was no sign that she registered these stimuli at all. If you think that the above things are rather unusual for a psychologist to inflict on a person, then you might be interested to know that they also inserted a stick through her nostril and injected histamine under her skin (usually regarded as forms of torture) to see whether she would feel pain. Fortunately, she did not.

This lack of pain was probably the major cause of Miss C.'s health problems which were very severe and led to her early death. She had problems with many of her joints, particularly her knees, hip and spine. People who *do* feel pain often have discomfort in their joints and this makes them change their behaviour. If we feel uncomfortable in a certain standing position then we will change it, and if we twist an ankle we will rest it. This allows the body to repair any tissue damage, but if it does not then the tissue around the joint deteriorates and becomes a breeding ground for infections. Miss C. died at the age of 29 when she developed massive infections that could not be controlled. Perhaps one of the most remarkable aspects of this case is that an examination of her nervous system after her death (around 1960) did not reveal any abnormalities.

Episodic analgesia

A much more common form of analgesia occurs when our sense of pain does not occur immediately after an injury, but some time later. The type of injury involved in this experience can range from minor abrasions to broken bones or even limb loss. The early observations of this were in soldiers wounded in battle who did not seem to feel the amount of pain that the severity of their wounds would indicate. A study by Carlen et al. (1978, cited in Melzack and Wall, 1988) described the reaction of Israeli soldiers during the Yom Kippur War when they experienced traumatic amputations (limbs blown off). Most of them described the initial injury as painless, and described the initial sensation as a 'bang', 'thump' or 'blow'. They did not seem to be in a state of shock and were fully aware of the state of their injuries. A number were understandably quite depressed by the experience of losing a limb and some felt guilty at having become wounded and letting their comrades down. The intriguing aspect of this observation is that depressed mood is usually associated with increased pain rather than reduced pain.

Melzack and Wall (1988) suggest there are six important characteristics of episodic analgesia:

1 The condition has no relation to the severity or the location of the injury.
2 There is no simple relationship to circumstances – sometimes it occurs in battle, but it also occurs in work situations.
3 The victim can be fully aware of the nature of the injury but still feel no pain.
4 The analgesia is instantaneous.
5 The analgesia lasts for a limited time.
6 The analgesia is localised to the injury, so although there is pain at the severed limb the patient might still complain about the needle prick for an injection.

Episodic analgesia is a puzzle for any theory of pain. The tissue damage is surely greatest at the time of the injury but the pain is delayed. This experience seems to be quite common because Melzack, Wall and Ty (1982) discovered that 37% of people arriving at the accident and emergency department of an urban American hospital with a range of injuries reported the experience of episodic analgesia.

Pain without injury

There are a number of examples of pain where there is no obvious physical cause, including neuralgia, causalgia, headache and phantom limb pain (see below). *Neuralgia* is a sudden sharp pain along a nerve pathway. It occurs after a nerve damaging disease (for example, herpes) has ended. *Causalgia* is a burning pain that often develops as a consequence of a severe wound – for example, from a knife. The remarkable thing about causalgia, like neuralgia, is that it develops after the wound has healed. Causalgia and neuralgia are not constant pains but they can be triggered by a simple stimulus in the environment like a breeze or the vibration of an air-conditioning unit.

Headaches are experienced by many but we really have very little idea about what causes them. Tension headaches, for example, have no known tissue damage and the early theories that they were the result of muscle contraction have been found to be inaccurate. Migraine is another form of headache which also has no obvious damage and no obvious cause. The common explanations of migraine refer to dilation of blood vessels but, according to Melzack and Wall (1988), these theories have been discounted because studies suggest that the changes in the blood vessels are more a result of the headache than a cause.

Pain out of proportion to the injury

The amount of pain does not always match the amount of injury. Some cancers cause massive injury to the body but produce very little pain until they are very advanced. On the other hand, some minor events that produce very little damage or threat can produce excruciating pain. For example, small kidney stones sometimes pass into the ureter that leads from the kidney to the bladder. This is a relatively trivial medical event but while it is occurring the person has agonising waves of pain that often cause them to collapse. The person obtains complete relief from the pain at the moment the stone leaves the ureter and enters the bladder.

The purpose of pain

Nobody wants pain but without it we would have serious problems. Pain seem to have three useful functions:

1 It can occur before a serious injury develops; for example, the pain experienced when picking up something hot will cause a person to immediately drop it.
2 It can aid learning and help people avoid harmful situations in the future.
3 When it occurs in damaged joints and muscles, pain sets a limit on activity and this helps the person to recover and also to avoid further damage.

This is not the whole story, though, and some pains serve no useful purpose. In fact, far from being the sign of a problem, pain can become the problem itself. Pain can become so severe and so feared that people would prefer to die than continue living with it. All these observations leave us with more questions than answers, although psychologists have attempted to respond to the puzzle of pain by developing explanations, and by developing interventions that relieve the suffering of pain.

SPECIAL ISSUE:
Phantom limb pain

Sometimes people who have lost a limb, or were born without a limb, experience all the sensations of having that limb. This experience is commonly referred to as having phantom limbs, and they have been recorded for over a century. One of the striking features about these phantom limbs is that people can experience very real pain from their phan- toms. This raises a number of questions about how we experience pain and, more generally, how our senses work, and how we interpret sensory information.

Melzack (1992) reviewed the evidence on phantom limbs and noted that they have the following remarkable features.

1 Phantom limbs have a vivid sensory quality and precise location in space – at first people sometimes try to walk on a phantom leg because it feels so real.
2 In most cases, a phantom arm will hang down at the side when the person sits or stands, but moves in co-ordination with other limbs when the person is walking.
3 Sometimes it gets stuck in an unusual position – for example, one person had a phantom arm bent behind them, and could not sleep on their back because the limb got in the way.
4 Wearing an artificial arm or leg enhances the phantom, and it often fills the extension like a hand fits a glove.
5 Phantoms have a wide range of sensations, including pressure, warmth, cold, dampness, itchiness and different kinds of pain (around 70% of amputees suffer pain in the phantom).
6 Patients perceive phantoms as an integral part of the body – even when a phantom foot is felt to be dangling in the air several inches below the stump and unconnected to the leg, it is still experienced as part of the body and moves appropriately.
7 Phantoms are also experienced by some people with spinal injury, and some paraplegics complain that their legs make continuous cycling movements producing painful fatigue, even though their actual legs are lying immobilised on the bed.

Explanations of phantom limbs

An early explanation was that the cut nerve ends, which grow into nodules called neuromas, continue to produce nerve impulses which the brain interprets as coming from the lost limb. Working on this hypothesis, various cuts have been made in the nerve pathways from the neuromas to the brain in an attempt to remove pain. These cuts, like other surgical attempts to relieve pain (see page 166),

sometimes bring about short-term relief, but the pain usually returns after a few weeks, and the cuts do not remove the phantom. Other theories have looked at nervous system activity in the spinal cord and in the brain. None of these approaches is able to account for all the phenomena associated with phantom limbs.

Melzack's model

Melzack suggests that the brain contains a neuromatrix – or network of neurones. This neuromatrix responds to information from the senses and also generates a characteristic pattern of impulses that indicate that the body is whole and is also your own. He calls this pattern the *neurosignature*. It is perhaps helpful to think of it as a mental hologram that builds up a picture of your body in the mind. If a limb is removed, the sensations cease from that region but the hologram is still created in the neuromatrix.

Melzack believes that this neuromatrix has nervous system pathways from the sensory systems, from the emotional and motivational systems and from the pathways associated with the recognition of self. Melzack suggests that the neuromatrix is largely pre-wired (or innate) and offers the evidence that very young children can experience phantoms after amputation, and people born with limbs missing can experience vivid phantoms. The matrix also responds to experience as shown by the gradual disappearance of some phantoms, though it is interesting to note that they can sometimes reappear years later.

Treating phantom limb pain

How do you stop the pain in a limb that isn't there? You obviously cannot use heat treatment, or kiss it better or apply anything that involves contact with the painful area. The only alternatives are to make surgical attacks on the nerve pathways (this produces very limited, if any, relief), or to use psychological and behavioural measures to control the pain. A summary of some of these methods is given on pages 166–168.

PSYCHOLOGICAL CONTRIBUTIONS

Theories of pain

Specificity theory

The traditional understanding of pain was described by specificity theory, which basically proposed that a special system of nerves carries messages from pain receptors in the skin to a pain centre in the brain. One of the points in favour of this approach was the discovery that there are specialised receptors in the skin for different sensations like heat and touch. The problem with the approach, as Melzack and Wall (1988) point out, is that the specialised receptors respond to certain unpleasant stimuli (a physiological event), but this does not mean that we always feel pain (a psychological experience). The examples of injury without pain, described above, show that there is not a direct connection between stimulation and pain. This point is reinforced by the evidence from neuralgia and causalgia, where a gentle touch can trigger a painful reaction.

A further argument against specificity theory comes from physiological evidence. For example, the technique of neurography allows us to record the activity of specific nerves and we can match up this activity to the sensations that people are feeling. This research found that there is not a close connection between the activity of certain nerves and particular sensations in the person. For example, Chery Croze and Duclaux (1980) found that the onset of pain was not connected with the onset of activity in the specialised nerves. Also, different painful stimuli such as chemicals, pressure and heat provoke activity in different groups of nerves, but people are unable to tell the difference between the different stimuli despite getting these different messages in their nervous system.

Pattern theories

Pattern theories, in contrast to specificity theories, suggest that there are no separate systems for perceiving pain, but instead the nerves are shared with other senses such as touch. According to these theories, the most important feature of pain is the pattern of activity in the nervous system which is affected by a number of factors including the amount of stimulation. For example, as the pressure of the touch increases, the sensation will develop into one of constriction and eventually to pain.

It is very difficult to build up an accurate 'wiring diagram' of the nervous system and to identify all the active bits of it. There is, however, a general belief that there are three types of receptor cells and nerve pathways that are important in pain. Firstly, there are *nociceptive cells*, which respond to pain but not to other stimuli. Secondly, there is another class of cells which respond to intense stimuli (in other words, pain) as well as weak stimuli like touch. Thirdly, there is a class of cells which respond just to touch and not to pain.

So how do we make sense of all this nervous system information and feel pain? This brings us to the best current model of the phenomena – the gate control theory.

Gate control theory

The gate control theory, first proposed by Melzack and Wall in the 1960s, combines the medical approach of previous theories with psychological and social factors that contribute to the experience of pain (the biopsychosocial approach). The theory suggests that there is a 'gate' in the nervous system that either allows pain messages to travel to the brain, or stops those messages (see Figure 11.1).

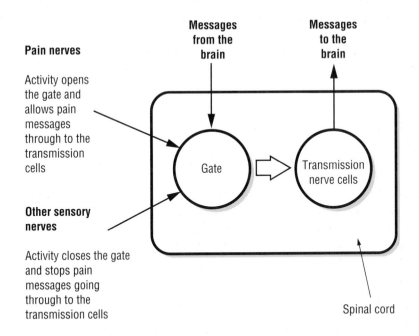

FIGURE 11.1 *The gate control theory of pain*

The gate control theory is biologically quite complex and the description of the nervous system pathways is beyond the scope of this text. The theory describes in some detail which nerves produce what reaction in the nervous system, and proposes a model for the control of the transmission of pain messages up the spinal cord to the brain. According to the theory, the gate is in the spinal cord and it is opened or closed by the following factors:

1 **Activity in the pain fibres**
   This is the 'specificity' part of the theory, and suggests that activity in the small diameter fibres, which respond specifically to pain, will open the gate.
2 **Activity in other sensory nerves**
   This is the 'pattern' part of the theory and refers to the large diameter nerves that carry information about harmless sensations such as touching, rubbing or scratching. Activity in these nerves will close the gate; this is in line with the observation that light rubbing around painful areas will reduce the pain.
3 **Messages from the brain**
   This is the central control mechanism and it responds to states such as anxiety or excitement to open or close the gate. The idea that the brain can influence the experience of pain explains why distracting people can help them not to notice the pain so much.

There are a number of factors that act to open or close the pain gate and a summary of these is shown in Table 11.1. The wiring diagram that is often presented with discussions of the gate control theory is a model based on the best available evidence. As yet, only some of the features of the model have been discovered in the nervous system and so it remains a model that explains the evidence rather than an accurate description of nervous system pathways. The model does, however, have a lot of support and it is accepted as a useful model for discussion and research about pain.

Table 11.1 Conditions that can open or close the pain gate (Source: Sarafino, 1994)

Conditions that open the gate	Conditions that close the gate
Physical conditions	**Physical conditions**
● Extent of the injury	● Medication
● Inappropriate activity level	● Counterstimulation, e.g. massage
Emotional conditions	**Emotional conditions**
● Anxiety or worry	● Positive emotions
● Tension	● Relaxation
● Depression	● Rest
Mental conditions	**Mental conditions**
● Focusing on the pain	● Intense concentration or distraction
● Boredom	● Involvement and interest in life activities

Factors affecting pain

As well as proposing there is a gate for pain in the spinal cord, Melzack and Wall also suggest that the experience of pain is made up of three components: sensation, emotion and cognition. *Sensation* refers to the information from our senses about the location of the pain and the type of pain it is. We have an *emotional reaction* to pain which can increase or diminish the experience of the pain. This emotional reaction is also connected with our motivation to try and escape it or try and tackle it head on. We also evaluate the pain and this is the *cognitive component*. This evaluation may tell us the pain is temporary and we just need to rest, but it might tell us that the pain will last a while and there is nothing we can do about it. The different interpretations of the same sensations will lead to a different experience of pain.

Measuring pain

'This won't hurt a bit,' says the doctor just before inflicting excruciating pain on you. How does the doctor know how much pain you will feel? It is important that we are able to know how much pain people are feeling, and it is also important to know what type of pain they are feeling. Like most personal experiences, it is difficult to make comparisons between what I experience and what you experience, and so psychologists have a problem when they try to measure pain.

One approach to pain measurement is that of Karoly (1985a) who suggests that we should not just focus on the immediate experience of pain but should examine all the factors that contribute to pain. Karoly identifies six key elements:

1 **Sensory:** for example, the intensity, duration, threshold, tolerance, location etc.
2 **Neurophysiological:** for example, brain-wave activity, heart rate etc.
3 **Emotional and motivational:** for example, anxiety, anger, depression, resentment etc.
4 **Behavioural:** for example, avoidance of exercise, pain complaints etc.
5 **Impact on lifestyle:** for example, marital distress, changes in sexual behaviour etc.
6 **Information processing:** for example, problem-solving skills, coping styles, health beliefs etc.

The methods that psychologists can use to collect information about pain include interviews, behavioural observation, psychometric measures, medical records and physiological measures. The main advantage of the interview method is that it can be used to cover most of the elements suggested by Karoly (see above). The problem is the time taken to obtain the information and the skill required to interpret the responses.

Questionnaires and rating scales

The more common way of obtaining information about pain is to use questionnaires and rating scales such as the McGill Pain Questionnaire (Melzack, 1975). This questionnaire, an extract of which is shown in Figure 11.2 has questions that refer to sensory elements of pain, emotional elements, evaluative (cognitive) elements and miscellaneous elements.

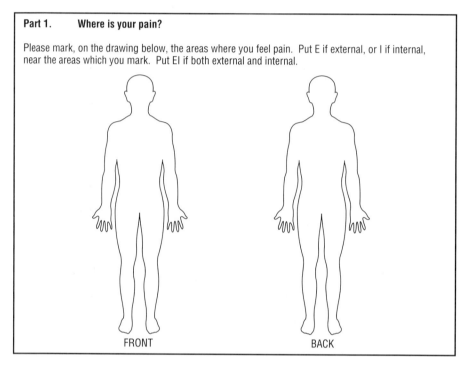

FIG 11.2 *Extract from the McGill Pain Questionnaire*

Part 2.   What does your pain feel like?

Some of the words below describe your *present* pain. Circle *ONLY* those words that best describe it. Leave out any category that is not suitable. Use only a single word in each appropriate category – the one that applies best.

1	2	3	4
Flickering	Jumping	Pricking	Sharp
Quivering	Flashing	Boring	Cutting
Pulsing	Shooting	Drilling	Lacerating
Throbbing		Stabbing	
Beating		Lancinating	
Pounding			
5	**6**	**7**	**8**
Pinching	Tugging	Hot	Tingling
Pressing	Pulling	Burning	Itchy
Gnawing	Wrenching	Scalding	Smarting
Cramping		Searing	Stinging
Crushing			
9	**10**	**11**	**12**
Dull	Tender	Tiring	Sickening
Sore	Taut	Exhausting	Suffocating
Hurting	Rasping		
Aching	Splitting		
Heavy			
13	**14**	**15**	**16**
Fearful	Punishing	Wretched	Annoying
Frightful	Gruelling	Blinding	Troublesome
Terrifying	Cruel		Miserable
	Vicious		Intense
	Killing		Unbearable
17	**18**	**19**	**20**
Spreading	Tight	Cool	Nagging
Radiating	Numb	Cold	Nauseating
Penetrating	Drawing	Freezing	Agonizing
Piercing	Squeezing		Dreadful
	Tearing		Torturing

FIGURE 11.2 (continued) *Extract from the McGill Pain Questionnaire*

A variation of this was developed by Varni, Thompson and Hanson (1987) for use with children (see Figure 11.3 overleaf). This illustrates one of the problems that we face when we are trying to measure experience, and that is the different language that different groups of people use. Children do not use adult descriptions of their experience so we are dependent on the observations of their parents and on any inventive ways we can develop to probe their thoughts and feelings. If we look back at the McGill Pain Questionnaire then it is possible to criticise it for the language it uses and the different ways that some groups of people will interpret it.

Measuring pain behaviour

Pain behaviour includes all the different ways to communicate pain, such as complaints, gestures and postures, etc. It also includes the numerous ways,

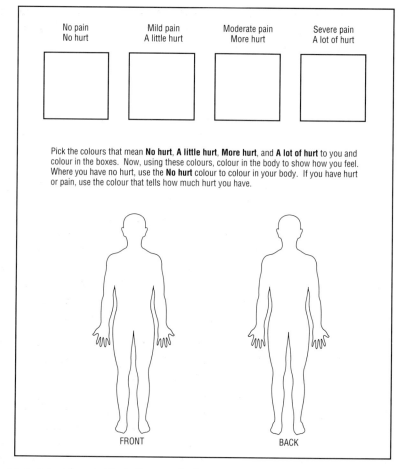

FIGURE 11.3 *Extract from the Varni, Thompson Paediatric Pain Questionnaire*

both adaptive and maladaptive, that we use to cope with pain, such as relaxation or behaviour to avoid the onset of a painful episode. One of the common methods of measuring these behaviours is to ask the patient to fill in a pain behaviour diary, which covers things such as sitting position, walking position, use of medication, and general movement during the day. Another method is to use a standard observation framework, such as the UAB Pain Behaviour Scale (Richards et al., 1982), which can be administered and scored quite quickly by health professionals. This scale asks the observer to rate such things as mobility, facial grimaces and the amount of time spent lying down.

INTERVENTIONS: CONTROLLING PAIN

There are numerous ways to alleviate pain and it is not possible in this text to do more than provide some examples from the range of different methods. We will look at some chemical treatments, surgical attempts, physical therapies, and psychological treatments.

Chemicals

A clergyman from Chipping Norton wrote to The Royal Society in 1763 to describe how useful the extract of willow was in the relief of rheumatism and bouts of fever. The active ingredient of willow extract is *acetylsalicylic acid* which we are more familiar with as aspirin. Aspirin, and other similar drugs such as ibuprofen, have three therapeutic actions: first, against pain; secondly, against inflammation; and thirdly, against fever. They appear to work on the damaged tissue that is causing the pain and inflammation, and they have no known effect on the nervous system. These drugs are heavily used today and the only drawback is the number of side-effects such as gastric irritation and bleeding and also (with large doses) deafness. There is another mild analgesic called *acetaminophen* (more commonly know as paracetamol) which has pain relief properties similar to those of aspirin. It does not, however, have the same anti-inflammatory action as aspirin and it is not known how it creates analgesia.

Another major set of chemicals used in pain relief come from the opium poppy. The medical value of the extract of this poppy has been known about for thousands of years and its use is recorded as far back as 1550 BC. A number of chemicals have been made from this poppy including *morphine, heroin* and *codeine*. Although the different chemicals vary in the amount of pain relief they produce, they all have a similar action, producing analgesia and, as the dose increases, also producing drowsiness, changes of mood and mental clouding. Opiates act on the central nervous system in the brain and also in the spinal cord. Their most likely action is to inhibit pain messages from travelling to the brain (in other words, they close the gate). The main reason that opiates are so effective in pain control is that the nervous system contains many nerves that respond to chemicals that are very similar to opiates. These nerves are involved in the experience of pain, though their action is complex and not yet fully understood.

We usually take drugs by injection or by swallowing pills, though if you're very unlucky then you might receive the medication by suppository. However, a recent development with pain control has been to allow patients to self-administer the drug by pressing a button on a small machine beside the bed. The machine is set up so that the patient cannot accidentally (or purposefully) give themselves too much medication. Patients do not take this opportunity to give themselves the largest possible amount of medication, but in fact use their control over the drug to balance the pain with the mental clouding that high doses produce. The overall result is a reduction in drug use in comparison with the amount given by medical staff (Keeri-Szanto, 1979).

Surgical attempts

Medical people have attempted to reduce pain through surgery by cutting nerve pathways or making lesions in special centres in the brain. One condition that has attracted surgery is *trigeminal neuralgia* which produces persistent and excruciating pain in the face. When medication fails to deal with the pain, surgeons will destroy the branch of sensory nerves to the facial area. This produces numbness in the face, but, sadly, only temporary relief from the pain, which recurs in many patients. The story is the same in other surgical interventions in that any pain relief that occurs is usually only temporary. This only goes to show how complex our pain senses are. On the whole, surgical techniques are only recommended for people with terminal illnesses who want medium-term relief from pain to make the rest of their lives more comfortable.

Physical therapies

There are a wide range of physical therapies that are used to relieve and control pain. These include *manual therapies* such as massage, *mechanical therapies* such as traction, *heat treatments* such as microwave diathermy and ultrasound, *cold treatments* such as ice packs, and *electrotherapy* such as electrical nerve stimulation.

Heat is widely used in the treatment of pain and is reported to be most effective for deep tissue injuries such as bruises, torn muscles and arthritis. It is generally considered doubtful that it speeds up the repair of these injuries. Given the extensive use of this treatment, it is remarkable that we do not know how it works. One hypothesis for the action of this treatment and many other physical treatments is that they produce sensory inputs that end up inhibiting the pain signals (they close the gate).

One method that has attracted a lot of research is the electrotherapy known as Transcutaneous Electrical Nerve Stimulation (TENS; *transcutaneous* means 'through the skin'). In this treatment the patient receives mild pulses of electricity in the painful area and this has been found to reduce chronic pain in a wide variety of conditions including neuralgia and arthritis.

Psychological treatments of pain

As we have seen in the previous sections of this chapter, psychological factors play a big role in the experience of pain. Over the past few years there has been a growing acceptance of the value of psychological interventions in the treatment of pain. Included in these interventions are relaxation, biofeedback (see pages 42–43), hypnosis, cognitive coping skills, operant techniques, mental imaging, self-efficacy and counselling.

Operant techniques

The idea behind operant techniques is to use the principles of operant conditioning to encourage behaviours that reduce pain and discourage behaviours that increase pain. Erskine and Williams (1989) suggest that these methods work by:

- using social reinforcement and periods of rest to gradually increase activity levels
- gradually decreasing the use of medication
- training people associated with the patient (medical staff and family) not to reinforce the pain behaviours through their sympathy and practical help.

This approach only deals with behavioural responses to pain and is most useful if someone has developed inappropriate behaviours for dealing with their pain. These behaviours might be the excessive use of drugs or the avoidance of activity. However, if someone has chronic pain from cancer, for example, then this approach is not likely to have much effect.

Coping training

Basler and Rehfisch (1990) looked at how coping training can be used to help people who were suffering from chronic pain. They developed a 12-week intervention package, which included training patients to reinterpret the pain experience, training in physical relaxation techniques, avoiding negative and catastrophic thinking, and training in how to use distraction at key times. They found that compared with an untreated waiting list control group, there were significant improvements for these patients at a six-month follow-up. The patients reported fewer general and pain-related symptoms, and a lower level of anxiety and depression. There was also a decline in the number of visits which they made to the doctor.

The implication of the study is that behavioural interventions to enhance coping skills in distressing medical conditions can be beneficial and relatively long-lasting. There are, of course, always problems with this type of study. For example, it is always possible that the patients were responding to the additional interest in their cases shown by those who had developed the training strategy; without the introduction of a third group who received just as much attention, it is not possible to be sure that this has not happened. (Although many of those working with chronic pain patients would argue that even if there was this type of 'placebo effect' going on, it wouldn't matter — the important thing is that the patients subjectively experienced less pain as a result of what happened to them!).

Self-efficacy

Self-efficacy (the sense of our ability to do something – see pages 176–177) may be a significant concept in the control of pain. Bandura et al. (1988) carried out an experimental study of the effect of self-efficacy on the ability to deal with pain. The psychologists took two groups of people and in one group they created a sense of high self-efficacy and in the other they created a sense of low self-efficacy. They did this by manipulating the demands of a mental arithmetic task. Half of each group were then given an injection of either a saline solution, which would have no effect, or naloxone. Naloxone blocks the action of opiates in the nervous system which means that it blocks the pain-killing response of the body. All of the research participants then immersed an arm in ice-cold water, and their pain thresholds were measured, partly by physiological stress measures, and partly by timing how long they could endure the pain.

Bandura et al. found that, among the research participants who were given the placebo injection (saline), those with low self-efficacy beliefs experienced higher levels of stress during the cognitive test, but could withstand more painful stimulation than those with high self-efficacy beliefs. The two groups given naloxone did not differ in their pain tolerance, which was low. The researchers suggested that because low self-efficacy beliefs are stressful for the body, it may be that such people secrete a higher level of natural pain-killers. While this might seem to be beneficial on the surface, in the long term it could have harmful effects on the immune system, rendering the person more vulnerable to illness. (Another possibility, of course, is that those with high self-efficacy beliefs were more ready to take action to change their situation and withdraw from the test, although this doesn't explain why there should be no difference between the two groups who received the 'real' injection.)

END NOTE

Psychologists and physiologists have discovered a lot about pain and its treatment but, as Youngson (1992) points out, this knowledge is rarely put into practice in medical treatment – particularly with respect to pain after surgery. According to a 1990 survey of attitudes to pain in British hospitals, staff chose pain-relieving drugs randomly, did not take account of the nature of the pain, and did not even believe that the relief of pain was one of their professional aims. Also, although there is clear evidence that post-operative pain can be relieved if an anaesthetic block is used before the operation, very few medical staff actually carried out this procedure.

SUMMARY

The study of pain illustrates the importance of the biopsychosocial model, since it is impossible to explain all the phenomena of pain without considering psychological and social factors as well as the more obvious biological factors. The theories of pain are still at a relatively early stage, though they have been useful in helping psychologists devise various treatments to help in the management of pain.

chapter twelve

CHRONIC DISORDERS

CHAPTER OVERVIEW

Each long-term health problem creates its own psychological issues. There are also, however, a number of features that are common to many disorders, and the INTRODUCTION looks at some of the aspects of developing chronic disorders and takes a special look at the role of uncertainty. Psychologists describe a number of COGNITIVE APPROACHES TO HEALTH including the experience of locus of control and self-efficacy. The SPECIAL ISSUE: END-STAGE RENAL DISORDER looks at the psychological response to dialysis and considers some psychological interventions. The INTERVENTIONS FOR CHRONIC ILLNESS include the role of self-help groups and the function of denial. There is also a brief look at some of the issues around the quality of life that we can hope for.

INTRODUCTION

Chronic disorders are ones that persist for a long period of time and probably get progressively worse. It is estimated (for example, see Taylor, 1986) that at any given time, around 50% of the general population has a chronic condition that requires medical management. These conditions range from mild disorders such as partial hearing loss, to serious life-threatening disorders such as diabetes, end-stage renal disease and heart disease. In fact, most of us will eventually develop a chronic disorder that will be a major factor in our death. What this means is that we are likely to have to deal with chronic disorders some time during our lives.

Each chronic disorder has a unique set of psychological effects and a range of possible psychological interventions. However, there are a number of key issues that are common to many chronic disorders so we will have a look at some of these in this chapter.

Developing chronic disorders

Psychologists are interested in whether the type of person we are and the way we behave have any connection with chronic disorders. In particular, they have looked at *negative affective styles*, which is a term attributed to people who are identifiably more depressed, more anxious and more hostile than the average. In a review of this area, Taylor and Aspinwall (1990) point out that research has found some weak associations between negative affective styles and several disorders such as coronary heart disease, asthma, headaches, ulcers and arthritis. They raise the possibility that there is a disease-prone personality type, or behaviour pattern. An example of this is the Type A behaviour pattern (described in Chapter 6, pages 82–84), but the evidence on this is very mixed, and the associations between illness and behaviour pattern are quite weak.

An alternative approach has been to look for behaviour that might enhance good health. There has been some interest in the protective role of *positive emotional states* such as optimism and perceived control. For example, Taylor and Aspinwall (1990) review a number of studies that suggest optimism is associated with people experiencing fewer symptoms, and with people making a better or speedier recovery. The down-side to this research is the growing belief that people who have chronic disorders should be cheerful all the time so that they can get better more quickly. It is not difficult to imagine the response of many people suffering pain when a health worker tells them to cheer up and 'put on a happy face'.

One of the many problems with research into the connections between behaviour patterns and illness is that chronic illness often develops long before it is visible to health workers. Many cancers, for example, develop over a period of years before they create discomfort to the patient. It is, therefore, difficult to examine the behaviour of the patient, and compare it to that of people without the disorder because their behaviour might already be affected by the long development of the cancer. The various attempts to relate cancers to psychological variables have produced very mixed results. The research has concentrated on the role of variables such as depression, social isolation, being passive and being unaggressive, though it is fair to say that no clear picture has developed.

The same lack of clear evidence is also the case for other chronic disorders such as diabetes and arthritis despite various attempts to identify behaviours that make the disorder more likely. This is also true for hypertension, though the exception is the behaviour pattern referred to as John Henryism described in Chapter 8 (page 122).

The response to chronic disorders

The two most obvious responses to the onset of a chronic disorder are anxiety and depression.

Some of the things that produce high levels of anxiety are (see Taylor and

Aspinwall, 1990):

- waiting for test results
- a diagnosis of cancer
- invasive procedures
- the side-effects of treatment
- changes to lifestyle
- dependency on health workers
- fear of recurrence
- uncertainty.

Depression is a disabling reaction to chronic illness, and it is estimated that between one quarter and one third of hospital admissions report these feelings (see Taylor and Aspinwall, 1990). Depression also appears to have an impact on recovery rates. It is difficult, however, to accurately identify depression in ill people since many of the symptoms such as fatigue, sleeplessness and weight loss might also be symptoms of the disease.

Uncertainty

One of the possible causes of anxiety and depression is the uncertainty that people have about their illness and what will happen to them.

Uncertainty is an important issue for chronically and terminally ill people, and a major source of stress in their lives. The feeling of uncertainty occurs when someone does not have a cognitive framework to understand their condition or situation, and when they cannot predict the outcomes of their behaviour or condition. Few people tolerate uncertainty well, and they deal with it in a variety of ways. The basic ways that people cope with uncertainty are by:

- **vigilance:** where people try and research possible diagnoses and so predict how their condition will develop
- **avoidance:** where people try and protect themselves against unpleasant knowledge by attributing symptoms to less harmful conditions, and not seeking medical advice.

These strategies create frameworks that allow the people to explain their situation to themselves and increase their sense of personal control.

Each chronic disorder has its own set of uncertainties, but there are some general themes common to many of them. We will look at uncertainty by considering a study on the lives of people with AIDS (see Box 12.1). Weitz (1989) carried out in-depth interviews with 25 people with AIDS from Arizona, USA and found seven main sources of uncertainty:

1 **Will I get AIDS?**
   Fear of contracting AIDS is a big issue for gay and bisexual men. Among the respondents, some assumed they had the infection long before diag-

nosis, whereas others developed theories that reduced their personal risk.

2 **What do my symptoms mean?**
People often feel 'under the weather' without necessarily being ill. If their symptoms persist, however, they have to make a decision at some point that they are no longer under the weather, but are, in fact, ill. The symptoms of AIDS build up gradually, and it is possible to blame the symptoms on a variety of causes. For example, several men initially blamed their night sweats and exhaustion on the Arizona heat.

3 **Why have I become ill?**
People like to blame illness on something. It might be their behaviour (for example, not wrapping up on a cold day), or another person (for example, 'you sneezed on me last week'), or a situation (for example, stress at work). The people with AIDS had all tried to come up with a reason for their illness, and although some had integrated it into religious experience (for example, believing that AIDS was a test from God), most of them had underlying attributions of personal guilt. On the whole, they blamed their promiscuity, homosexuality, lack of forethought, or drug use, but they were still left with the question, 'Why me?'

4 **Will I be able to function tomorrow?**
Most people can make accurate predictions about their likely state of health in the short- to medium-term future. This is not so for many people with chronic disorders. AIDS causes unpredictable flare-ups and remissions. This made it very difficult for the respondents in the Weitz study to plan anything, even as simple as going shopping with someone the following Tuesday, because they did not know how they would feel on that day. The result of this was that they tended to avoid plans, both long and short term, to avoid disappointment. This meant their social world became smaller and less active.

5 **Will I be able to live with dignity?**
Fear of death is minimal compared to the fear of what life may become. In particular the respondents feared neurological impairment (which is common in people with AIDS), and disfigurement by Kaposi's sarcoma (a disfiguring skin cancer which occurs in 10% of people with AIDS). They especially feared the unusual illnesses whose effects they could not predict. One respondent said, 'I'm not [as] afraid of getting infections from people as I am from inanimate objects like fruits and moldy tile ... I know what a cold is like ...[It's] something I have experienced. I've never experienced a mold infection' (page 277).

6 **Will I be able to 'beat' AIDS?**
Can we beat death and live forever? The simple answer is 'no', but it did not stop the respondents from wondering whether God or medicine would be able to cure them.

7 **Will I be able to die with dignity?**
The end stage of many chronic disorders can be painful, uncomfortable and humiliating. Life can be prolonged by medical means far beyond a

time when it retains any meaning or dignity. Concern about this issue led some of the people with AIDS to sign living wills which would prevent physicians keeping them alive by extraordinary means (it is not possible to do this in the UK).

Managing uncertainty, then, is one of the major issues for people with AIDS. It is also a chronic problem for people with other disorders. Other common themes include dealing with disfigurement (for example, fear of loss of femininity after a mastectomy), sexual problems (for example, see the section on end-stage renal disease, pages 177–179), and changes in social life (for example, see point 4 above).

Box 12.1 AIDS

AIDS stands for Acquired Immune Deficiency Syndrome.

HIV stands for Human Immunodeficiency Virus.

It is generally believed that AIDS is caused by HIV. It attacks one type of white blood cell (the T helper lymphocytes), reduces the competence of the immune system, and makes the body vulnerable to attacks by malignancies and infections.

If someone is infected with HIV they can continue without any symptoms for several years. Alternatively, they might develop a number of symptoms including swollen glands, weight loss, diarrhoea, fever and fatigue. This collection of symptoms are referred to as AIDS-related Complex (ARC).

The diagnosis of AIDS also requires identification of malignancy or infection not associated with a healthy immune system.

COGNITIVE APPROACHES TO HEALTH

Locus of control

How much control do you think you have over your behaviour, your environment or your health? Psychologists believe that the amount of control that we perceive ourselves to have is very important to us. Rotter (1966) first described the concept of locus of control and applied it to range of activities such as gambling, political activism and hospitalisation. He suggested that people differ in the way they experience their locus of control – in other words, where the control over events in their life comes from. Some people experience themselves as having an *external locus of control*, which means they do not feel in control of events. They perceive their lives as being controlled by outside forces; things happen to them. On the other hand, some people experience themselves as having an *internal locus of control*, which means they experience themselves as having personal control over themselves and events; they do things.

Health locus of control

The concept of locus of control was measured using a series of statements that people could either agree or disagree with. However, it soon became apparent that people's control beliefs about their health were quite different from their control beliefs about other aspects of their behaviour. So, health psychologists such as Wallston, Wallston and Devellis (1978) expanded the original scale beyond the simple external–internal dimension to develop health-specific psychometric tests. The multidimensional health locus of control scale measures three dimensions of health locus of control:

1 **Internality:** the extent to which locus of control for health is internal (example statement: 'If I become sick, I have the power to make myself well again.')
2 **Chance:** the belief that chance or external factors are affecting the outcome of health problems (example statement: 'Often I feel sick no matter what I do, if I am going to get sick, I will get sick.')
3 **Powerful others:** the belief in the control of powerful others (such as doctors) over our health (example statement: 'Following doctor's orders to the letter is the best way for me to stay healthy.')

The health locus of control scales provide a simple way of investigating the effect of beliefs on health outcomes. Consequently, there has been a large amount of research using these scales, though the relationship between health locus of control and health outcome has not been as strong as we might have expected. One reason for this is that people have very different perceptions of their control over different areas of their health. For example, I may feel in control of my diet but unable to control my alcohol consumption. To deal with this problem, some scales have been developed that are even more specific, and look at such detailed beliefs as perceived control over pain.

Breast self-examination

An example of research on this topic is an investigation into the cancer-screening behaviour of women carried out by Murray and McMillan (1993). One way of screening for breast cancer is to carry out breast self-examination (see Chapter 4, pages 60–61), but many women do not perform this procedure as often as they are recommended to. Murray and McMillan looked at whether various psychological approaches, including the health belief model and health locus of control, could be used to predict whether women would carry out the procedure or not. Their questionnaire study of over 400 women in Northern Ireland found that the dimension of powerful others was a predictor of breast examination. The findings suggested that women were more likely to carry out breast self-examination if they believed that the health care system did not have a prominent role to play in their health.

These findings show how some aspects of health locus of control can be applied to our behaviour. The same study, however, found that health locus of control had no effect on whether women would choose to attend a clinic for a cervical smear (another method of screening for cancer), and this illustrates how specific these effects are. In fact, the most important predictor of breast examination discovered in this study was not the women's locus of control but their confidence in how to carry out self-examination. This is an example of self-efficacy which we will now look at.

Self-efficacy

Self-efficacy is a belief that you can perform adequately in a particular situation. Your sense of personal competence influences your perception, motivation and performance. Bandura (1977) suggested that self-efficacy beliefs are important to us, because they are concerned with what we believe we are capable of. If we believe that we are able to engage in certain types of actions successfully, then we are more likely to put effort into carrying them out, and therefore we are more likely to develop the necessary skills.

It seems likely that beliefs about our self-efficacy will affect how much effort we put into any activity. In the area of health, if we do not believe that we can change our lifestyle and, for example, give up smoking, then we will probably not even try. Bandura suggested that it is a good thing if people have beliefs about their self-efficacies which are slightly higher than the evidence would suggest (in other words, they think they are more capable than they really are), because this encourages them to aim high, and, by doing so, to try harder and so develop their skills and abilities even further.

We make judgements of self-efficacy primarily on the bases of our achievements. Other sources of these judgements include:

- observations of the performance of others ('Well, if she can do it, then so can I')
- social and self-persuasion ('Oh, you know you can do it really')
- monitoring our emotional states, for example, if we are feeling anxious then this would suggest low expectations of efficacy ('I don't feel up to it today').

An example of a study that looks at the role of self-efficacy was an investigation into the use of condoms by college students (Wulfert and Wan, 1993). They found that their sample of students were well-informed about the health risks of unprotected sex, and the facts and myths of AIDS transmission. They found that knowledge had little effect on sexual behaviour and many of the students made inconsistent use of condoms. The factor that was the best predictor of condom use was, in fact, self-efficacy, or in other words, whether the students felt they could use a condom and still have a successful sexual encounter. This suggests that health education on the use of condoms should not concentrate on the health risks of unprotected sex but on encouraging a sense of self-efficacy in potential condom users.

SPECIAL ISSUE:
End-stage renal disease

Kidney failure, or end-stage renal disease (ESRD) to use its technical name, used to be fatal. However, with modern medicine techniques, patients can now survive for a long time either with regular dialysis or with a transplant. In 1960 the longest that anyone had continued to live with dialysis was only 181 days (cited in Long, 1989), whereas today survival can be well over ten years. The problem for the dialysis patient is to adjust their lifestyle to deal with this long-term condition. This adjustment involves strict adherence to a fairly unpleasant diet, and dealing with the physical discomfort which grows between each dialysis which has to take place two or three times a week.

Psychological responses to dialysis

The most frequently cited psychological problems (see Long, 1989) reported by haemodialysis patients are:

1 **Anxiety**
   Patients sometimes experience a general state of anxiety, and sometimes develop phobic responses to aspects of the dialysis such as having needles stuck into them.
2 **Depression**

3 **Suicidal reactions**
   Dialysis patients have a much higher suicide rate than the general population though this might be partly because they have the means to do it.
4 **Passive non-compliance with medical demands**
   Diet control is an important ingredient of the treatment, but a survey by Britton et al. (1982, cited in Long, 1989) found that 50% of patients report difficulty with dietary restrictions, and 15% confessed to non-compliance with important parts of the diet.
5 **Depressive reactions**
   Such as anorexia and sleep disturbance.
6 **Sexual dysfunction**
   The three most common types of sexual problem are (i) a decrease or loss of libido in men and women, (ii) partial or total impotence in men, (iii) men reported difficulties in ejaculating; women reported insufficient or absent lubricant, accompanied by less frequent orgasm or loss of orgasmic response.
7 **Psychosocial problems**
   Some patients develop stronger relationships with their family and friends following the disease, but many experience relationship problems. One immediate problem is that many patients are unable to continue working and so their standard of

living drops dramatically. This loss of work also changes the role the patient has in the family, and they might experience a loss of control over their lives. Other family members also take some of the strain, and Long (1989) reports that 30% of the children of patients show high levels of anxiety, depression, and psychosomatic problems. Also, a survey of the patient's partners found that 61% felt depressed at how their partner had changed during the first year of dialysis, and 54% were exhausted at the effort of coping.

A brief look at this list makes depressing reading, so it should be said that many people on dialysis are able to live productive and positive lives even though they have to adjust to the many stresses of their condition. These stresses, however, are very real and they make the lives of people with ESRD very different from what they were before they developed the disease. The stresses they experience include the following:

1 **A heightened sense of mortality**
   Many healthy people live their lives as if they are going to live for ever, and in this country we pay little attention to our inevitable death and so make little preparation for it. People on dialysis, however, are constantly aware of their own mortality, partly because if they do not adhere to the treatment programme they will put their lives at risk. Another reason for the sense of mortality is that they are often treated in a group and so, over a period of time, they will witness other patients dying.

2 **Feeling ill**
   People receiving dialysis often experience a reduction in their energy level and often have feelings of illness including nausea, fatigue, restlessness, dizziness, itching and an inability to concentrate.

3 **Changed social life**
   The loss of employment and money, combined with the reduced mobility, can all create stress. Chronic disorders can lead to lessened interest in social activities and family holidays. The patient has to develop interests that require only a little money and a minimal amount of mobility. Some people find this easier than others.

4 **Treatment**
   The regular treatment of being connected to a dialysis machine for several hours can create feelings of helplessness and dependency. It can also create a loss of personal power and a reduced sense of personal control and self-efficacy.

Psychological interventions

There are clearly a number of issues with this condition where psychologists could make a positive contribution. However, there are also some obstacles to their involvement in the treatment. One is the resistance of patients to any psychological treatment. This might be because they see their condition as entirely physical, and they do not want to be labelled as someone who needs psychological treatment. Alternatively, it might be because they want to avoid any discussion about their adherence to the treatment programme. Patients are reluctant to admit to adherence problems if they believe that the psychologists might inform the medical staff, since this might then reduce their chances of receiving a transplant. Another obstacle to psychological intervention is the treatment setting itself. Patients spend many hours on dialysis machines and many of them will only agree to see a psychologist while they are dialysing since they do not want to extend their treatment time any further. This inhibits the interaction because of the lack of privacy and the dominating and distracting presence of the dialyser.

Despite the obstacles to treatment, psychologists have made a number of interventions with renal dialysis patients, including:

- progressive muscle relaxation and bio-feedback for anxiety, panic attacks, and tension headaches
- operant methods to control the gagging and vomiting that often accompany the dialysis treatment
- token economies and behavioural con-tracting to help patients improve their diet control
- hypnotherapy for the excessive thirst cre-ated by the restricted diet
- sex therapy
- counselling and cognitive-behavioural therapy for depression
- ecological intervention to improve the psychosocial environment.

INTERVENTIONS FOR CHRONIC ILLNESS

There are a number of interventions that psychology can make in the treatment of chronic illness. Some of these are dealt with elsewhere in this text – for example, in the sections on improving the communication between patient and health worker (see Chapter 9), changing smoking habits (see Chapter 7), adjusting lifestyles (see Chapter 6) and developing coping skills (see Chapter 3). In this section we will look at three examples of interventions: self-help groups, the role of denial, and the effects of increasing personal control.

Self-help groups

People with chronic disorders sometimes get support from membership of a self-help group. This sort of group usually consists of other people with the disorder and sometimes includes their close relatives and friends. The group can provide social support and information about the disorder; it can also provide role models for new patients on how to cope with the disorder and function as normally as possible. Research studies into self-help groups for a variety of disorders such as cancer, hypertension and epilepsy (see Taylor and Aspinwall, 1990) found that the groups were effective in helping members to cope with the stigma of the disorder, and helping members to develop their motivation to cope and their motivation to adhere to the treatment programme. Interestingly, it has been impossible to identify why these groups are successful.

Health professionals are generally supportive of self-help groups because they are quite convenient and relatively cheap. Unfortunately, these groups only reach a very small proportion of the people with chronic disorders, and they also tend to attract mainly professional white women to the exclusion of other groups. Furthermore, according to Taylor and Aspinwall (1990), the people who join these groups are already in contact with the health services, and the large number of people who are relatively invisible to the health services are not helped by this means.

Denial

Sometimes we deny the evidence of our own eyes, and this can be useful if we want to avoid things that might cause anxiety or pain (see Chapter 3). It appears that denial can sometimes be useful in helping people to gradually come to terms with their chronic illness. However, the suggestion that health workers should encourage someone to deny the reality of their health is very controversial. The relationship between denial and health is complex, as shown in the research by Levine et al. (1988, cited in Taylor and Aspinwall, 1990). Their study looked at people who had just experienced myocardial infarction (MI – 'heart attack' to you and me) and found that people who had high levels of denial had fewer days in intensive care and fewer signs of cardiac dysfunction than people with low levels of denial. However, in the year following their discharge from hospital, the high denial patients showed less adaptation to the disorder, they were less likely to adhere to the treatment programme and required more days back in hospital. So, although denial seems to help recovery in the short term, it hinders it in the long term.

Locus of control: improving health in a nursing home

The chronic condition we all share is ageing. We are all getting older, but is our decline inevitable and are there any interventions that can help us continue to live rich and productive lives?

A study by Langer and Rodin (1976) investigated whether it is possible to enhance the health of patients by changing the environment and organisation of their nursing home. In particular, Langer and Rodin wanted to find out whether the ability to make specific choices would have a general effect on their experience of their own level of control and competence (see the section on locus of control, above). The study was based in a nursing home in the USA, and it compared the patients living on two different floors of the same building. The aim of the study was to encourage a sense of responsibility and control in the residents on one floor and compare their long-term progress and general level of health with the control residents on the other floor. The two sets of patients were similar in age and health status.

The nursing home administrator gave a talk to both groups which he introduced as some information about the nursing home (Arden House). The experimental group were told:

- you have the responsibility of caring for yourselves
- you can decide how you want your rooms arranged
- you can decide how you want to spend your time
- it's your life
- it's your responsibility to make complaints known.

They were also offered a plant as a present, told that there was a movie showing in the home on Thursday and Friday, and asked which night, if any, they would like to go.

The control group were given a similar talk, the difference being that their personal responsibility and control was not emphasised. So, for example, they were given the present of a plant rather than offered it, and told that they would be scheduled to see the movie one night or the other, and told how the staff tried to make their rooms nice.

The researchers measured the sense of responsibility in the residents using questionnaires which were given one week before the communication and three weeks after. A summary of some of the results is shown in Table 12.1 These indicate some substantial differences between the two groups after three weeks. When the scores for the individual residents were examined, it showed that 93% of the experimental group, but only 21% of the control group, were judged to have improved. Sadly, the researchers did not measure the plants to see how they were doing.

Table 12.1 Change scores of residents in the nursing home

Average scores for self-report, interviewer ratings and nurse ratings for the experimental and control groups. The data is presented as change scores which are calculated by subtracting the second assessments from the first assessments.

	EXPERIMENTAL GROUP Change score	CONTROL GROUP Change score
SELF-REPORT		
Happy	+0.28	−0.12
Active	+0.2	−1.28
PERCEIVED CONTROL		
Have	+0.16	+0.41
Want	−0.05	+0.17
INTERVIEWER RATING		
Alertness	+0.29	−0.37
NURSE RATINGS		
General improvement	+3.97	−2.37
CHANGE IN TIME SPENT		
visiting patients	+6.78	−3.29
visiting others	+2.25	−4.17
talking to staff	+8.22	+1.6
watching staff	−2.14	+4.64

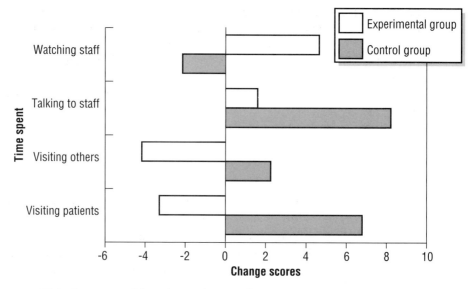

FIGURE 12.1 *Change scores of the residents in the nursing home*

The researchers went back to the home after 18 months (Rodin and Langer, 1977) and found that the experimental group were still improved in comparison with the control group. They were in better health and fewer had died. Overall, the authors' work suggests that this minor intervention had a substantial effect on the health and well-being of the residents in the old people's home.

Quality of life

A final point to consider concerns the quality of life. The aim of any treatment for chronic illness is to improve the patient's quality of life. The problem lies in how we measure quality of life, and our assumptions about what improves and what impairs our quality of life. For example, doctors and patients rarely agree about this issue. One study (Jachuck et al., 1982) asked doctors, patients and family members to rate the patient's quality of life after they had started on a treatment programme for hypertension. The doctors estimated that 100% of the patients had an improved quality of life, but only 49% of the patients perceived any improvement, and 96% of the relatives perceived no change or a slight deterioration.

One of the findings in this area that goes against our intuitive judgements is the observation that chronic disorders can have positive consequences for the patient. In a study of cancer patients by Collins (cited in Taylor and Aspinwall, 1990), over 90% of the patients reported that the cancer had brought about some beneficial changes in their lives. For example, they reported that they were more likely to appreciate each day, and they were less likely put things off to another time. They also reported that they put more effort into their personal relationships and believed they had acquired a greater understanding and sympathy for the needs of others. Perhaps most surprisingly, they also reported feeling stronger, more self-assured and more compassionate to those they perceived as being less fortunate than themselves. Similar results have been found for patients with other life-threatening disorders.

END NOTE

All of this brings us full circle in this book. We started off by looking at the problems of how to define good health, and discovered that there can be no clear definition. Now we close by acknowledging that our quality of life can occasionally be enhanced, in some ways, when we develop a chronic disorder. So, it is difficult to know what illness means, and even when someone has a serious health disorder, it does not mean that their quality of life is inevitably damaged. The conclusion we have to draw is that it is very difficult to accurately describe any person's experience of their state of health. We can, however, through psychological research, gain a better understanding of the processes that enhance health and prevent illness, and we can devise programmes that will improve the health of all people.

appendices

APPENDIX 1:
THE HERALD OF FREE ENTERPRISE

Chain of events and active failures	Contributing conditions and latent failures
The Herald is docked at No. 12 berth in Zeebrugge's inner harbour and is loading passengers and vehicles before making the crossing to Dover.	This berth is not capable of loading both car decks (E and G) at the same time, having only a single ramp. Due to high water spring tides, the ramp could not be elevated sufficiently to reach E deck. To achieve this, it was necessary to trim the ship nosedown by filling trim ballast tanks Nos. 14 and 3. Normal practice was to start filling No. 14 tank 2 hours before arrival. *(System failure)*
At 18.05 on 6 March 1987, *The Herald* goes astern from the berth, turns to starboard, and proceeds to sea with both her inner and outer bow doors fully open.	The most immediate cause is that the assistant bosun (whose job it was to close the doors) was asleep in his cabin, having just been relieved from maintenance and cleaning duties. *(Supervisory failure and unsuitable rostering)* The bosun, his immedite superior, was the last man to leave G deck. He noticed that the bow doors were still open, but did not close them, since he did not see that as part of his duties. *(Management failure)*
Chief officer checks that there are no passengers on G deck, and thinks he sees assistant bosun going to close doors (though testimony is confused on this point).	The chief officer, responsible for ensuring door closure, was also required (by company orders) to be on the bridge 15 minutes before sailing time. *(Management failure)* Because of delays at Dover, there was great pressure on crews to sail early. Memo from operations manager: 'Put pressures on your first officer if you don't think he's moving fast enough … sailing late out of Zeebrugge isn't on. It's 15 minutes early for us.' *(Management failure)* Company standing orders (ambiguously worded) appear to call for 'negative reporting' only. If not told otherwise, the master should assume that all is well. Chief officer did not make a report, nor did the master ask him for one. *(Management failure)*

Chain of events and active failures	Contributing conditions and latent failures
On leaving harbour, master increases speed. Water enters open bow doors and floods into G deck. At around 18.27, *Herald* capsizes to port.	Despite repeated requests from the masters to the mangement, no bow door indicators were available on the bridge, and the master was unaware that he had sailed with bow doors open. Estimated cost of indicators was £400–500. *(Management failure)* Ship had chronic list to port. *(Management and technical failure)* Scuppers inadequate to void water from flooded G deck. *(Design and maintenance failure)* Top-heavy design of *The Herald* and other 'ro ro' ships in its class was inherently unsafe. *(Design failure)*

Source: Reason, 1990

APPENDIX 2: NOTES AND ANSWERS FOR THE AWARENESS OF BLACK NEEDS CHECKLIST (SEE BOX 8.1, PAGE 113)

1 The statement 'I and I' made by a black person should be interpreted as
   A Speech disorder ☐
   B Thought disorder ☐
   C Schizophrenia ☐
   D Culturally specific language ☒
   E Collective identity ☒

Notes: The identity of a black person might be less individualistic than a white European's (see Nobles, 1976), and the phrase 'I and I' refers to a collective identity. It is also an example of culturally specific language.

2 An Iranian woman gives her religion as Muslim. Her diet will therefore be
   A Vegetarian diet ☐
   B Non-vegetarian diet ☐
   C Halal meat ☐
   D None of these necessarily ☒
   E Vegan diet ☐

Notes: The answer to the question about religion does not mean that the patient can be stereotyped. Imagine if someone gave the response 'Church of England'. This response tells us very little about the person since they might be very active in their church or they may not have been in it since they were christened. Minority groups are often stereotyped, and health workers then make inappropriate generalisations about their health needs and treatment.

3   To die in dignity a practising Muslim patient would want to
   A   Sit or lie facing the sun ☐
   B   Sit or lie with their back to the sun ☐
   C   Not be touched by a non-Muslim ☐
   D   Sit or lie facing Mecca ☒
   E   Prepare by eating fish ☐

Notes: Death is associated with a number of customs for different religious and cultural groups. The British Health Service is relatively blind to diversity of needs in this area.

4   The term 'soul food' refers to
   A   Traditional Asian foods ☐
   B   Meals with lots of spices ☐
   C   Traditional black foods ☒
   D   Special religious meals ☐
   E   Fruit from the Caribbean ☐

Notes: People from different ethnic backgrounds have their own particular diet. Black food has a deep emotional significance and provides a sense of satisfaction. Any health care programme that requires the patient to modify their diet must take account of their cultural diet and the social significance they attach to food and eating.

5   Hair care of a white person is
   A   Similar to the hair care for a black person ☐
   B   Different to the hair care for a black person ☒

6   When a black person gets chicken pox they have
   A   No noticeable symptoms ☐
   B   Black spots ☒
   C   Red spots ☐

Notes: Hair care for black people is very different from that of white people. The issue about the spots is a little more debatable, though the central issue is that physical symptoms can look very different on people with different skin tones and skin types. For example, a black person does not go 'red in the face' when they are hot or embarrassed in the same way that a white person does. However, this checklist should not lead you to think that it is possible to make simple generalisations about the visible symptoms of different ethnic groups. There is a massive amount of diversity within groups as well as between groups.

7   When a black African woman claims that she is sometimes able to hear voices even though no one is actually talking, the most likely explanation is
   A   She is schizophrenic ☐
   B   She is taking some form of psycho-active drug ☐
   C   She is talking about a religious or spitirual experience ☒

Notes: Many people are aware of an internal dialogue, and of 'voices'. For example when they are going out on a Friday night, many people can hear their mother saying, 'You'll catch your death dressed like that!', even though she is 200 miles away. Some cultures describe their spiritual experiences in terms of voices, and although this sounds strange to Europeans, it just represents another way of describing our experience.

Adapted from Hylton (1994), used with permission.

References

Abraham, S. and Llewellyn-Jones, D (1987) *Eating Disorders: The Facts*, 2nd ed. Oxford: Oxford University Press.

Abraham, S.C.S., Sheeran, P., Spears, R. and Abrams, D. (1992) Health beliefs and the promotion of HIV-preventive intentions among teenagers: A Scottish perspective. *Health Psychology*, 11, 363–370.

American Psychiatric Association (1991) *DSM-IV Options Book: Diagnostic and Statistical Manual of Mental Disorders*. Washington, D.C.: APA.

Argyle, M. (1975) *Bodily Communication*. London: Methuen.

Arnold, J., Robertson, I.T. and Cooper, C.L. (1991) *Work Psychology*. London: Pitman Publishing.

Asch, S.E. (1955) Opinions and social pressure. *Scientific American*, 193, 31–35.

Asken, M. and Raham, D. (1983) Resident performance and sleep deprivation: A review. *Journal of Medical Education*, 58, 382–388.

Baggaley, J. (1991) Media health campaigns: Not just what you say, but the way you say it. In World Health Organisation, *AIDS Prevention through Health Promotion: Facing Sensitive Issues* 24–32. Geneva: World Health Organisation.

Bandura, A. (1977) Self-efficacy. *Psychological Review*, 84, 191–215.

Bandura, A., Cioffi, D., Barr Taylor, C. and Brouillard, M.E. (1988) Perceived self-efficacy in coping with cognitive stressors and opioid activation. *Journal of Personality and Social Psychology*, 55 479–488.

Basler, H.D. and Rehfisch, H.P. (1990) Follow-up results of a cognitive–behavioural treatment for chronic pain in a primary care setting. *Psychology and Health*, 4, 293–304.

Bauer, R.M., Greve, K.W., Besch, E.L., Schramke, C.J., et al. (1992) The role of psychological factors in the report of building-related symptoms in sick building syndrome. *Journal of Consulting and Clinical Psychology*, 60 213–219.

Becker, M.H. and Rosenstock, I.M. (1984) Compliance with medical advice. In Steptoe, A. and Matthews, A. (eds) *Health Care and Human Behaviour*. Academic Press.

Bell, P.A., Fisher, J.D., Baum, A. and Greene, T.C. (1990) *Environmental Psychology*, 3rd ed. Fort Worth, Texas: Holt, Rinehart and Winston.

Bennett, P. and Murphy, S. (1994) Psychology and health promotion. *The Psychologist*, 7, 126–128.

Berry, J., Pootinga, Y.H., Segall, M.H. and Dasen, P.R. (1992) *Cross-cultural Psychology*. Cambridge: Cambridge University Press.

Billings, A.G. and Moos, R.H. (1981) The role of coping responses and social resources in attenuating the stress of life events. *Journal of Behavioural Medicine*, 4, 139–157.

Birch, L.L., Zimmerman, S.I. and Hind, H. (1980) The influence of social–affective context on the formation of children's food preferences. *Child Development*, 51 856–861.

Boyle, C.M. (1970) Differences between patients' and doctors' interpretations of common medical terms. *British Medical Journal*, 2, 286–289.

Bradley, C. (1994) Contributions of psychology to diabetes management. *British Journal of Clinical Psychology*, 33, 11–21.

Breakwell, G. (1994) The echo of power: A framework for social psychological research. *The Psychologist*, 7, 65–72.

Bridge, L.R., Benson, P., Pietroni, P.C. and Priest, R.G. (1988) Relaxation and imagery in the treatment of breast cancer. *British Medical Journal*, 297. 1169-72.

British Psychological Society (1993) *Response to The Health of the Nation*. Leicester: British Psychological Society.

Broome, A. (ed) (1989) *Health Psychology: Process and Applications*. London: Chapman and Hall.

Brown, G.W. and Harris, T.O. (1989) *Life Events and Illness*. London: Unwin Hyman.

Brownell, K.D. and Foreyt, J. (eds) (1986) *Handbook of Eating Disorders: Physiology, Psychology and the Treatment of Obesity, Anorexia and Bulimia*. London: Harper Collins.

Budzynski, T.H., Stoyva, J. and Adler, C.S. (1970) Feedback-induced muscle relaxation: Application to tension headache. *Journal of Behaviour Therapy and Experimental Psychiatry*, 1, 205–211.

Cairns, E. and Wilson, R. (1984) The impact of political violence on mild psychiatric morbidity in Northern Ireland. *British Journal of Psychiatry*, 145, 631–635.

Carroll, D., Davey Smith, G. and Bennett, P. (1994) Health and socio-economic status. *The Psychologist*, 7, 122–125.

Central Statistical Office (1994) *Social Trends*. London: HMSO.

Cherek, R.D. (1985) Effect of acute exposure to increased levels of background industrial noise on cigarette smoking behaviour. *International Archives of Occupational and Environmental Health*, 56, 23–30.

Chery Croze, S. and Duclaux, R. (1980) Discrimination of painful stimuli in human beings. *Journal of Neurophysiology*, 44, 1–10.

Cluss, P.A. and Epstein, L.H. (1985) The measurement of medical compliance in the measurement of disease. In Karoly, P. (ed) *Measurement Strategies in Health Psychology*. New York: Wiley.

Cohen, S. and Wills, T.A. (1985) Stress, social support and the buffering hypothesis. *Psychological Bulletin*, 98, 310–357.

Cohen, S., Kamarck, T. and Mermelstein, R. (1983) A global measure of perceived stress. *Journal of Health and Social Behavior*, 24, 385–96.

Cohen S., Evans G.W., Krantz, D.S. and Stokols, D. (1980) Physiological, motivational and cognitive effects of aircraft noise on children. *American Psychologist*, 35, 231–243.

Colman, A.M. (1987) *Facts, Fallacies and Frauds in Psychology*. London: Unwin.

Concar, D. (1994) Prisoners of pleasure? *New Scientist*, 1 October, 26–31.

Cooper, C.L., Cooper, R.D. and Eaker, L.H. (1988) *Living with Stress*. Harmondsworth: Penguin.

Cooper, P.J. (1995) Eating disorders. In Lazarus, A.A. and Colman, A.M. (eds) (1995) *Abnormal Psychology*. Harlow: Longman.

Costa, P.T. and Vandenbos G.R. (eds) (1990) *Psychological Aspects of Serious Illness: Chronic Conditions, Fatal Diseases and Clinical Care*. Washington, D.C.: American Psychological Association.

Cowpe, C. (1989) Chip pan fire prevention, 1976–1984. In Channon, C. (ed) *Twenty Advertising Case Histories*. 2nd series. London: Cassell.

Czander, W. M. (1994) The sick building syndrome: A psychoanalytic perspective. *International Forum of Psychoanalysis*, 3 139–149.

Deal, T.E. and Kennedy, A.A. (1988) *Corporate Cultures: The Rites and Rituals of Corporate Life*. London: Penguin.

Department of Health (1992) *The Health of the Nation*. London: HMSO.

Department of Health (1993) *The Effect of Tobacco Advertising on Tobacco Consumption*. London: Economics and Operational Research Division.

Department of Health (1995) *Fit for the Future: Second Progress Report on the Health of the Nation*. London: HMSO.

DiMatteo, M.R. and DiNicola, D.D. (1982) *Achieving Patient Compliance: The Psychology of the Medical Practitioner's Role*. New York: Pergamon Press.

Dolecek, T.A. et al. (1986) A long-term nutrition intervention experience: Lipid responses and dietary adherence patterns in the Multiple Risk Factor Intervention Trial. *Journal of the American Dietetic Association*, 86, 752–758.

Douglas, R.B., Blanks, R., Crowther, A. and Scott, G. (1988) A study of stress in West Midlands firemen, using ambulatory electrocardiograms. Special Issue: Stress in the public services. *Work and Stress*, 2, 309–318.

Erskine, A. and Williams, A.C. (1989) Chronic pain. In Broome, A.K. (ed) *Health Psychology: Processes and Applications*. London: Chapman and Hall.

Ewles, L. and Simnett, I. (1992) *Promoting Health: A Practical Guide*, 2nd ed. London: Scutari Press.

Fallon, A.E. and Rozin, P. (1985) Sex differences in perceptions of desirable body shape. *Journal of Abnormal Psychology*, 94, 102–105.

Farquhar, J.W., Maccoby, N., Wood, P.D., Alexander, J.K. et al. (1977) Community education for cardiovascular health. *Lancet*, 1192–1195.

Feuerstein, M., Labbe, E., and Kuczmierczyk, A. (1986) *Health Psychology: A Psychobiological Perspective*. New York: Plenum.

Flora, J. and Thoresen, C. (1988) Reducing the risk of AIDS in adolescents. *American Psychologist*, 43, 965–970.

Folkman, S. and Lazarus, R.S. (1990) Coping and emotion. In Monat, A. and Lazarus, R. (eds) *Stress and Coping*, 3rd ed. New York: Columbia University Press.

Folkman, S., Lazarus, R.S., Dunkel-Schetter, C., Delongis, A. and Gruen, R.J. (1986) The dynamics of a stressful encounter. *Journal of Personality and Social Psychology*, 50, 992–1003.

Fox, D., Hopkins, B. and Anger, W. (1987) The long-term effects of a token economy on safety performance in open-pit mining. *Journal of Applied Behaviour Analysis*, 20, 215–224.

Friedman, M. and Rosenman, R.H. (1959) Association of specific overt behaviour pattern with blood cardiovascular findings. *Journal of American Medical Association*, 169, 1286–1296.

Friedman, M. and Rosenman, R.H. (1974) *Type A Behaviour and Your Heart*. New York: Knopf.

Friedman, M., Thorensen, C.E., Gill, J.J., Ulmer, D. et al. (1986) Alteration of Type A behaviour and its effect on cardiac recurrences in post-myocardial infarction patients: Summary results in the Recurrent Coronary Prevention Project. *American Heart Journal*, 112, 653–665.

Glasgow, R.E., McCaul, K.D. and Schafer, L.C. (1987) Self-care behaviour and glycemic control in Type 1 diabetes. *Journal of Chronic Diseases*, 40, 399–412.

Grier, E.H. and Cobbs, P.M. (1968) *Black Rage*. New York: Basic Books.

Griffiths, M.D. (1995a) *Adolescent Gambling*. London: Routledge.

Griffiths, M.D. (1995b) Scratch-card gambling: A potential addiction? *Education and Health*, 13, 1–3.

Gulian, E. Glendon, A.I., Matthews, G., Davies, D. et al. (1990) The stress of driving: A diary study. *Work and Stress*, 4, 7–16.

Harkness, S., Wyon, J. and Super, C. (1988) The relevance of behavioural sciences to disease prevention and control in developing countries. In Dasen, P., Berry, J. and Sartorius, N. (eds) *Cross-cultural Psychology and Health: Towards Applications*. London: Sage.

Harris, P. (1984) Assessing burn-out: The organisational and individual perspective. *Family and Community Health*, 6, 32-43.

Herman, C.P., Olmstead, M.P. and Polivy, J. (1983) Obesity, externality, and susceptibility to social influence: An integrated analysis. *Journal of Personality and Social Psychology*, 45, 926–934.

Herzlich, C. (1973) *Health and Illness: A Social Psychological Analysis*. London: Academic Press.

Hodgkinson, P.E. and Stewart, M. (1991) *Coping with Catastrophe*. London: Routledge.

Hofstede, G. (1980) *Culture's Consequences*. London: Sage.

Holmes, T.H. and Rahe, R.H. (1967) The social readjustment rating scale. *Journal of Psychosomatic Research*, 11, 213–218.

Horsford, B. (1990) Cultural issues and psychiatric diagnosis. Paper delivered at Abnormal Psychology Study Day, Nottingham University, 18 December.

Horton, R. (1967) African traditional thought and Western science. In Young, M.F.D. (ed) (1971) *Knowledge and Control*. Cambridge, Mass.: Addison-Wesley.

Hylton, P. (1994) *Checklist: Awareness of Black Needs*. Training materials for Black Psychology Workshop, Nottingham: Nottingham Psychology Conferences.

Jachuck, S.J., Brierley, H., Jachuck, S. and Willcox, P.M. (1982) The effect of hypotensive drugs on the quality of life. *Journal of the Royal College of General Practitioners*, 32, 103–105.

Jahoda, M. (1958) *Current Concepts of Positive Mental Health*. New York: Basic Books.

James, S.A., Strogatz, D.S., Wing, S.B. and Ramsey, D.L. (1987) Socioeconomic status, John Henryism, and hypertension in blacks and whites. *American Journal of Epidemiology*, 126, 664–673.

Janis, I. and Feshbach, S. (1953) Effects of fear-arousing communications, *Journal of Abnormal and Social Psychology*, 48, 78–92.

Jeffs, B. and Saunders, W. (1983) Minimising alcohol-related offences by enforcement of the existing licensing legislation. *British Journal of Addiction*, 78, 67–77.

Johnston, M., Wright, S. and Weinman, J. (1995) *Measures in Health Psychology*. Windsor: NFER-Nelson.

Jourard, S.M. (1966) An exploratory study of body accessibility. *Journal of Social and Clinical Psychology*, 5, 221–231.

Kanner, A.D., Coynes, J.C., Schaefer, C. and Lazarus, R.S. (1981) Comparison of two modes of stress measurement: Daily hassles and uplifts versus major life events. *Journal of Behavioural Medicine*, 4, 1–39.

Kaplan, R.M., Sallis, J.F. and Patterson, T.L. (1993) *Health and Human Behaviour*. New York: McGraw-Hill.

Karoly, P. (1985a) The assessment of pain: Concepts and Procedures. In Karoly, P. (ed) *Measurement Strategies in Health Psychology*. New York: Wiley.

Karoly, P. (1985b) *Measurement Strategies in Health Psychology*. New York: Wiley.

Keeri-Szanto, M. (1979) Drugs or drums: What relieves post-operative pain? *Pain*, 6, 217–230.

Kinsey, A.C. et al. (1948) *Sexual Behaviour in the Human Male*. Philadelphia: Saunders.

Kinsey, A.C. et al. (1953) *Sexual Behaviour in the Human Female*. Philadelphia: Saunders.

Kobasa, S.C. (1979) Stressful life events, personality and health: An inquiry into hardiness. *Journal of Personality and Social Psychology*, 37, 1–11.

Korsch, B.M., Gozzi, E.K. and Francis, V. (1968) Gaps in doctor–patient communication. *Pediatrics*, 42, 855–871.

Krause, N. (1992) Stress, religiosity, and psychological well-being among older blacks. *Journal of Ageing and Health*, 4 412–439.

Kübler-Ross, E. (1969) *On Death and Dying*. New York: Macmillan.

Kübler-Ross, E. (1975) *Death: The Final Stage of Growth*. Englewood Cliffs, N.J.: Prentice-Hall.

Kunz, L. (1987) Stress intervention programs for reducing medical costs and accident claims in a hospital. *Journal of Business and Psychology*, 1, 257–263.

Langer, E.J. and Rodin, J. (1976) The effects of choice and enhanced personal responsibility for the aged: A field experiment in an institutional setting. *Journal of Personality and Social Psychology*, 34, 191–198.

Lashley, K. and Watson, J.B. (1921) A psychological study of motion pictures in relation to venereal disease. *Social Hygiene*, 7, 181–219.

Lazarus, R. and Folkman, S. (1984) The concept of coping. In Monat, A. and Lazarus, R. (eds) (1991) *Stress and Coping*, 3rd edn, 189–206. New York: Columbia University Press.

Lewin, B., Robertson, I.H., Cay, E.L., Irving,

J.B. and Campbell, M. (1992) A self-help post-MI rehabilitation package – the heart manual: Effects on psychological adjustment, hospitalisation and GP consultation. *Lancet*, 339, 1036–1040.

Ley, P. (1988) *Communicating with Patients*. London: Croom Helm.

Ley, P. (1989) Improving patients' understanding, recall, satisfaction and compliance. In Broome, A.K. (ed) *Health Psychology: Processes and Applications*. London: Chapman and Hall.

Ley, P., Bradshaw, P.W., Eaves, D. and Walker, C.M. (1973) A method for increasing patients' recall of information presented by doctors. *Psychological Medicine*, 3 217–220.

Littlewood, R. and Lipsedge, M. (1989) *Aliens and Alienists*, 2nd ed. London: Unwin Hyman.

Long, C. (1989) Renal care. In Broome, A. (ed) *Health Psychology: Processes and Applications*. London: Chapman and Hall.

Lundberg, U. (1976) Urban commuting: Crowdedness and catacholamine excretion. *Journal of Human Stress*, 2, 26–32.

Marteau, T.M. (1990a) Attitudes to doctors and medicine: The preliminary development of a new scale. *Psychology and Health*, 4, 351–356.

Marteau, T.M. (1990b) Framing of information: Its influence upon decisions of doctors and patients. Proceedings of the second conference of the Health Psychology Section. BPS Occasional Papers No.2. Leicester: British Psychological Society.

Maslach, C. (1982), *Burn-out: The Cost of Caring*. Englewood Cliffs, N.J.: Prentice-Hall.

Maslow, A. (1968) *Towards a Psychology of Being*, 2nd edn. Princeton, N.J.: Van Nostrand.

Matarazzo, J.D. (1982) Behavioural health's challenge to academic, scientific and professional psychology. *American Psychologist*, 37, 46–51

Matlin, M.W. (1987) *The Psychology of Women*. London: Holt, Rinehart and Winston.

McKinlay, J.B. (1975) Who is really ignorant – physician or patient? *Journal of Health and Social Behaviour*, 16, 3-11.

McKinstry, B. and Wang, J. (1991) Putting on the style: What patients think of the way their doctor dresses. *British Journal of General Practice*, 41, 275-278.

McNaught, A. (1987) *Health Action and Ethnic*

Minorities. London: Bedford Square Press.

Meichenbaum, D. (1977) Cognitive-Behaviour Modification: An Integrative Approach. New York: Plenum Press.

Melzack, R. (1975) The McGill Pain Questionnaire: Major properties and scoring methods. Pain, 1, 277–299.

Melzack, R. (1992) Phantom limbs. Scientific American, April, 90–96.

Melzack, R. and Wall, P. (1965) Pain mechanisms: a new theory. Science, 150, 971–979.

Melzack, R. and Wall, P. (1988) The Challenge of Pain. London: Penguin.

Melzack, R., Wall, P.D. and Ty, T.C. (1982) Acute pain in an emergency clinic: Latency of onset and descriptor patterns. Pain, 14, 33–43.

Mestel, R. and Concar, D. (1994) How to heal the body's craving. New Scientist, 1 October, 32–37.

Meyerowitz, B.E. and Chaiken, S. (1987) The effect of message framing on breast self-examination attitudes, intentions and behaviour. Journal of Personality and Social Psychology, 52, 500–510.

Milgram, S. (1963) Behavioural study of obedience. Journal of Abnormal and Social Psychology, 67, 371–378.

Monat, A. and Lazarus, R. (eds) (1991) Stress and Coping. New York: Columbia.

Moos, R.H. (1973) Conceptualisations of human environments. American Psychologist, 28, 652–665.

Moos, R.H. and Moos, B.S. (1981) Family Environment Scale Manual. Palo Alto, Calif.: Consulting Psychologists Press.

Murphy, L. and Sorenson, S. (1988) Employee behaviours before and after stress management. Journal of Organisational Behaviour, 9, 173–182.

Murray, M. and McMillan, C. (1993) Health beliefs, locus of control and women's cancer screening behaviour. British Journal of Clinical Psychology, 32, 87–100.

Nobles, W. (1976) Extended self: Rethinking the so-called Negro self-concept. Journal of Black Psychology, 2.

Oakley, A. (1984) Doctor knows best. In Black, N., et al. Health and Disease: A Reader, 170–175. Milton Keynes: Open University Press.

Olds, J. and Milner, P. (1954) Positive reinforcement produced by electrical stimulation of the septal area and other regions of the rat brain. Journal of Comparative and Physiological Psychology, 47, 419–427.

Oliphant, J. (1995) Sick building syndrome? Occupational Safety and Health, 25, 14–15.

Orford, J. (1985) Excessive Appetites: A Psychological View of Addictions. Chichester: John Wiley.

Parrott, A. (1991) Social drugs: Their effects on health. In Pitts, M. and Phillips, K. (eds) The Psychology of Health: An Introduction. London: Routledge.

Paulus, P., McCain, G. and Cox, V. (1978) Death rates, psychiatric commitments, blood pressure and perceived crowding as a function of institutional crowding. Environmental Psychology and Nonverbal Behaviour, 3, 107–116.

Pilkington, E. (1995) Work till you drop. The Guardian, 23 May.

Pinel, J.P.J. (1993) Biopsychology, 2nd edn. Needham Heights, Mass.: Allyn and Bacon.

Pitts, M. (1991a) The medical consultation. In Pitts, M. and Phillips, K. (eds) The Psychology of Health, 3–14. London: Routledge.

Pitts, M. (1991b) An Introduction to Health Psychology. In Pitts, M. and Phillips, K. (eds) (1991) The Psychology of Health. London: Routledge.

Pitts, M. and Phillips, K. (eds) (1991) The Psychology of Health. London: Routledge.

Prochaska, J.O., DiClemente, C.C. and Norcross, J.C. (1992) In search of how people change: Applications to addictive behaviours. American Psychologist, 47, 1102–1114.

Rack, P. (1982) Migration and mental illness: A review of recent research in Britain. Transcultural Psychiatric Research Review, 19, 151–169.

Ragland, D. R. and Brand, R. J. (1988) Type A behavior and mortality from coronary heart disease. New England Journal of Medicine, 318, 65–70.

Ramseur, H.P. (1991) Psychologically healthy black adults. In Jones, R. (ed) Black Psychology, 3rd edn, 353–378. Berkeley, Calif.: Cobb and Henry.

Reason, J. (1990) Human Error. Cambridge: Cambridge University Press.

Richards, J.S., Nepomuceno, C., Riles, M. and Suer, Z. (1982) Assessing pain behaviour: The UAB Pain Behaviour Scale. *Pain*, 14, 393–398.

Riggio, R. (1990) *Introduction to Industrial/Organisational Psychology*. Glenview, Illinois: Scott, Foresman and Company.

Ritzer, G. (1993) *The McDonaldization of Society*. Thousand Oaks, Calif.: Pine Forge.

Robinson, R. and West, R. (1992) A comparison of computer and questionnaire methods of history-taking in a genitourinary clinic. *Psychology and Health*, 6, 77–84.

Rodin, J. and Langer, E.J. (1977) Long-term effects of a control relevant intervention with the institutionalised aged. *Journal of Personality and Social Psychology*, 35, 897–902.

Rosenhan, D.L. and Seligman, M.E.P. (1989) *Abnormal Psychology*, 2nd edn. New York: Norton.

Rotter, J. B. (1966) Generalised expectancies for internal vs. external control of reinforcement. *Psychological Monographs*, 80, 1–28.

Sarafino, E. (1994) *Health Psychology: Biopsychosocial Interactions*, 2nd edn. New York: Wiley.

Sarason, I.G., Levine, H.M., Basham, R.B. and Sarason, B.R. (1983) Assessing social support: The Social Support Questionnaire. *Journal of Personality and Social Psychology*, 44, 127–139.

Sayal, A. (1990) Black women and mental health. *The Psychologist*, 3, 24–27.

Scambler, G. and Scambler, A. (1984) The illness iceberg and aspects of consulting behaviour. In Fitzpatrick, R., Hinton, J., Newman, S., Scambler, G. and Thompson, J. (eds) *The Experience of Illness*. London: Tavistock Publications.

Selye, H. (1973) The evolution of the stress concept. *American Scientist*, 61 692–699.

Selye, H. (1982) History and the present status of the stress concept. In Goldberger, L. and Breznitz, S. (eds) *Handbook of Stress: Theoretical and Clinical Aspects*. London: Macmillan.

Sheridan, C. and Radmacher, S. (1992) *Health Psychology: Challenging the Biomedical Model*. New York: Wiley.

Shillitoe, R.W. and Miles, D.W. (1989) Diabetes mellitus. In Broome, A. (ed) *Health Psychology: Process and Applications*. London: Chapman and Hall.

Slobin, D.I. (1971) *Psycholinguistics*. Glenview, Illinois: Scott Foresman.

Smith, P.B. and Harris Bond, M. (1993) *Social Psychology Across Cultures*. Hemel Hempstead: Harvester Wheatsheaf.

Soden, M. and Stewart, M. (1984) The repositioning of Lucozade. In Broadbent, S. (ed) *Twenty Advertising Case Histories*. Eastbourne: Holt Rinehart Winston.

Stokes, J.P. (1983) Predicting satisfaction with social support from social network structure. *American Journal of Community Psychology*, 11, 141–152.

Sutherland, V. and Cooper, C.L. (1987) *Man and Accidents Offshore*. London: Lloyds.

Tapper-Jones, L., Smail, S.A., Pill, R. and Harvard Davies, R. (1988) General practitioners' use of written materials during consultations. *British Medical Journal*, 296, 908–909.

Taylor, S. (1986) *Health Psychology*. New York: Random House.

Taylor, S. (1990) Health psychology: The science and the field. *American Psychologist*, 45, 40–50.

Taylor, S.E. and Aspinwall, L.G. (1990) Psychosocial aspects of chronic illness. In Costa, P.T. and Vandenbos, G.R. (eds) *Psychological Aspects of Serious Illness: Chronic Conditions, Fatal Diseases and Clinical Care*, 3–60. Washington, D.C.: American Psychological Association.

Torkington, P. (1991) *Black Health: A Political Issue*. Liverpool: Catholic Association for Racial Justice.

Townsend, J. (1993) Policies to halve smoking deaths. *Addiction*, 88, 43–52.

Turner, C., Anderson, P., Fitzpatrick, R., Fowler, G. and Mayon-White, R. (1988) Sexual behaviour, contraceptive practice and knowledge of AIDS of Oxford University students. *Journal of Biosocial Science*, 20, 445–451.

Varni, J.W., Thompson, K.L. and Hanson, V. (1987) The Varni–Thompson Paediatric Pain Questionnaire: I. Chronic musculoskeletal pain in juvenile rheumatoid arthritis. *Pain*, 28 27–38.

Wadden, T.A. and Brownell, K.D. (1984) The development and modification of dietary practices in individuals, groups and large populations. In Matarazzo, J.D. and Weiss, S.M. (eds) *Behavioural Health: A Handbook of Health Enhancement and Disease Prevention*. New York: Wiley.

Wade, C. and Tavris, C. (1990) *Psychology*, 2nd edn. New York: Harper and Row.

Wallston, K.A., Wallston, B.S. and Devellis, R. (1978) Development of the multi-dimensional health locus of control (MHLC) scales. *Health Education Monographs*, 6, 161–170.

Warner, R. (1976) The relationship between language and disease concepts. *International Journal of Psychiatry in Medicine*, 7, 57–68.

Waxler-Morrison, N., Hislop, T.G., Mears, B. and Can, L. (1991) The facts on social relationships on survival with women with breast cancer: A prospective study. *Social Science and Medicine*, 3, 177–183.

Weinman, J. (1981) *An Outline of Psychology as Applied to Medicine*. Bristol: John Wright and Sons Ltd.

Weinstein, N.D. (1987) Unrealistic optimism about susceptibility to health problems: Conclusions from a community-wide sample. *Journal of Behavioural Medicine*, 10, 481–500.

Weinstein, N.D. (1993) Testing four competing theories of health-protective behaviour. *Health Psychology*, 12, 324–333.

Weitz, R. (1989) Uncertainty and the lives of persons with AIDS. *Journal of Health and Social Behaviour*, 30, 270–281.

Wener, R. E. and Keys, C. (1988) The effects of changes in jail population densities on crowding, sick call, and spatial behaviour. *Journal of Applied Social Psychology*, 18, 852–866.

Williamson, J. and Chapin, J.M. (1980) Adverse reactions to prescribed drugs in the elderly: A multicare investigation. *Age and Ageing*, 9, 73–80.

Wilson, R. and Cairns, E. (1992) Trouble, stress and psychological disorder in Northern Ireland. *The Psychologist*, 5, 347–350.

Wing, R. R., Epstein, L.H., Nowalk, M.P. and Lamparski, D.M. (1986) Behavioural self-regulation in the treatment of patients with diabetes mellitus. *Psychological Bulletin*, 99, 78–89.

World Health Organisation (1984) Health Promotion: a WHO discussion document on concepts and principles. *Journal of the Institute of Health Education*, 23.

World Health Organisation (1991) *AIDS Prevention through Health Promotion: Facing Sensitive Issues*. Geneva: World Health Organisation.

Wortman, C.B and Silver, R.L. (1987) Coping with irrevocable loss. In Vandenbos, G. and Bryant, B. (eds) *Cataclysms, Crises and Catastrophes: Psychology in Action* 185–235. Washington, D.C.: American Psychological Association.

Wulfert, E. and Wan, C.K. (1993) Condom use: A self-efficacy model. *Health Psychology*, 12, 346–353.

Youngson, R. (1992) Pathways to pain control. *New Scientist*, 21 March.

Zeigler, S.G., Klinzing, J. and Williamson, K. (1982) The effects of two stress management programs on cardiorespiratory efficiency. *Journal of Sport Psychology*, 4, 280–289.

Zimbardo, P., Ebbesen, E. and Maslach, C. (1977) *Influencing Attitudes and Changing Behaviour*, 2nd edn. Reading Mass.: Addison-Wesley.

Index

Picture credits

The author and publisher would like to thank the following copyright holders for their permission to use material in this book:

Dan Addelman for Figures 8.1c and 8.1d (p. 117); **Associated Press/ Topham** for Figures 5.3 (p. 74), 8.1b (p. 117) and 10.3 (p. 148); **Cambridge University Press** for the extract (Appendix 1, pp 184–185) from Reason, J. (1990) *Human Error*; **Harcourt Brace and Company Limited** for Figure 5.1 (p. 69) from Becker, M.H. and Rosenstock, I.M. (1984) 'Compliance with medical advice', Steptoe, A. and Matthews, A. (eds) *Health Care and Human Behaviour*; **Office for National Statistics** for adaptation of Figures 1.3 (p. 10), 6.1 (p. 80) and Table 8.1 (p. 112), Crown copyright (1994), reproduced with the permission of the Controller of HMSO and the Office for National Statistics; **Plenum Publishing** for Box 2.3 (pp 29-30) from Kanner et al. (1981) 'Comparison of two modes of stress measurement: Daily hassles and uplifts versus major life events', *Journal of Behavioural Medicine*, 4; **Ogilvy and Mather** on behalf of Smithkline & Beecham for Figure 4.3 (p. 57); **QUIT** for Figure 7.4 (p. 107); **Richard Powers** for Figure 8.1a (p. 117); **Roger Ressmeyer, Starlight/Science Photo Library** for Figure 7.3 (p. 105); **The Royal College of General Practitioners** for Figure 9.2 (p. 130) from McKinstry, B. and Wang, J. (1991) 'Putting on the style: What patients think of the way their doctor dresses,' *British Journal of General Practice*, 41 (reprinted with permission).

Every effort has been made to obtain necessary permission with reference to copyright material. The publishers apologise if inadvertently any sources remain unacknowledged and will be glad to make the necessary arrangements at the earliest opportunity.